D0287339

of
LIGHT

story and art by
SEIKO ERISAWA

vol. 1

BOUNDARY STORE

CONTENTS

Ep3

Cream Dorayaki @130x3 ¥390

Green Tea 380 mL ¥140

Subtotal ¥530

...ndary Tax ¥42

¥572

Ep6

Corn Menchi-Katsu

Hot Coffee M

Subtotal

Total

Episode 1
Workaholic Misaki

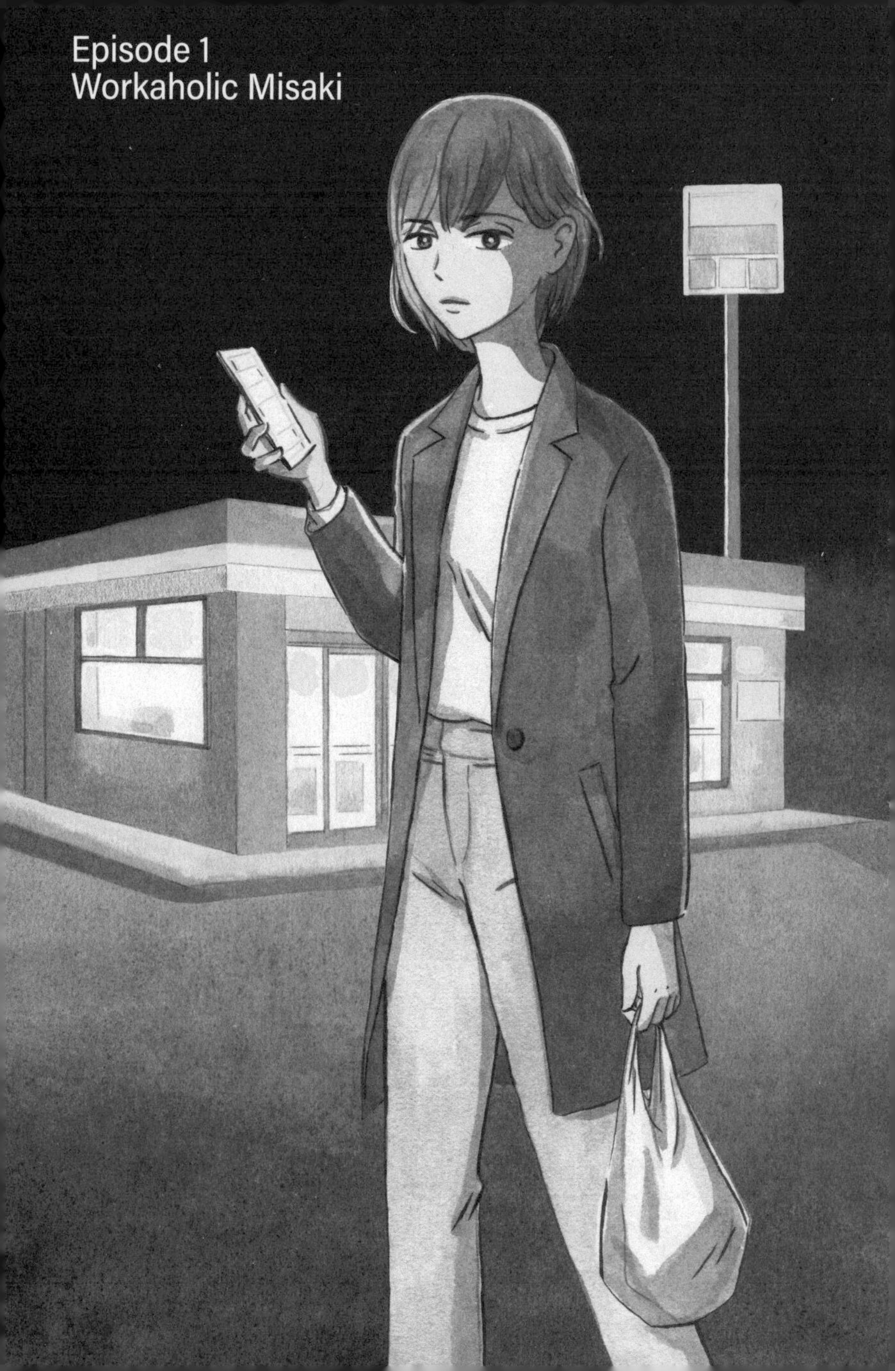

WELL, I SUPPOSE THERE'S NO CHOICE THEN.

TOK

TOK

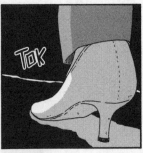

TOK

SHIF

SHIF

I WAS ON MY WAY HOME, BUT I'LL RETURN TO THE OFFICE AND DEAL WITH IT.

YES, I'LL MAKE SURE IT'S DONE BEFORE THE MEETING TOMORROW MORNING.

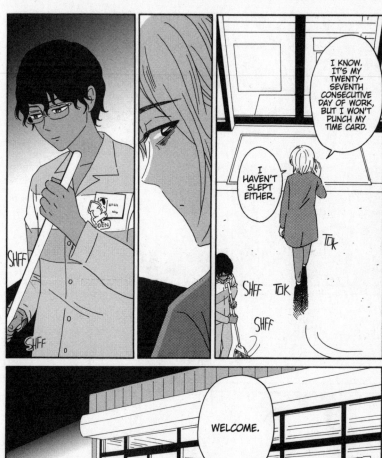

I KNOW. IT'S MY TWENTY-SEVENTH CONSECUTIVE DAY OF WORK, BUT I WON'T PUNCH MY TIME CARD.
I HAVEN'T SLEPT EITHER.
TOK
SHFF TOK
SHFF
ODEN
SHFF
SHFF
WELCOME.
SHFF
SHFF

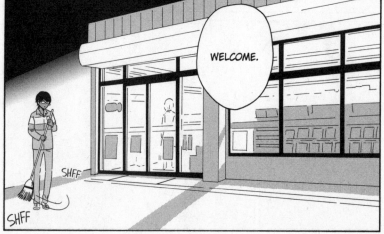

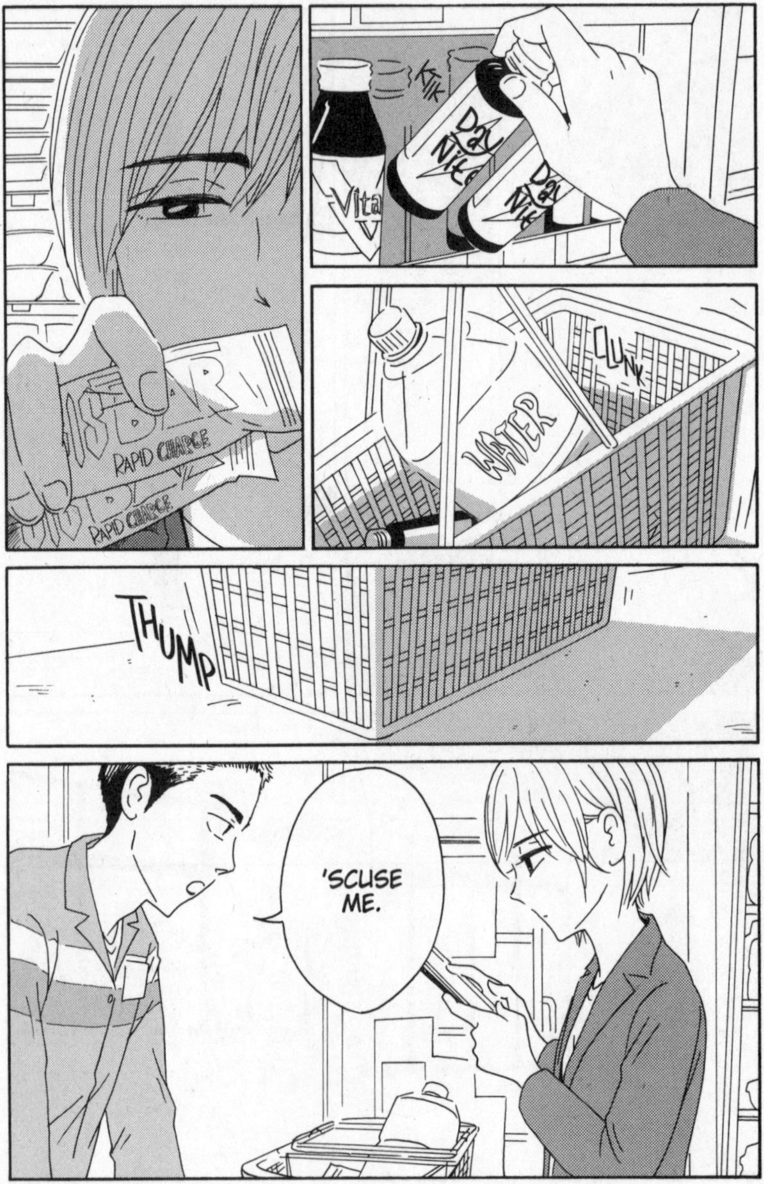
KIK
Day Nite
Day Nite
CLUNK
WATER
RAPID CHARGE
RAPID CHARGE
THUMP
'SCUSE ME.

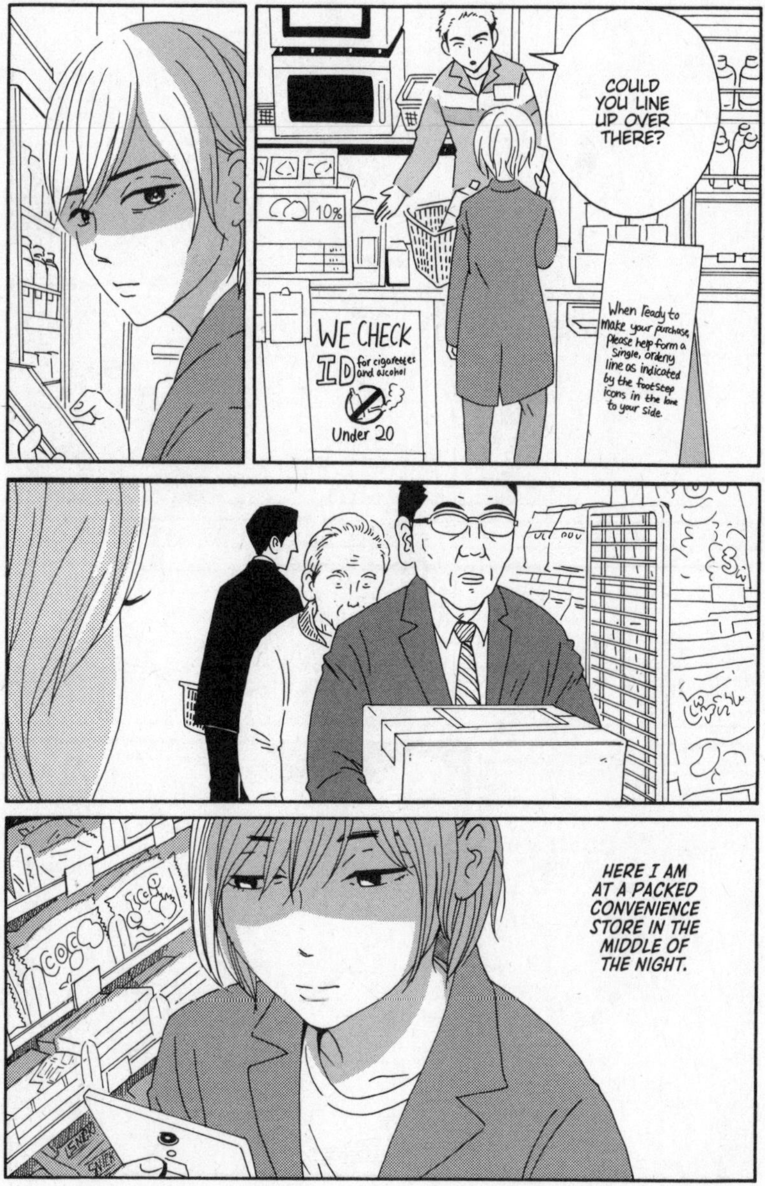
COULD YOU LINE UP OVER THERE?
When ready to make your purchase, please help form a single, orderly line as indicated by the footstep icons in the lane to your side.
WE CHECK ID for cigarettes and alcohol
Under 20
10%
HERE I AM AT A PACKED CONVENIENCE STORE IN THE MIDDLE OF THE NIGHT.

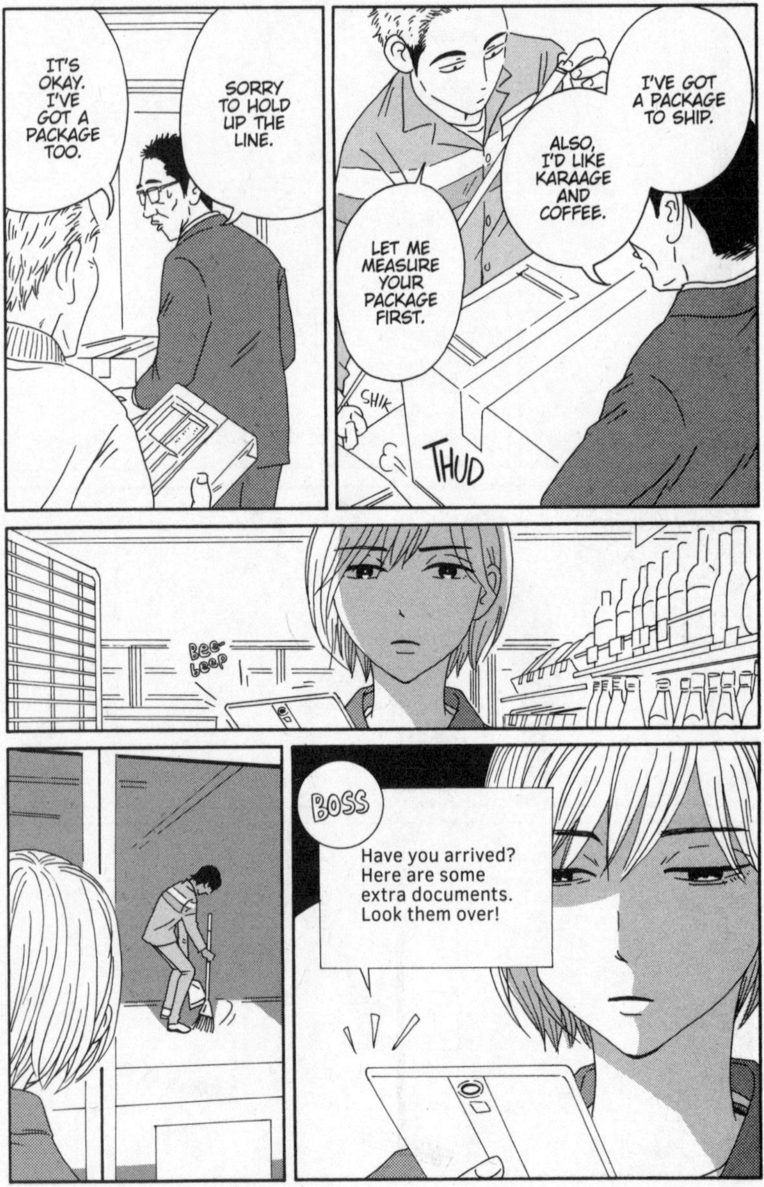
I'VE GOT A PACKAGE TO SHIP.
ALSO, I'D LIKE KARAAGE AND COFFEE.
LET ME MEASURE YOUR PACKAGE FIRST.
SHIK
THUD
SORRY TO HOLD UP THE LINE.
IT'S OKAY. I'VE GOT A PACKAGE TOO.
Bee-beep
BOSS
Have you arrived? Here are some extra documents. Look them over!

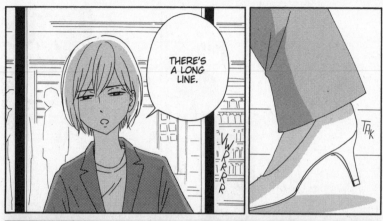

TAK
THERE'S A LONG LINE.
VWRRRR
NOD
SHF
SHF
SO OPEN ANOTHER REGISTER.
STILL BUSY CLEANING, YOU KNOW.

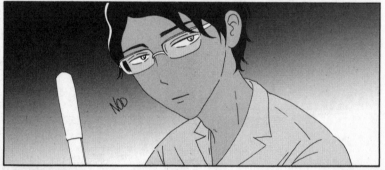

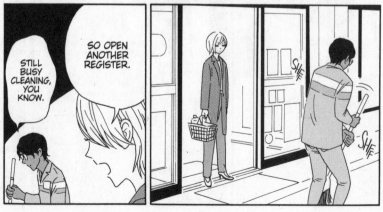

Shuffle

Beep

Beep

WAIT, WHEN DID...?

NEXT CUSTOMER.

So buy it.

I need beer!

YES.

Hee hee hee!

bee bee bee

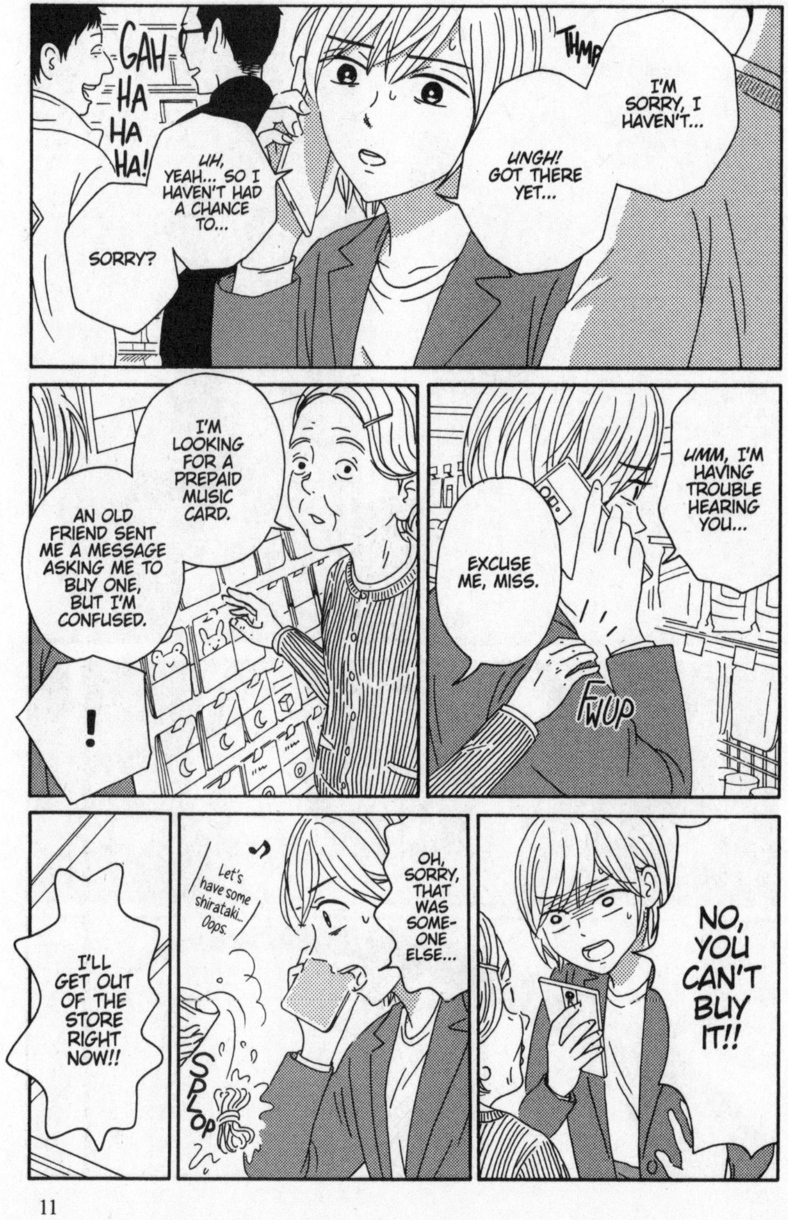
THMP
I'M SORRY, I HAVEN'T...
UNGH! GOT THERE YET...
GAH HA HA HA!
UH, YEAH... SO I HAVEN'T HAD A CHANCE TO...
SORRY?
UMM, I'M HAVING TROUBLE HEARING YOU...
EXCUSE ME, MISS.
FWUP
I'M LOOKING FOR A PREPAID MUSIC CARD.
AN OLD FRIEND SENT ME A MESSAGE ASKING ME TO BUY ONE, BUT I'M CONFUSED.
!
NO, YOU CAN'T BUY IT!!
OH, SORRY, THAT WAS SOMEONE ELSE...
Let's have some shirataki... Oops.
SPLOP
I'LL GET OUT OF THE STORE RIGHT NOW!!

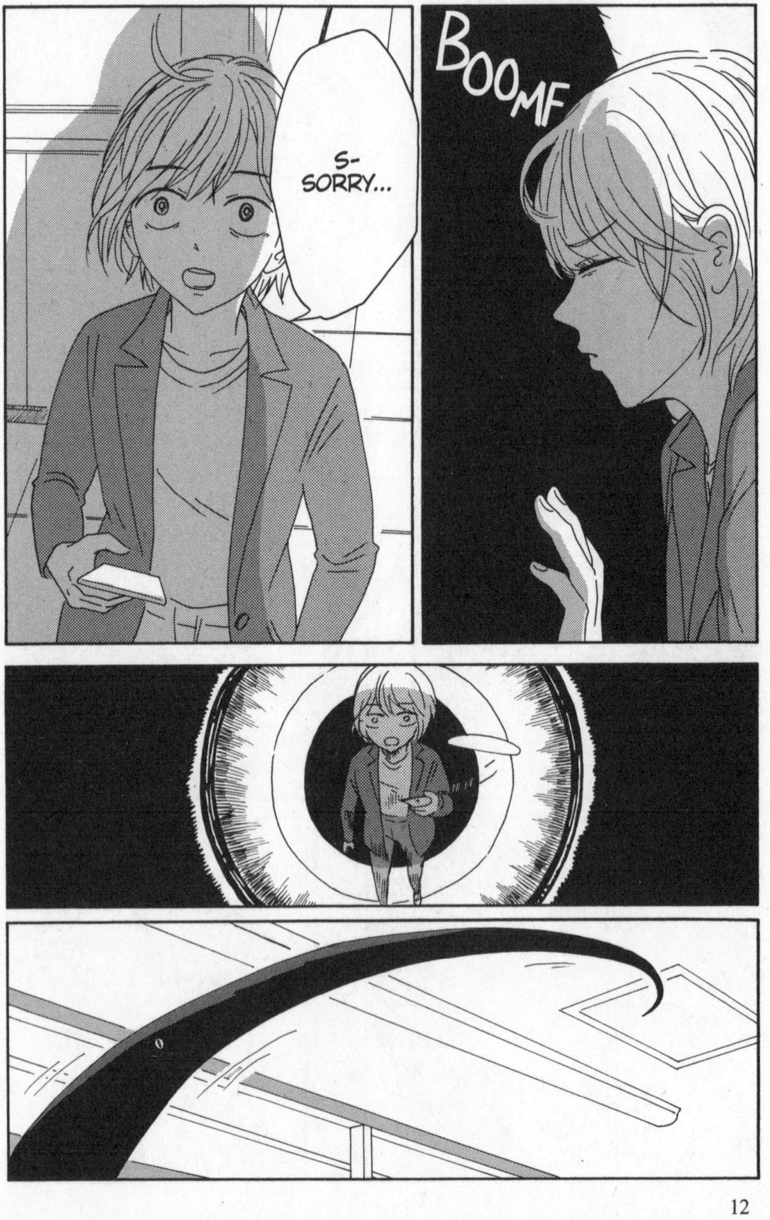
BOOMF
S-SORRY...

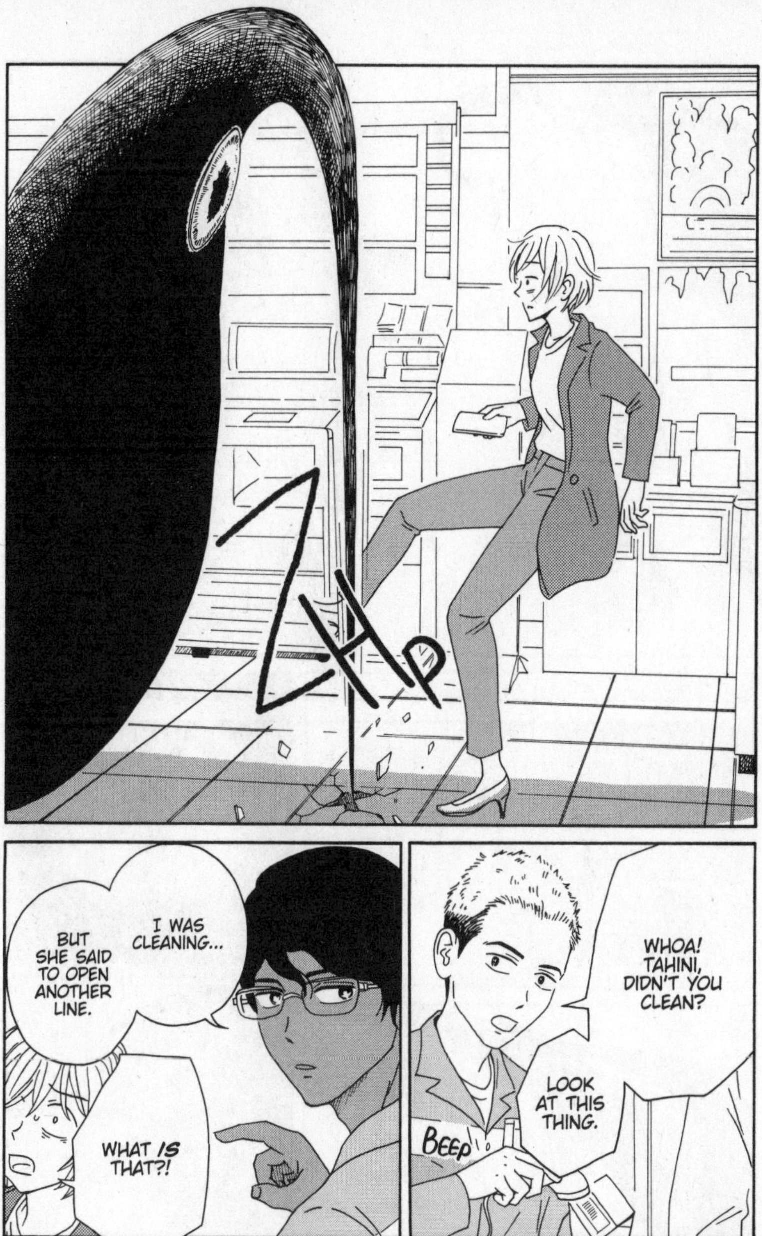
ZHP
WHOA! TAHINI, DIDN'T YOU CLEAN?
LOOK AT THIS THING.
BEEP
I WAS CLEANING...
BUT SHE SAID TO OPEN ANOTHER LINE.
WHAT *IS* THAT?!

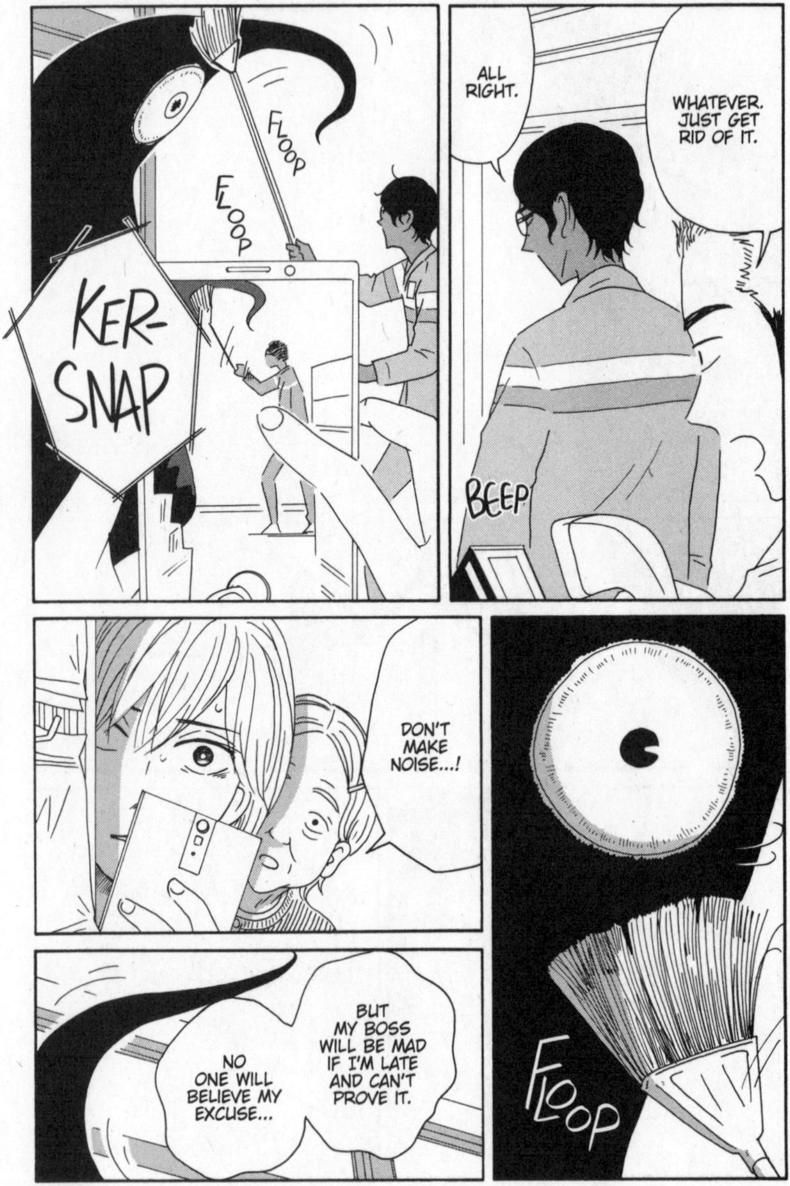
WHATEVER. JUST GET RID OF IT.
ALL RIGHT.
BEEP
FLOOP
FLOOP
KER-SNAP
FLOOP
DON'T MAKE NOISE...!
BUT MY BOSS WILL BE MAD IF I'M LATE AND CAN'T PROVE IT.
NO ONE WILL BELIEVE MY EXCUSE...

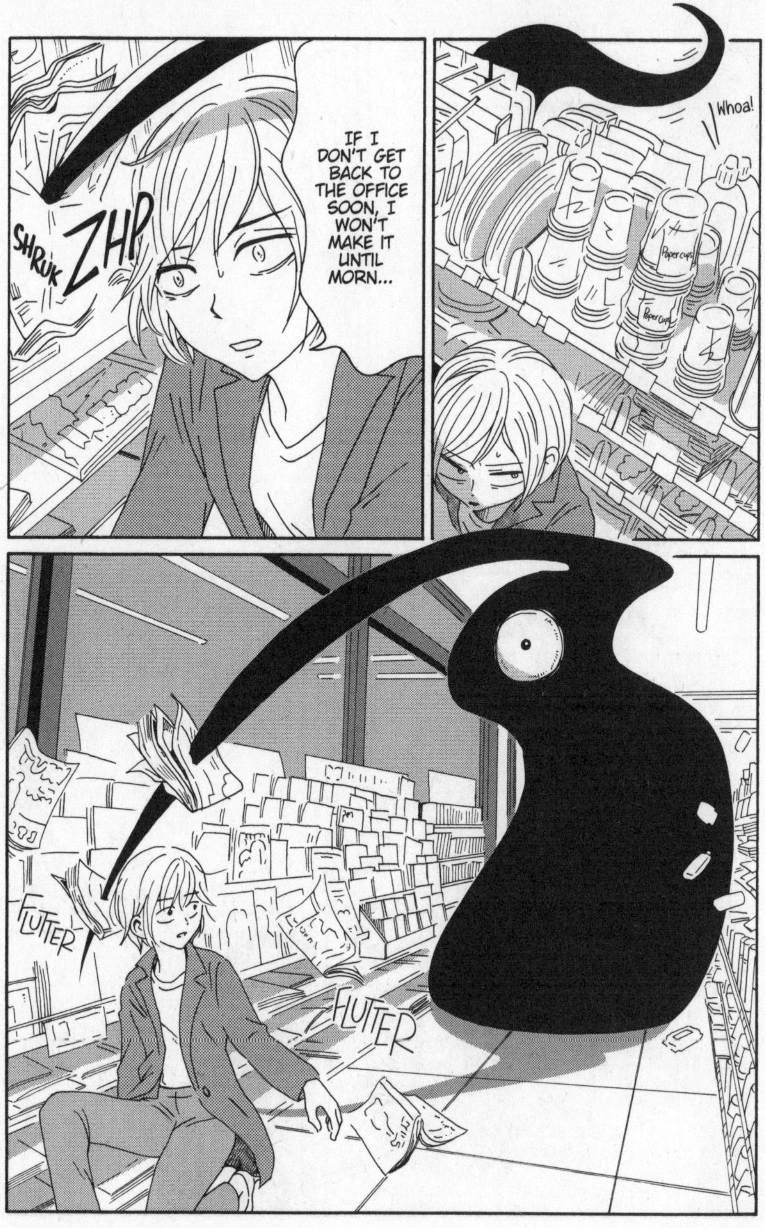
Whoa!
Paper cups
Paper cups
IF I DON'T GET BACK TO THE OFFICE SOON, I WON'T MAKE IT UNTIL MORN...
SHRUK
ZHP
FLUTTER
FLUTTER

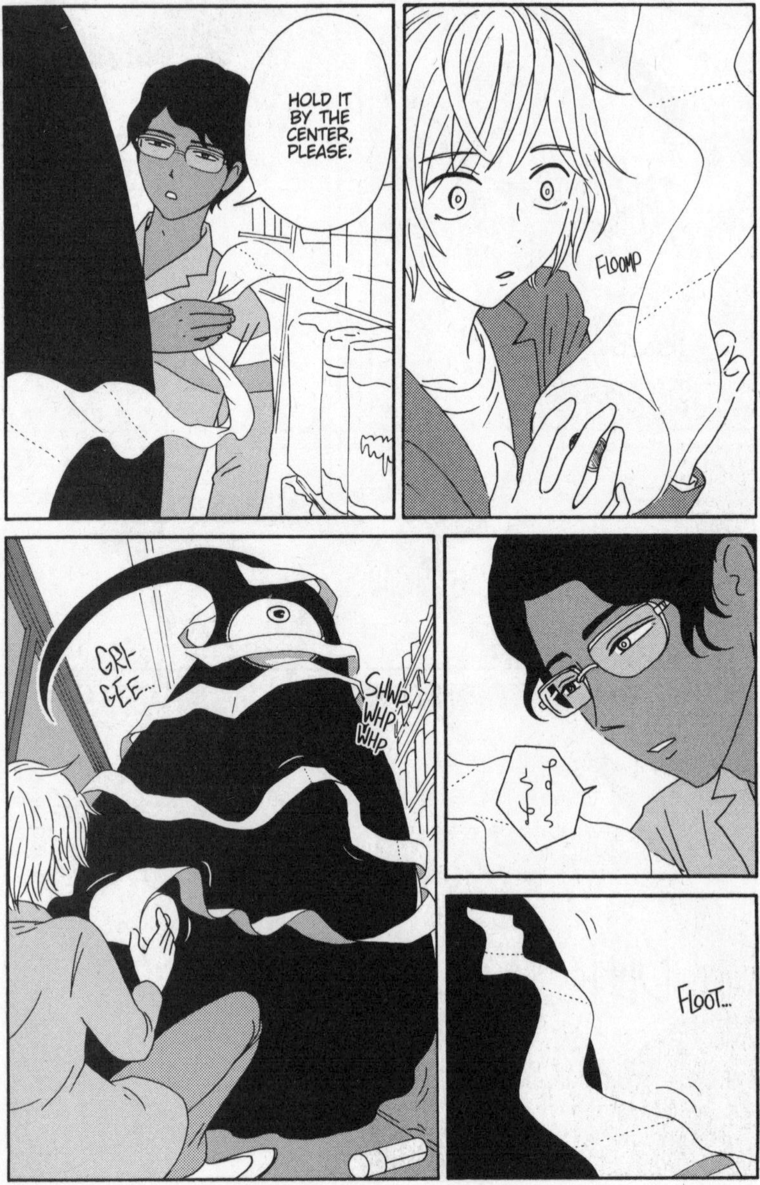
FLOOMP
HOLD IT BY THE CENTER, PLEASE.
FLOOT...
GRI-GEE...
SHWP WHP WHP

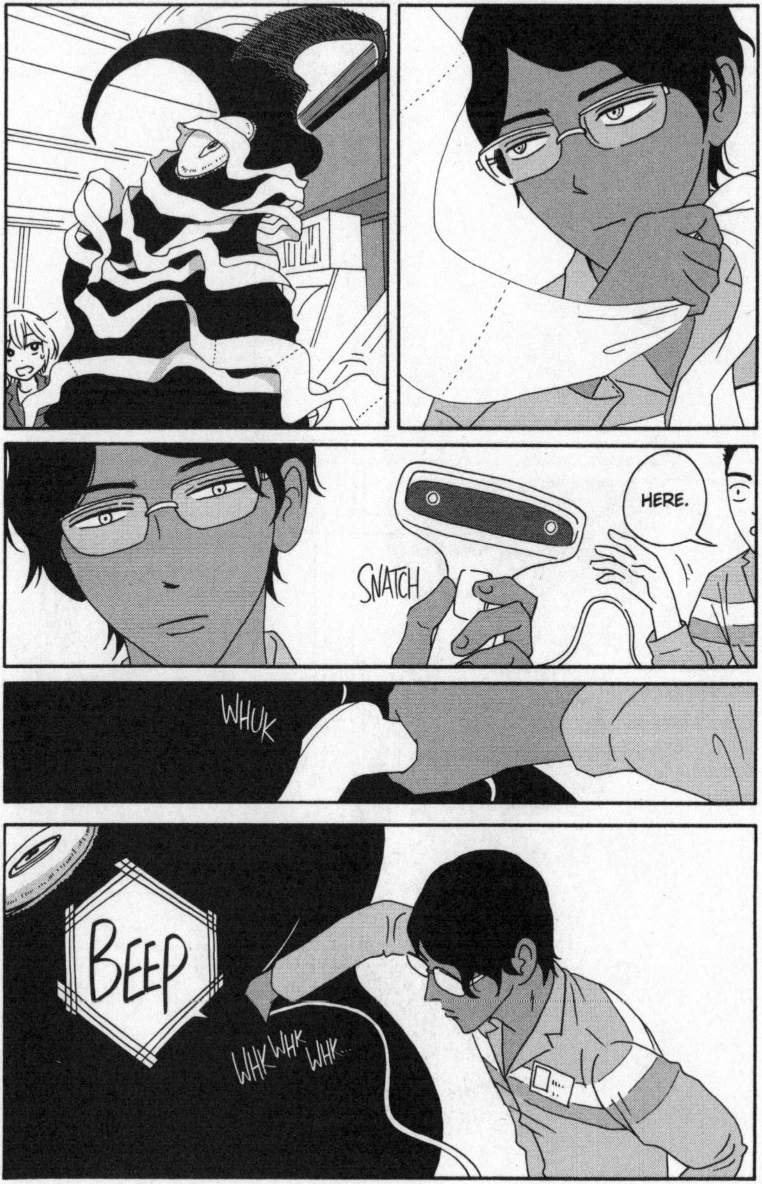
HERE.
SNATCH
WHUK
BEEP
WHK WHK WHK...

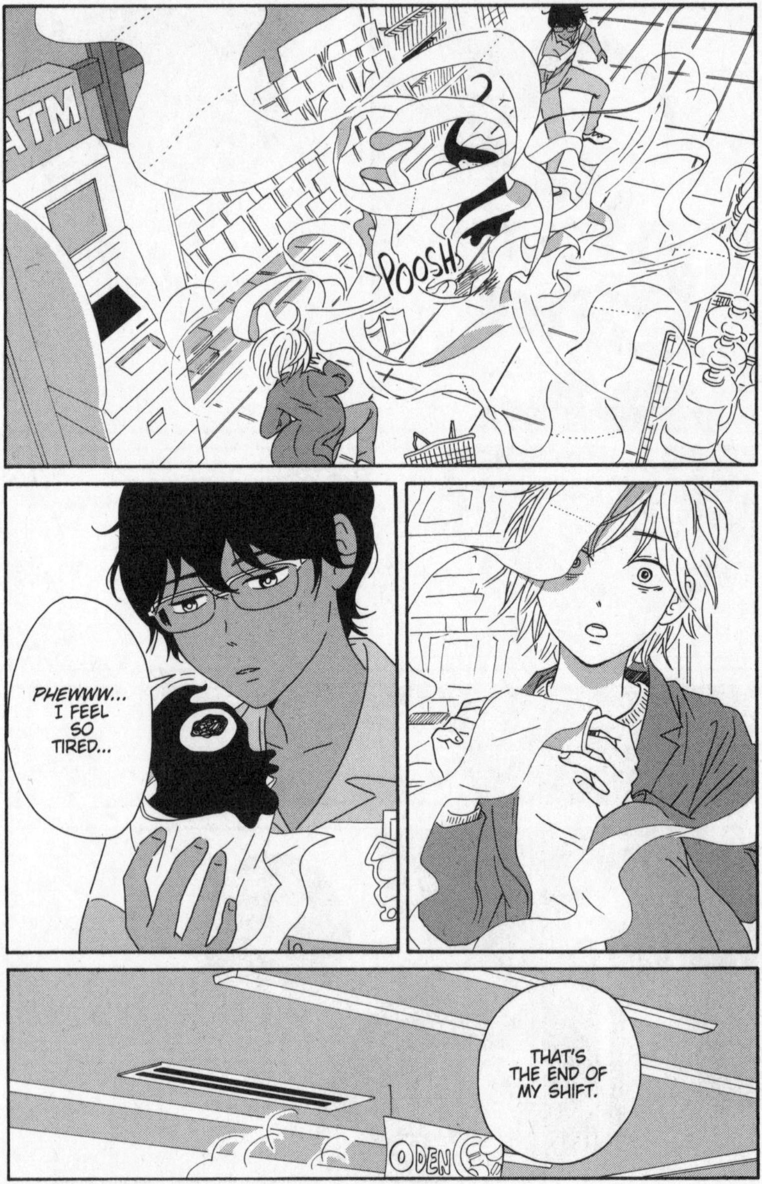
ATM
POOSH
PHEWWW... I FEEL SO TIRED...
THAT'S THE END OF MY SHIFT.
ODEN

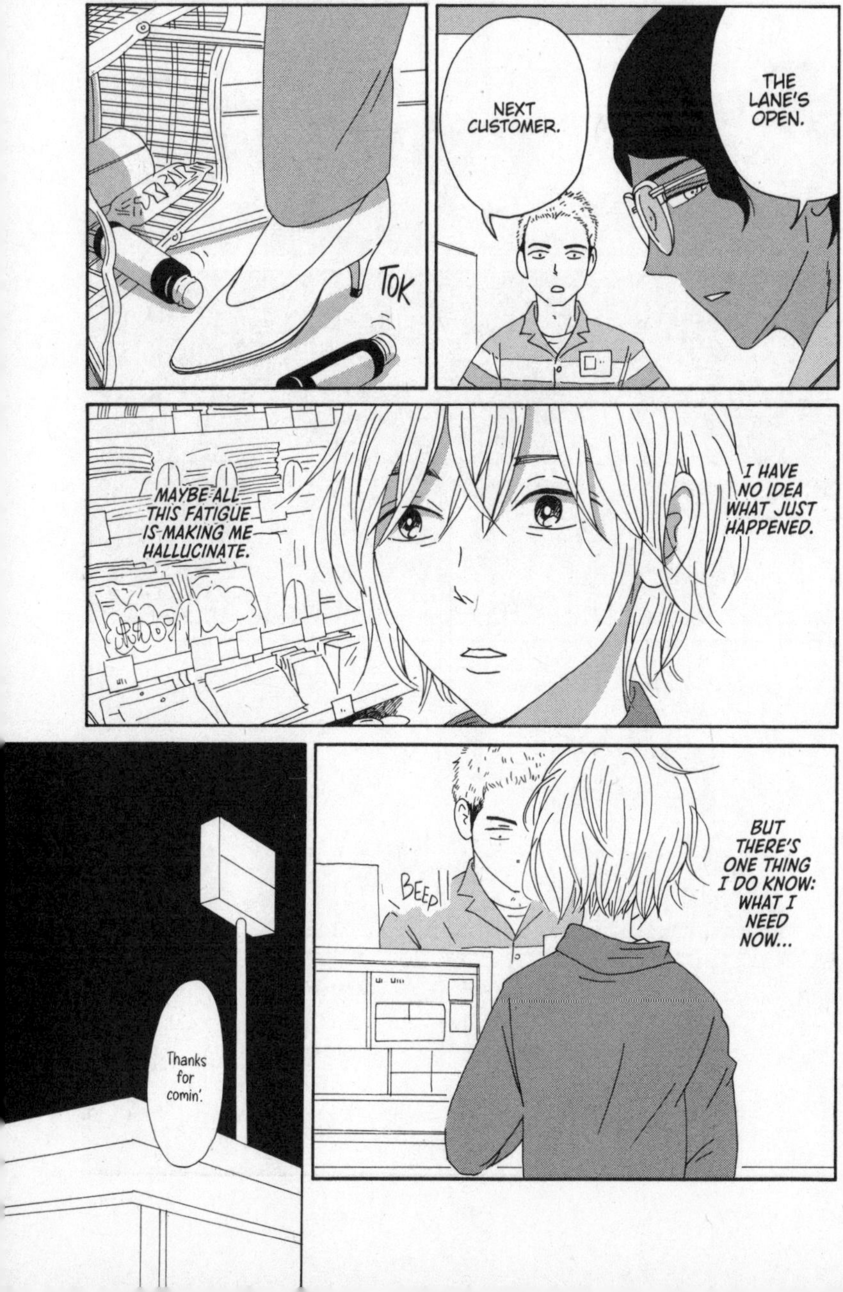
THE LANE'S OPEN.
NEXT CUSTOMER.
TOK
I HAVE NO IDEA WHAT JUST HAPPENED.
MAYBE ALL THIS FATIGUE IS MAKING ME HALLUCINATE.
BUT THERE'S ONE THING I DO KNOW: WHAT I NEED NOW...
BEEP
Thanks for comin'.

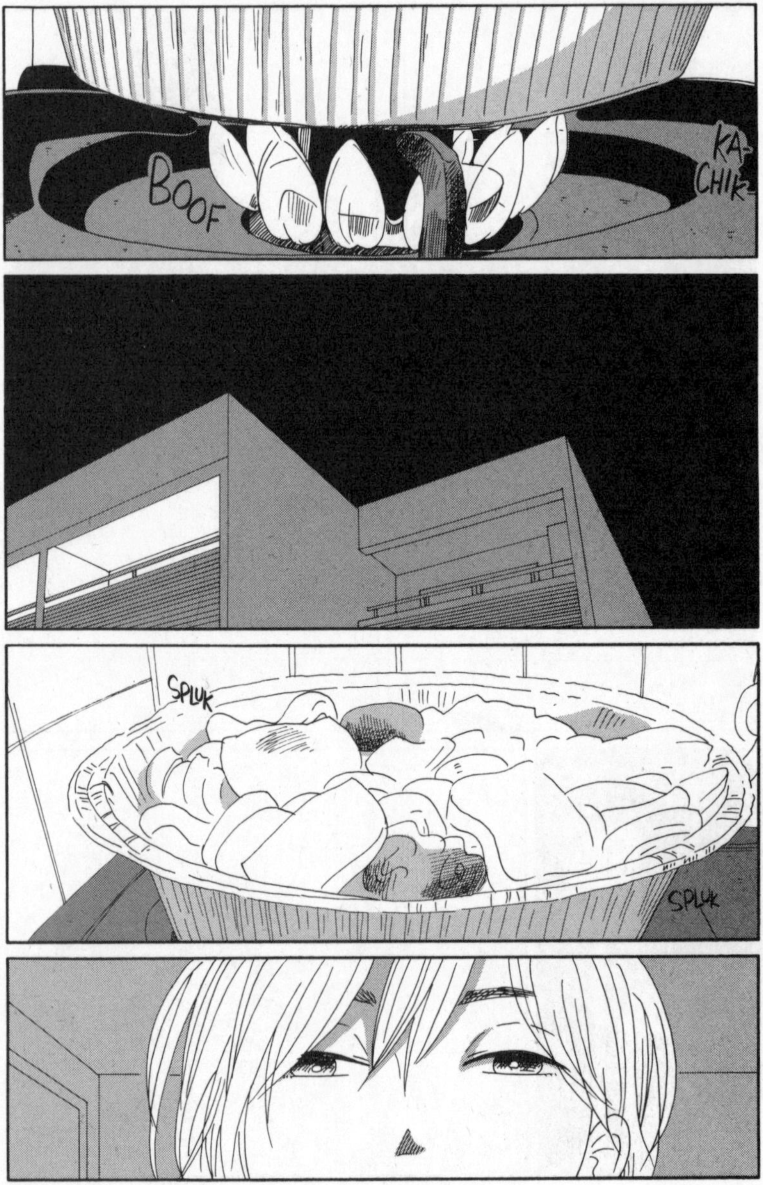
KA-CHIK
BOOF
SPLUK
SPLUK

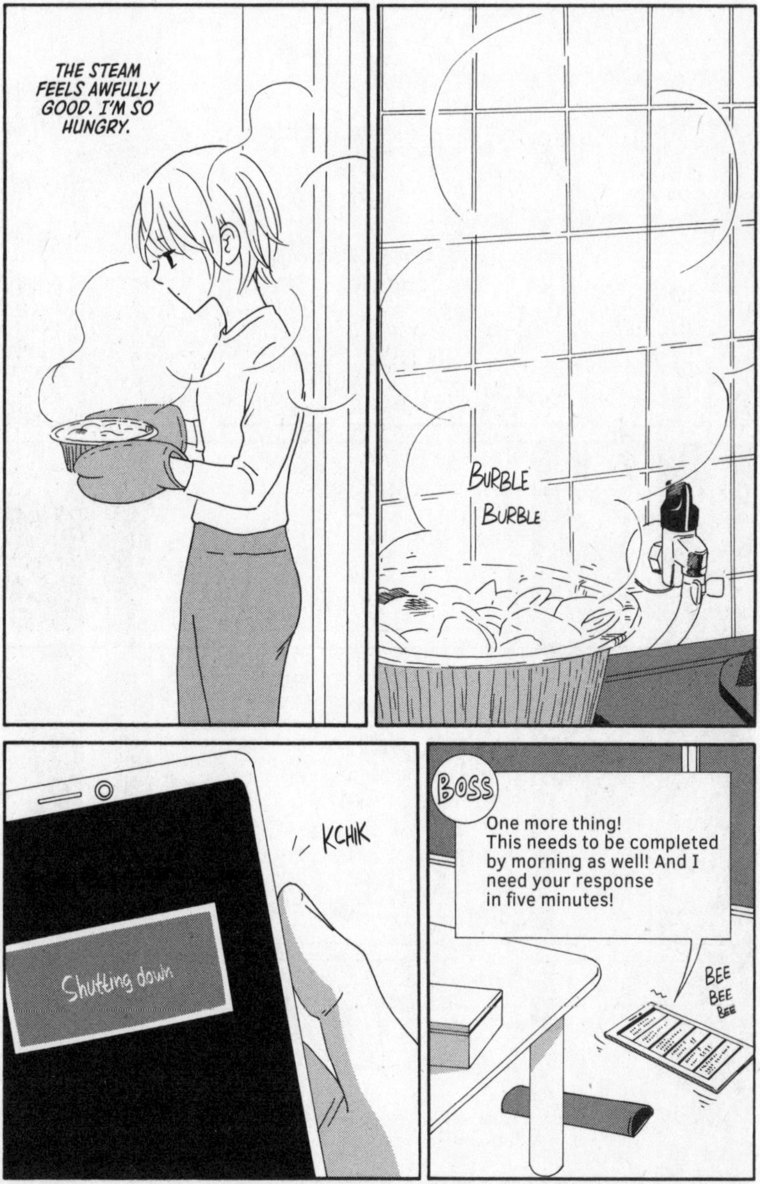
BURBLE
BURBLE
THE STEAM FEELS AWFULLY GOOD. I'M SO HUNGRY.
BOSS
One more thing!
This needs to be completed
by morning as well! And I
need your response
in five minutes!
BEE
BEE
BEE
KCHIK
Shutting down

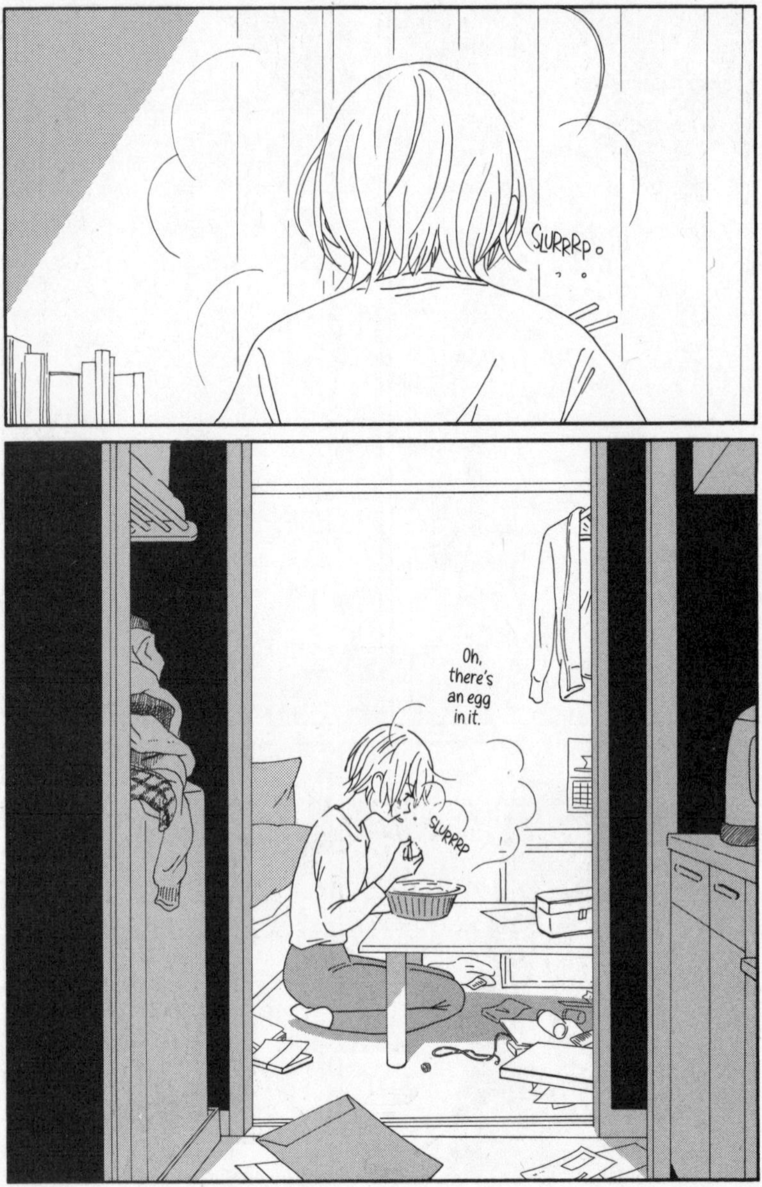
SLURRRP
Oh, there's an egg in it.
SLURRRP

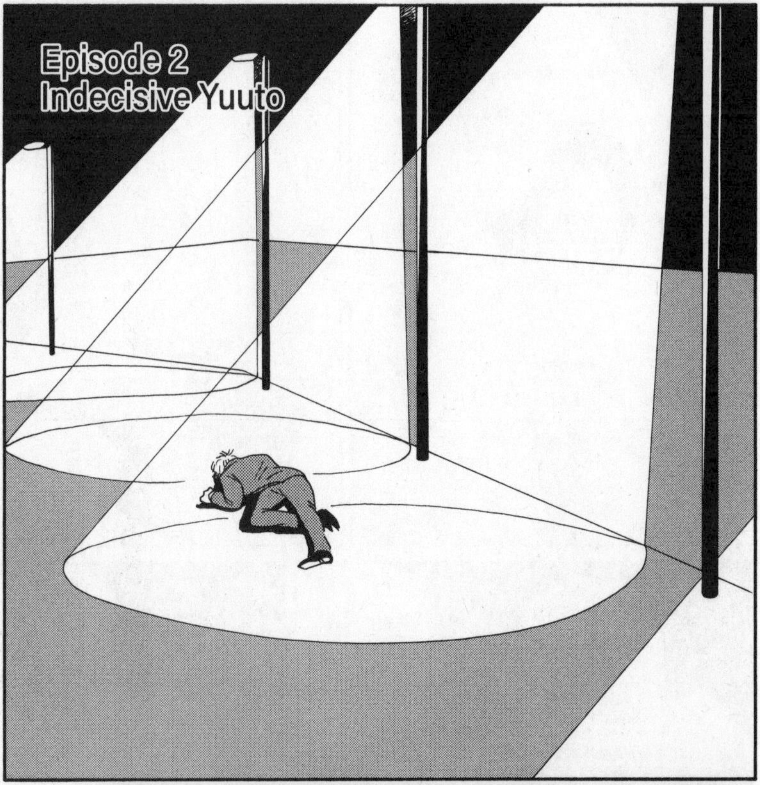
Episode 2
Indecisive Yuuto

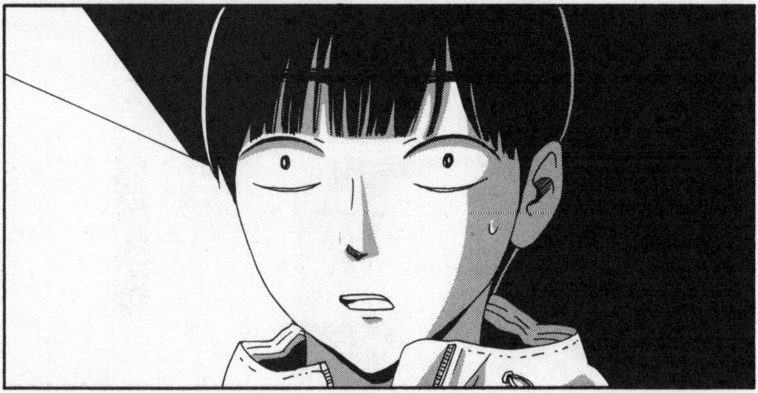

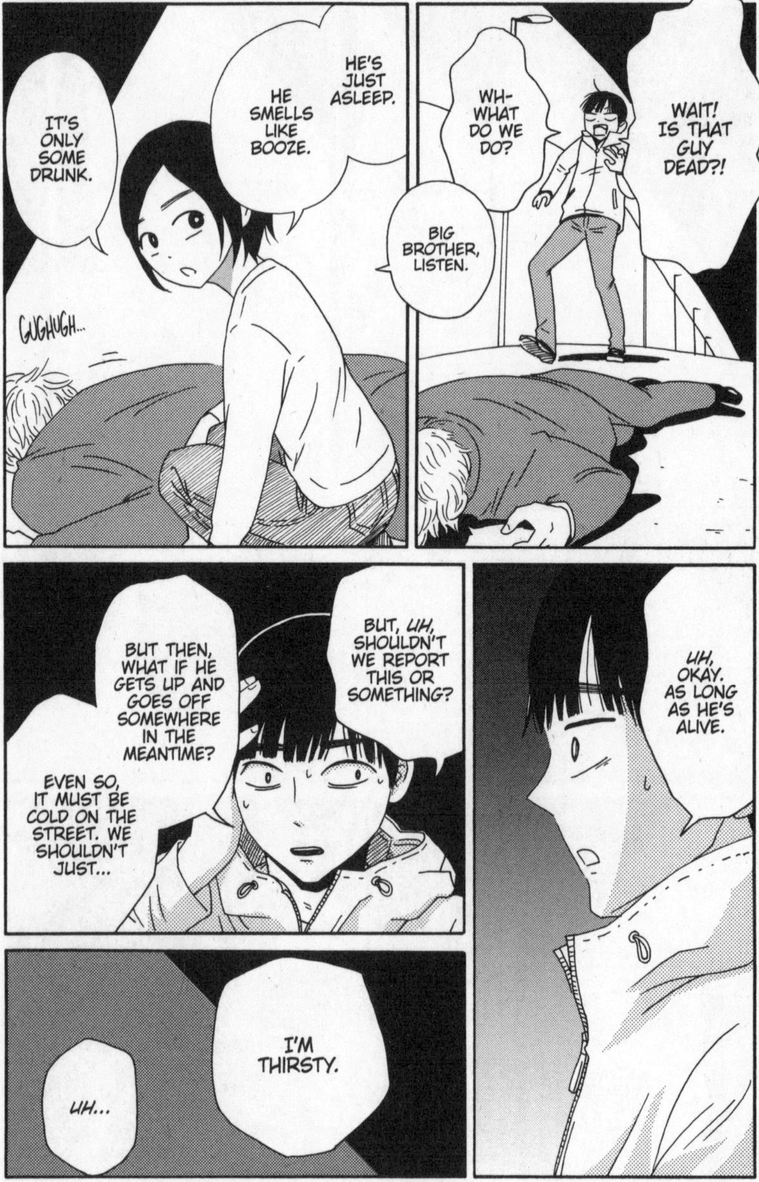
WAIT! IS THAT GUY DEAD?!
WH- WHAT DO WE DO?
BIG BROTHER, LISTEN.
HE'S JUST ASLEEP.
HE SMELLS LIKE BOOZE.
IT'S ONLY SOME DRUNK.
GUGHUGH...
UH, OKAY. AS LONG AS HE'S ALIVE.
BUT, UH, SHOULDN'T WE REPORT THIS OR SOMETHING?
BUT THEN, WHAT IF HE GETS UP AND GOES OFF SOMEWHERE IN THE MEANTIME?
EVEN SO, IT MUST BE COLD ON THE STREET. WE SHOULDN'T JUST...
I'M THIRSTY.
UH...

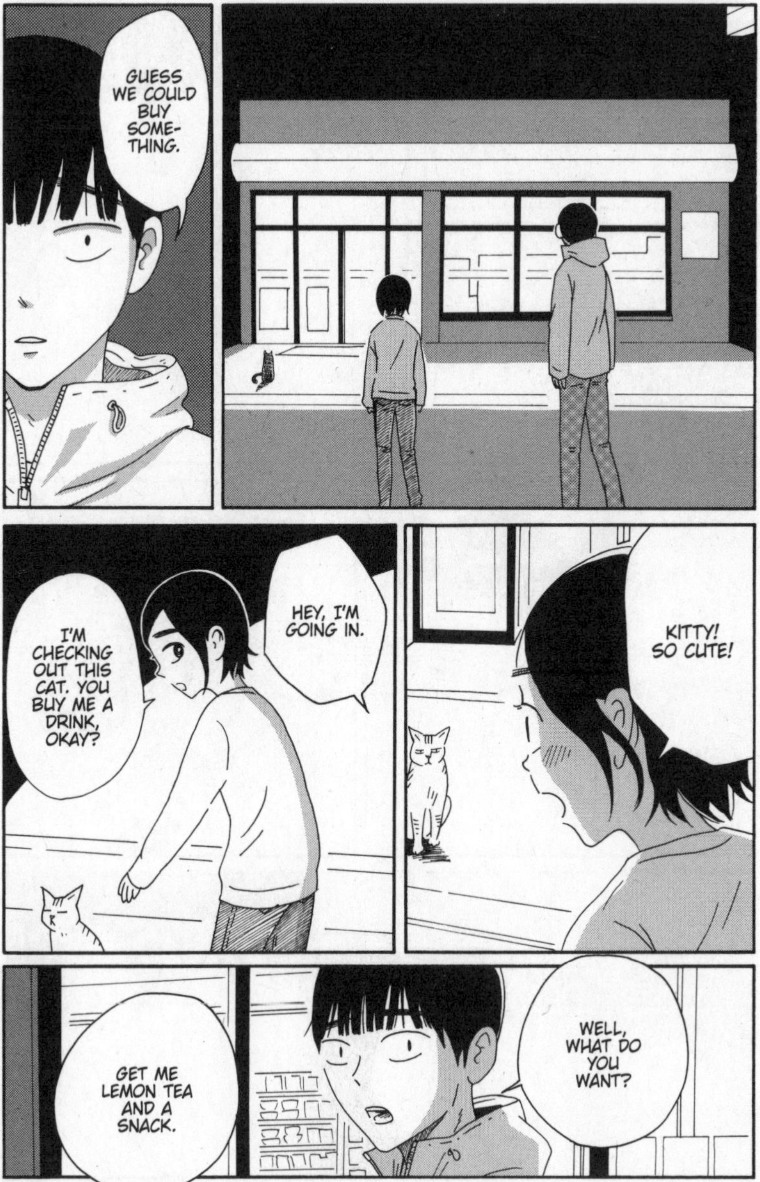
GUESS WE COULD BUY SOME-THING.
KITTY! SO CUTE!
HEY, I'M GOING IN.
I'M CHECKING OUT THIS CAT. YOU BUY ME A DRINK, OKAY?
WELL, WHAT DO YOU WANT?
GET ME LEMON TEA AND A SNACK.

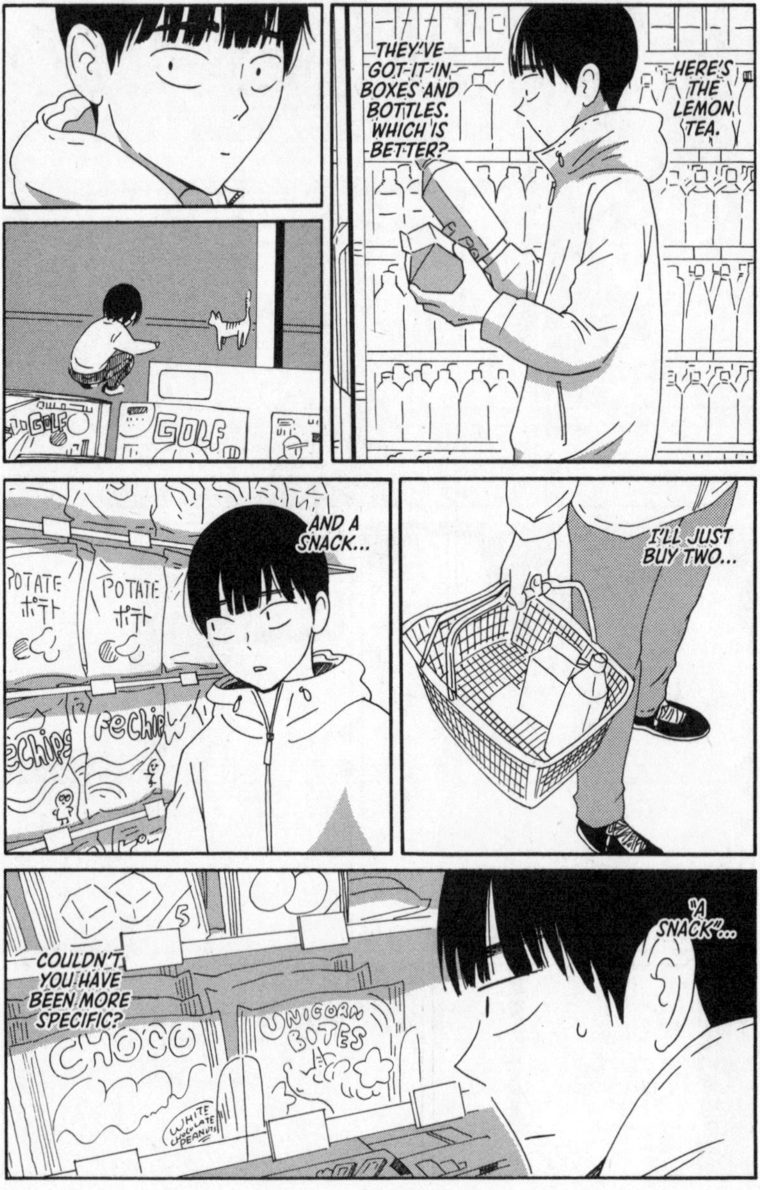
HERE'S THE LEMON TEA.
THEY'VE GOT IT IN BOXES AND BOTTLES. WHICH IS BETTER?
GOLF
GOLF
I'LL JUST BUY TWO...
AND A SNACK...
POTATE ポテト
POTATE ポテト
fechips
"A SNACK"...
COULDN'T YOU HAVE BEEN MORE SPECIFIC?
CHOCO
UNICORN BOTES
WHITE CHOCOLATE PEANUTS

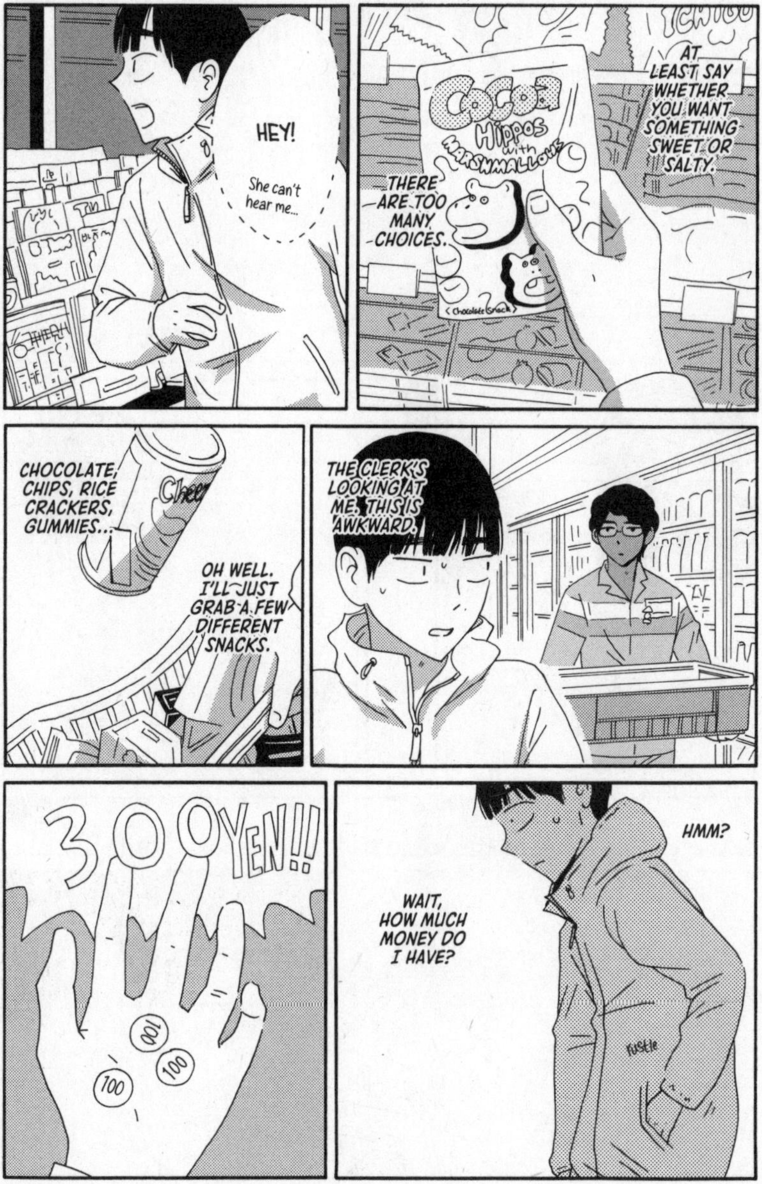

AT LEAST SAY WHETHER YOU WANT SOMETHING SWEET OR SALTY.
COCOA Hippos with MARSHMALLOWS
THERE ARE TOO MANY CHOICES.
Chocolate Snack
HEY!
She can't hear me...
THE CLERK'S LOOKING AT ME. THIS IS AWKWARD.
CHOCOLATE, CHIPS, RICE CRACKERS, GUMMIES...
OH WELL. I'LL JUST GRAB A FEW DIFFERENT SNACKS.
HMM?
WAIT, HOW MUCH MONEY DO I HAVE?
rustle
300 YEN!!
100
100
100

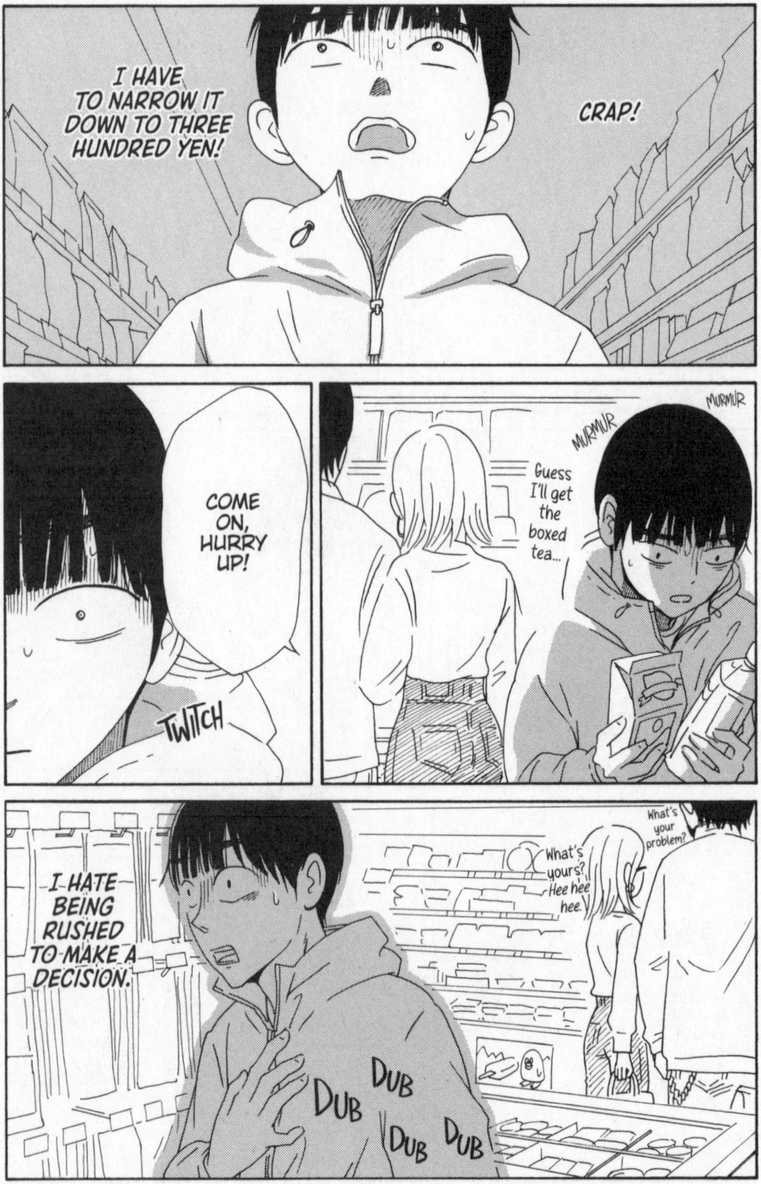
CRAP!
I HAVE TO NARROW IT DOWN TO THREE HUNDRED YEN!
MURMUR
MURMUR
Guess I'll get the boxed tea...
COME ON, HURRY UP!
TWITCH
What's your problem?
What's yours? Hee hee hee.
I HATE BEING RUSHED TO MAKE A DECISION.
DUB
DUB
DUB
DUB

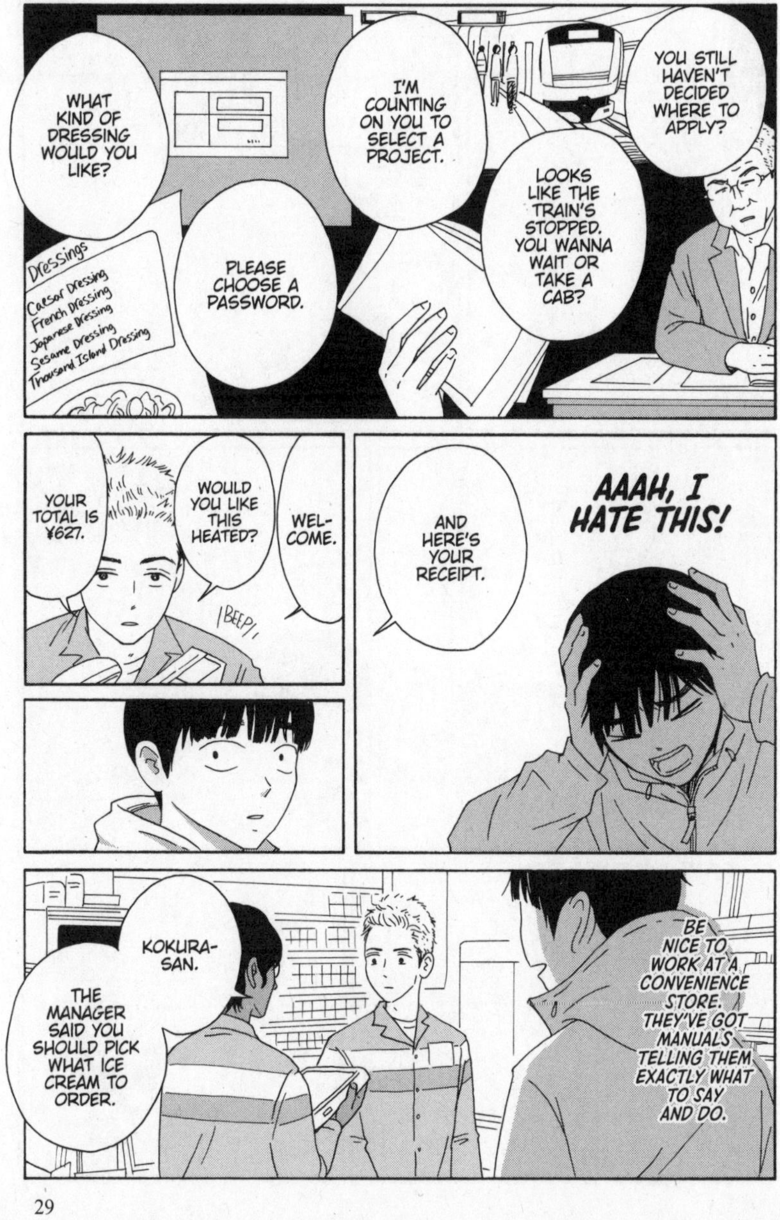
YOU STILL HAVEN'T DECIDED WHERE TO APPLY?
LOOKS LIKE THE TRAIN'S STOPPED. YOU WANNA WAIT OR TAKE A CAB?
I'M COUNTING ON YOU TO SELECT A PROJECT.
PLEASE CHOOSE A PASSWORD.
WHAT KIND OF DRESSING WOULD YOU LIKE?
Dressings
Caesar Dressing
French Dressing
Japanese Dressing
Sesame Dressing
Thousand Island Dressing
AAAH, I HATE THIS!
AND HERE'S YOUR RECEIPT.
WEL-COME.
WOULD YOU LIKE THIS HEATED?
BEEP
YOUR TOTAL IS ¥627.
BE NICE TO WORK AT A CONVENIENCE STORE. THEY'VE GOT MANUALS TELLING THEM EXACTLY WHAT TO SAY AND DO.
KOKURA-SAN.
THE MANAGER SAID YOU SHOULD PICK WHAT ICE CREAM TO ORDER.

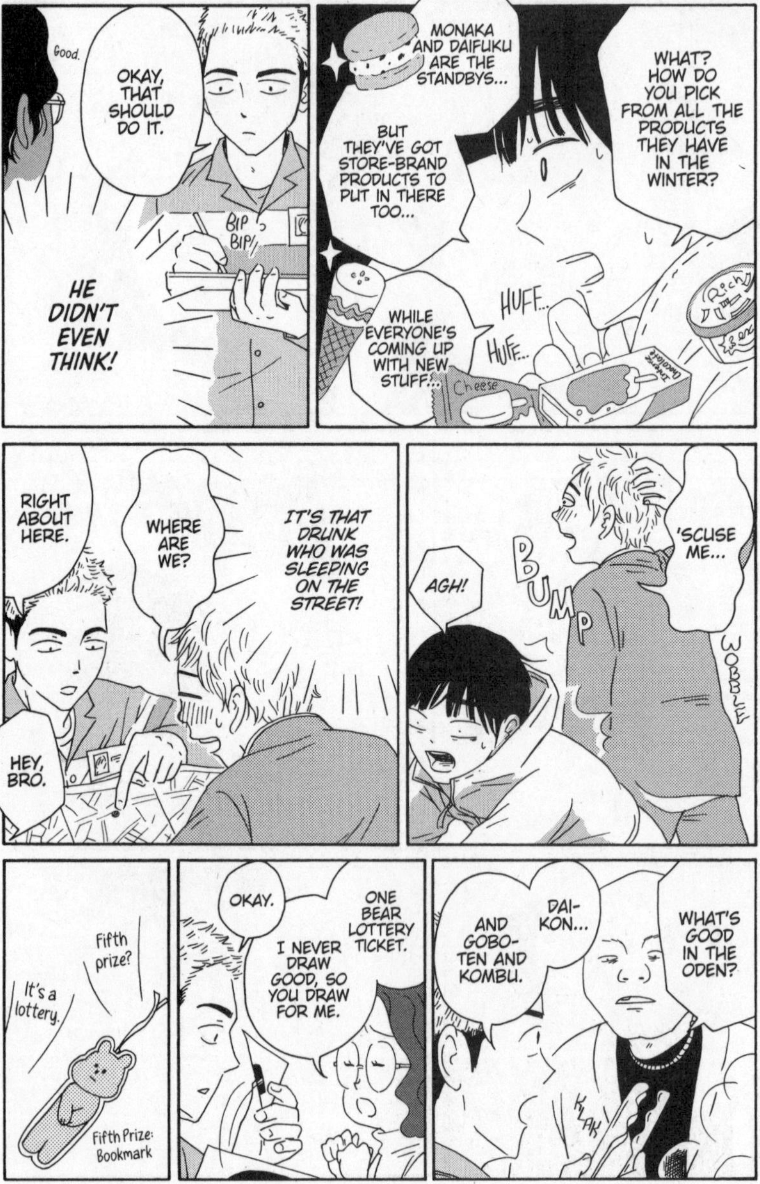
WHAT? HOW DO YOU PICK FROM ALL THE PRODUCTS THEY HAVE IN THE WINTER?
MONAKA AND DAIFUKU ARE THE STANDBYS...
BUT THEY'VE GOT STORE-BRAND PRODUCTS TO PUT IN THERE TOO...
HUFF...
HUFF...
WHILE EVERYONE'S COMING UP WITH NEW STUFF...
Cheese
OKAY, THAT SHOULD DO IT.
Good.
BIP BIP
HE DIDN'T EVEN THINK!
'SCUSE ME...
BUMP
WOBBLE
AGH!
IT'S THAT DRUNK WHO WAS SLEEPING ON THE STREET!
WHERE ARE WE?
RIGHT ABOUT HERE.
HEY, BRO.
WHAT'S GOOD IN THE ODEN?
DAI-KON...
AND GOBO-TEN AND KOMBU.
KLAK
ONE BEAR LOTTERY TICKET.
OKAY.
I NEVER DRAW GOOD, SO YOU DRAW FOR ME.
Fifth prize?
It's a lottery.
Fifth Prize: Bookmark

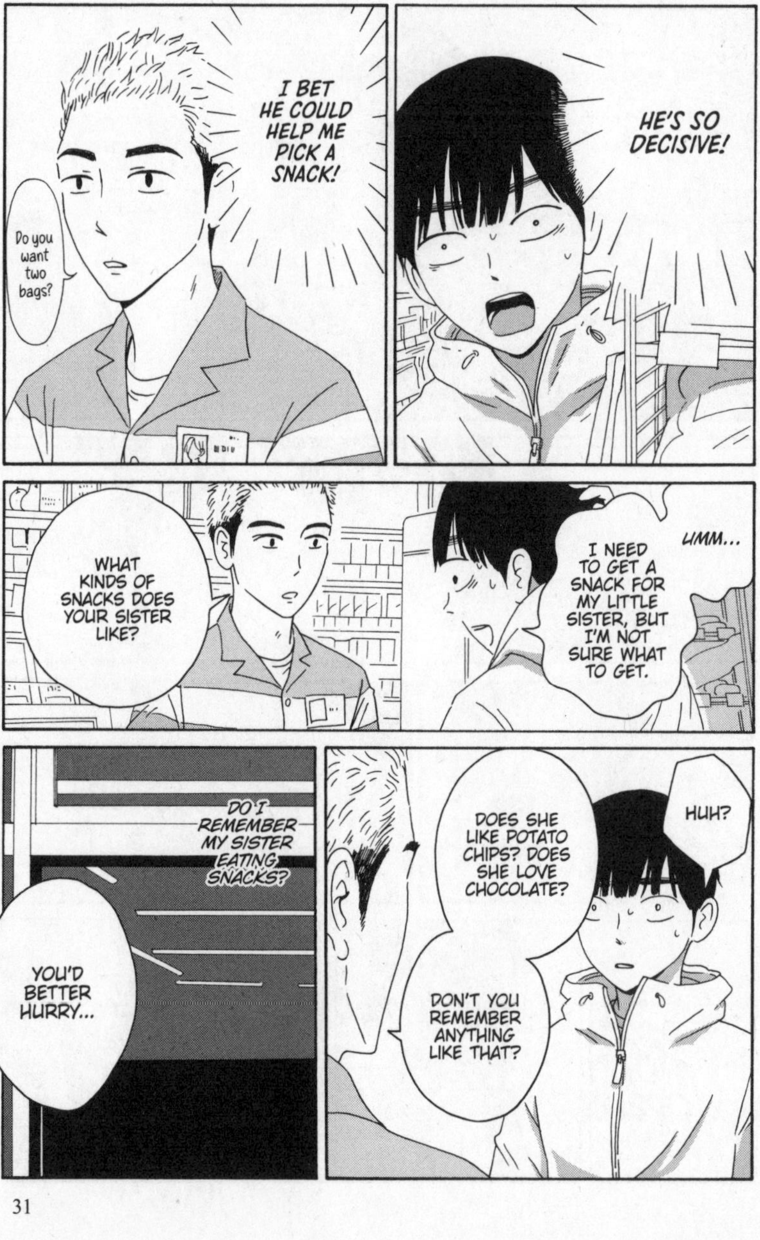
HE'S SO DECISIVE!
I BET HE COULD HELP ME PICK A SNACK!
Do you want two bags?
UMM...
I NEED TO GET A SNACK FOR MY LITTLE SISTER, BUT I'M NOT SURE WHAT TO GET.
WHAT KINDS OF SNACKS DOES YOUR SISTER LIKE?
HUH?
DOES SHE LIKE POTATO CHIPS? DOES SHE LOVE CHOCOLATE?
DON'T YOU REMEMBER ANYTHING LIKE THAT?
DO I REMEMBER MY SISTER EATING SNACKS?
YOU'D BETTER HURRY...

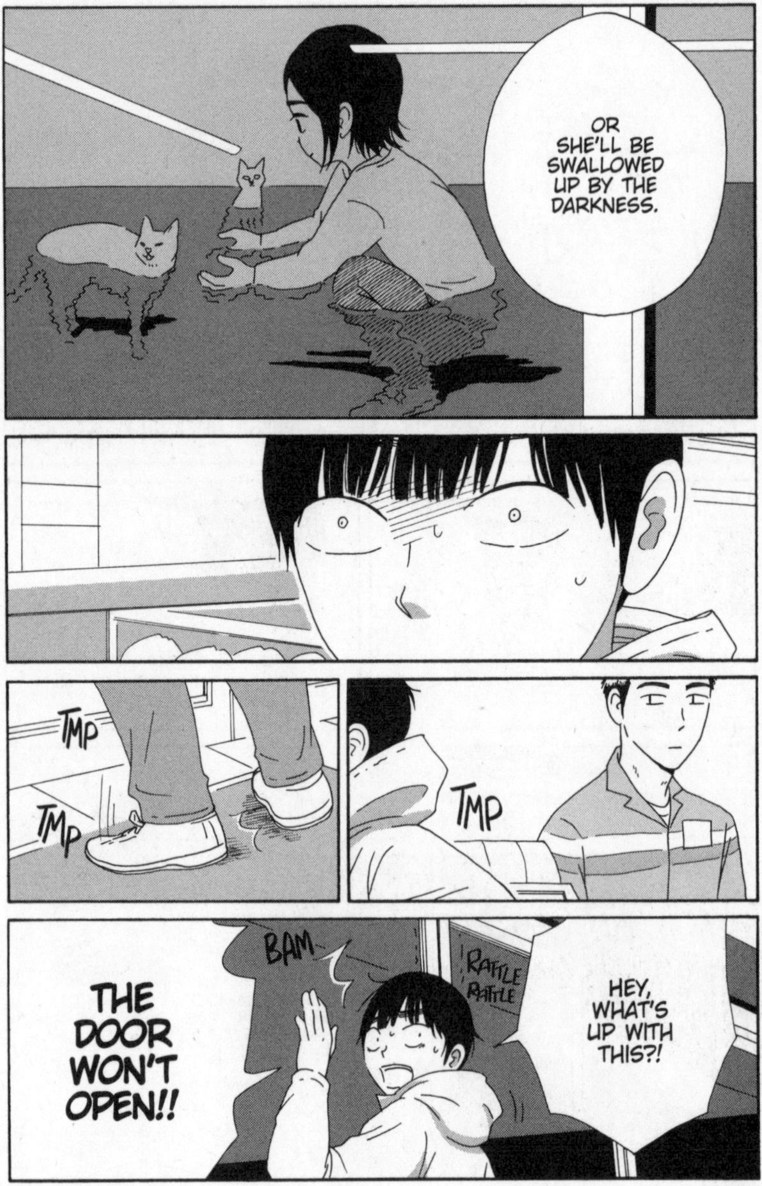
OR SHE'LL BE SWALLOWED UP BY THE DARKNESS.
TMP
TMP
TMP
HEY, WHAT'S UP WITH THIS?!
RATTLE RATTLE
BAM
THE DOOR WON'T OPEN!!

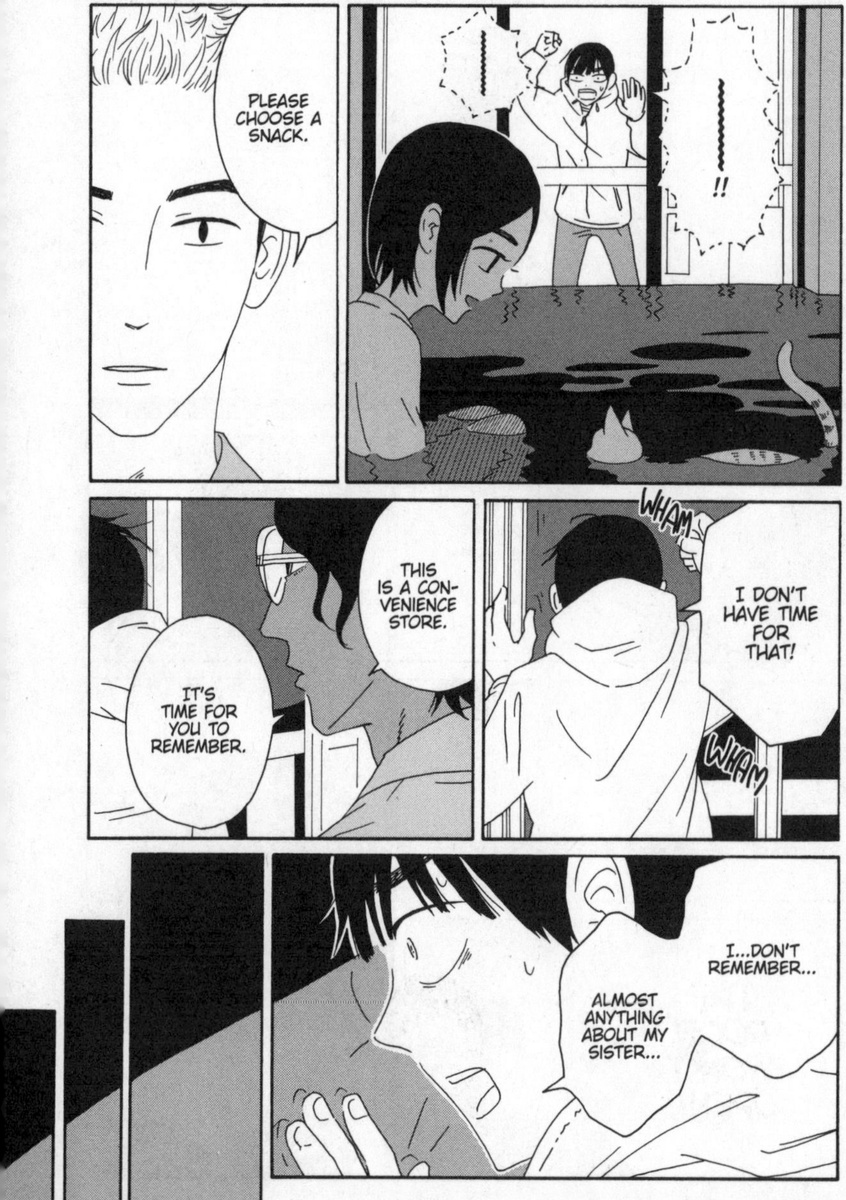
!!
PLEASE CHOOSE A SNACK.
WHAM
I DON'T HAVE TIME FOR THAT!
WHAM
THIS IS A CON-VENIENCE STORE.
IT'S TIME FOR YOU TO REMEMBER.
I...DON'T REMEMBER...
ALMOST ANYTHING ABOUT MY SISTER...

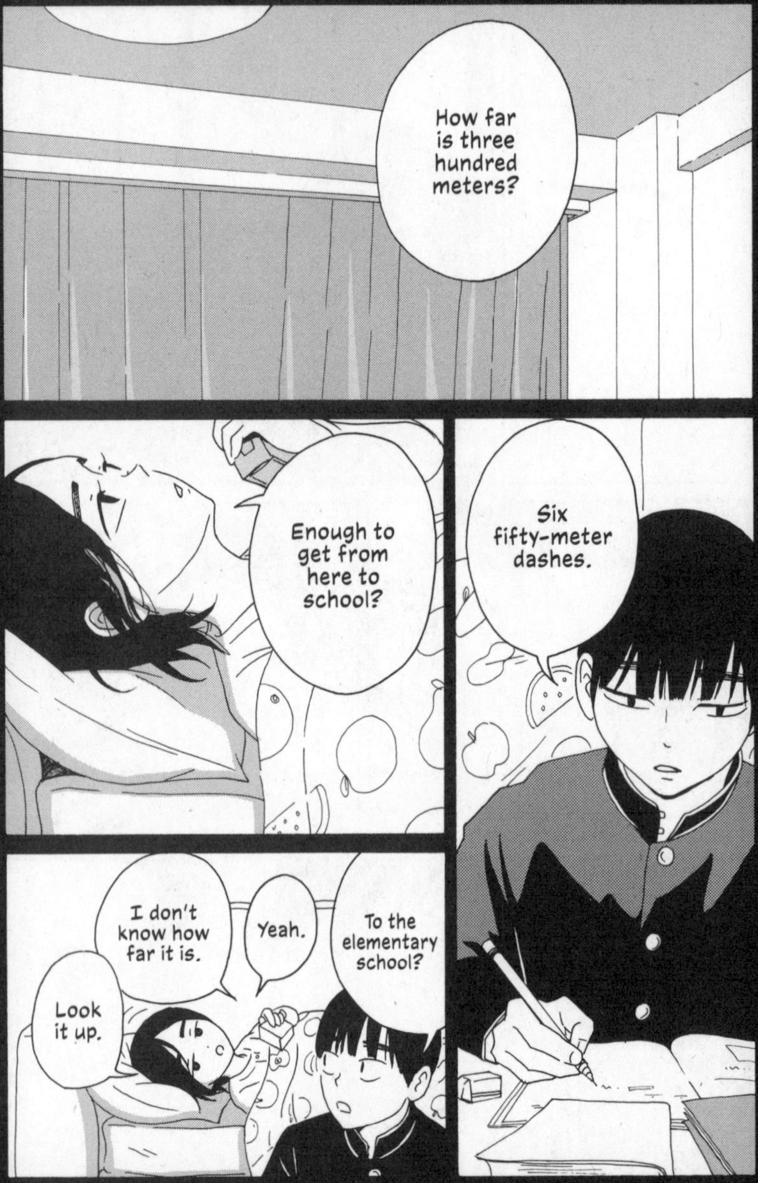
How far is three hundred meters?
Six fifty-meter dashes.
Enough to get from here to school?
To the elementary school?
Yeah.
I don't know how far it is.
Look it up.

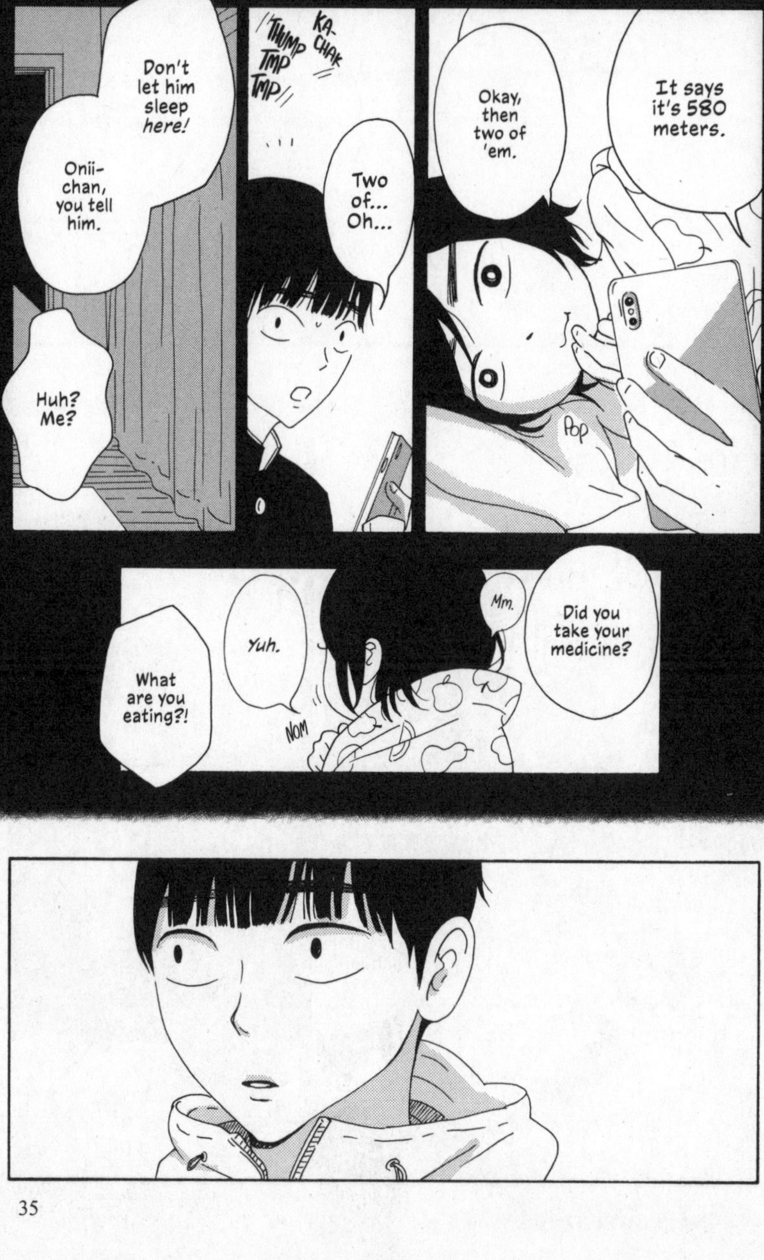
It says it's 580 meters.
Okay, then two of 'em.
POP
KA-CHAK
THUMP TMP TMP
Two of... Oh...
Don't let him sleep *here!*
Onii-chan, you tell him.
Huh? Me?
Did you take your medicine?
Mm.
Yuh.
NOM
What are you eating?!

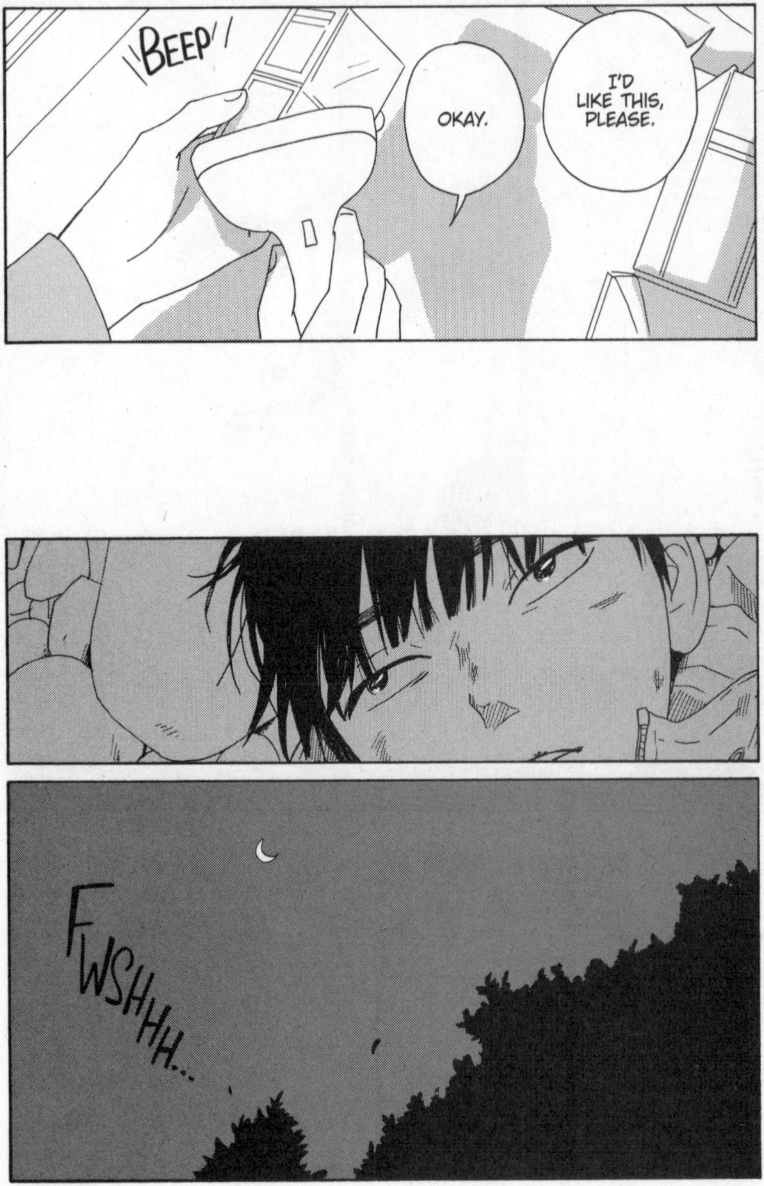
I'D LIKE THIS, PLEASE.
OKAY.
BEEP
FWSHHH...

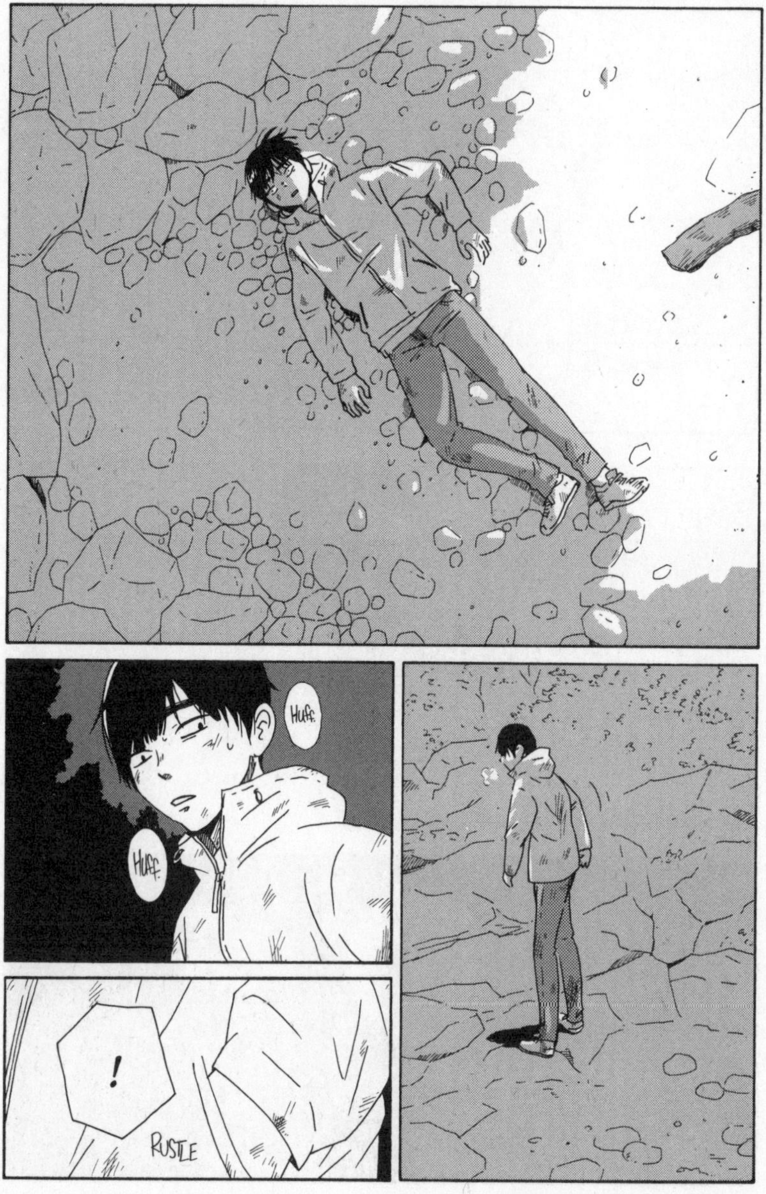
Huff.
Huff.
!
RUSTLE

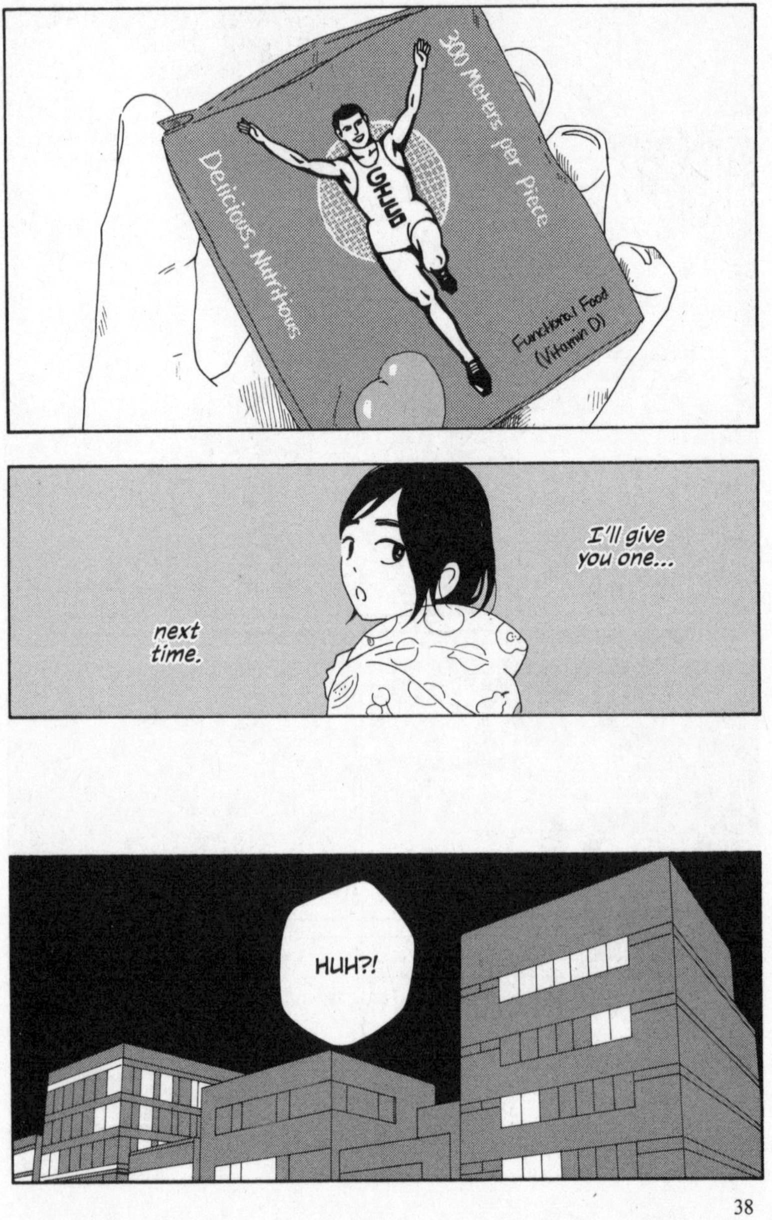
300 Meters per Piece
Delicious, Nutritious
Functional Food
(Vitamin D)
I'll give you one...
next time.
HUH?!

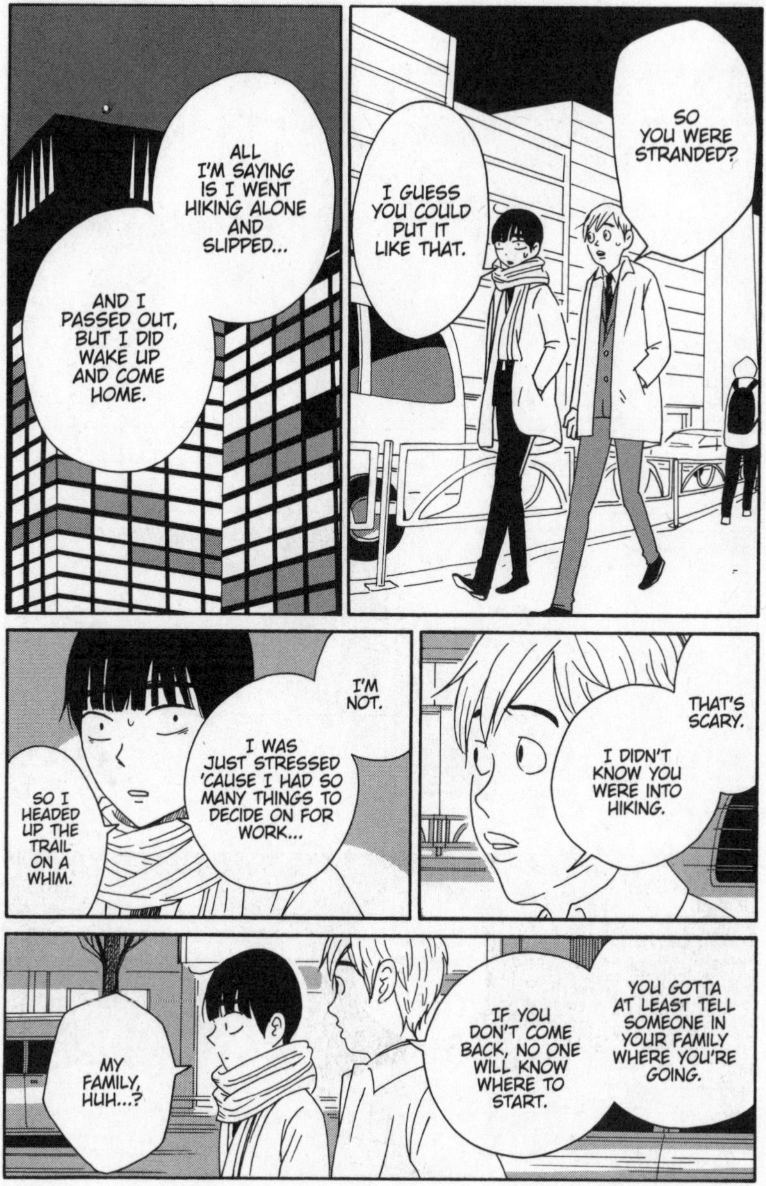
SO YOU WERE STRANDED?
I GUESS YOU COULD PUT IT LIKE THAT.
ALL I'M SAYING IS I WENT HIKING ALONE AND SLIPPED...
AND I PASSED OUT, BUT I DID WAKE UP AND COME HOME.
THAT'S SCARY.
I DIDN'T KNOW YOU WERE INTO HIKING.
I'M NOT.
I WAS JUST STRESSED 'CAUSE I HAD SO MANY THINGS TO DECIDE ON FOR WORK...
SO I HEADED UP THE TRAIL ON A WHIM.
YOU GOTTA AT LEAST TELL SOMEONE IN YOUR FAMILY WHERE YOU'RE GOING.
IF YOU DON'T COME BACK, NO ONE WILL KNOW WHERE TO START.
MY FAMILY, HUH...?

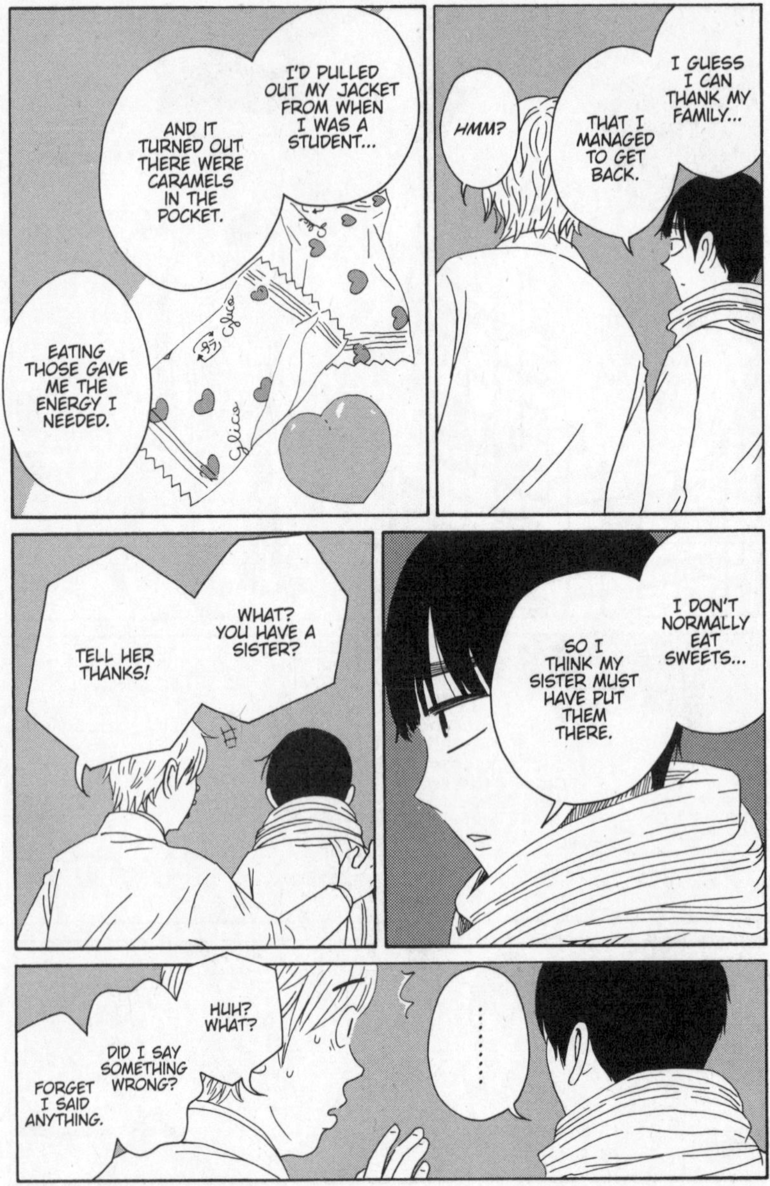
I GUESS I CAN THANK MY FAMILY...
THAT I MANAGED TO GET BACK.
HMM?
I'D PULLED OUT MY JACKET FROM WHEN I WAS A STUDENT...
AND IT TURNED OUT THERE WERE CARAMELS IN THE POCKET.
EATING THOSE GAVE ME THE ENERGY I NEEDED.
I DON'T NORMALLY EAT SWEETS...
SO I THINK MY SISTER MUST HAVE PUT THEM THERE.
WHAT? YOU HAVE A SISTER?
TELL HER THANKS!
......
HUH? WHAT?
DID I SAY SOMETHING WRONG?
FORGET I SAID ANYTHING.

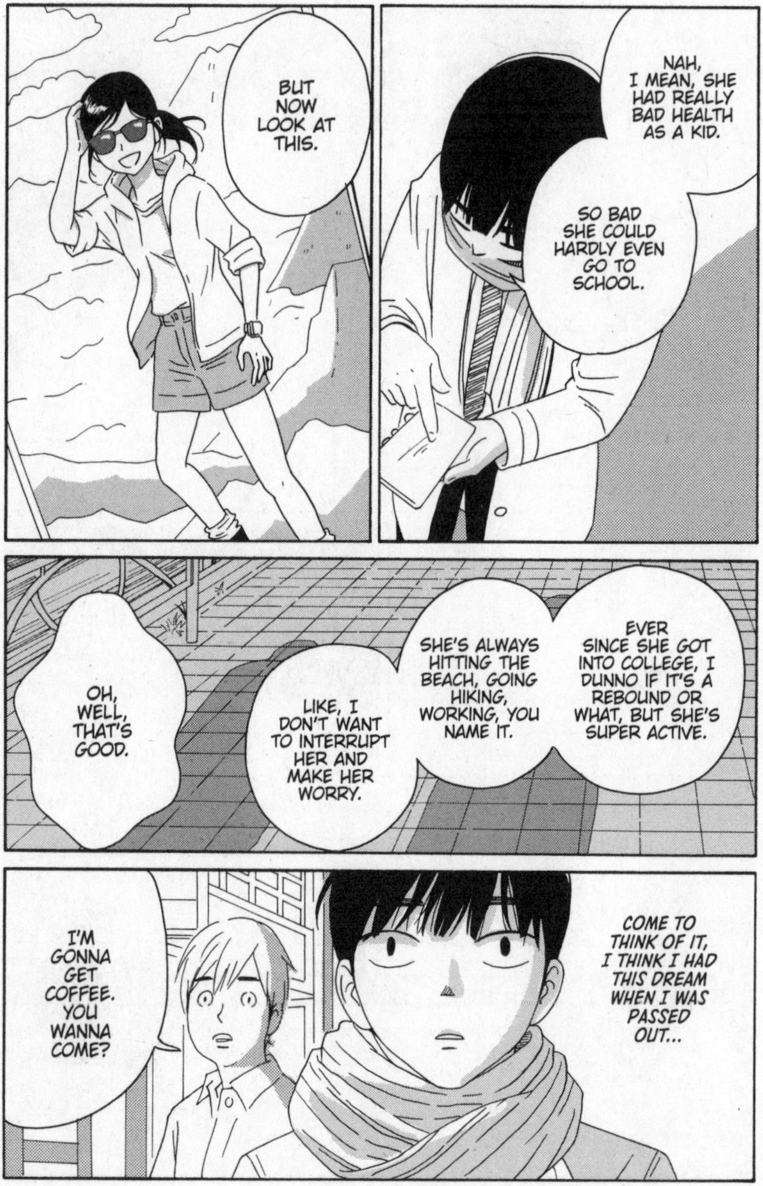
NAH, I MEAN, SHE HAD REALLY BAD HEALTH AS A KID.
SO BAD SHE COULD HARDLY EVEN GO TO SCHOOL.
BUT NOW LOOK AT THIS.
EVER SINCE SHE GOT INTO COLLEGE, I DUNNO IF IT'S A REBOUND OR WHAT, BUT SHE'S SUPER ACTIVE.
SHE'S ALWAYS HITTING THE BEACH, GOING HIKING, WORKING, YOU NAME IT.
LIKE, I DON'T WANT TO INTERRUPT HER AND MAKE HER WORRY.
OH, WELL, THAT'S GOOD.
COME TO THINK OF IT, I THINK I HAD THIS DREAM WHEN I WAS PASSED OUT...
I'M GONNA GET COFFEE. YOU WANNA COME?

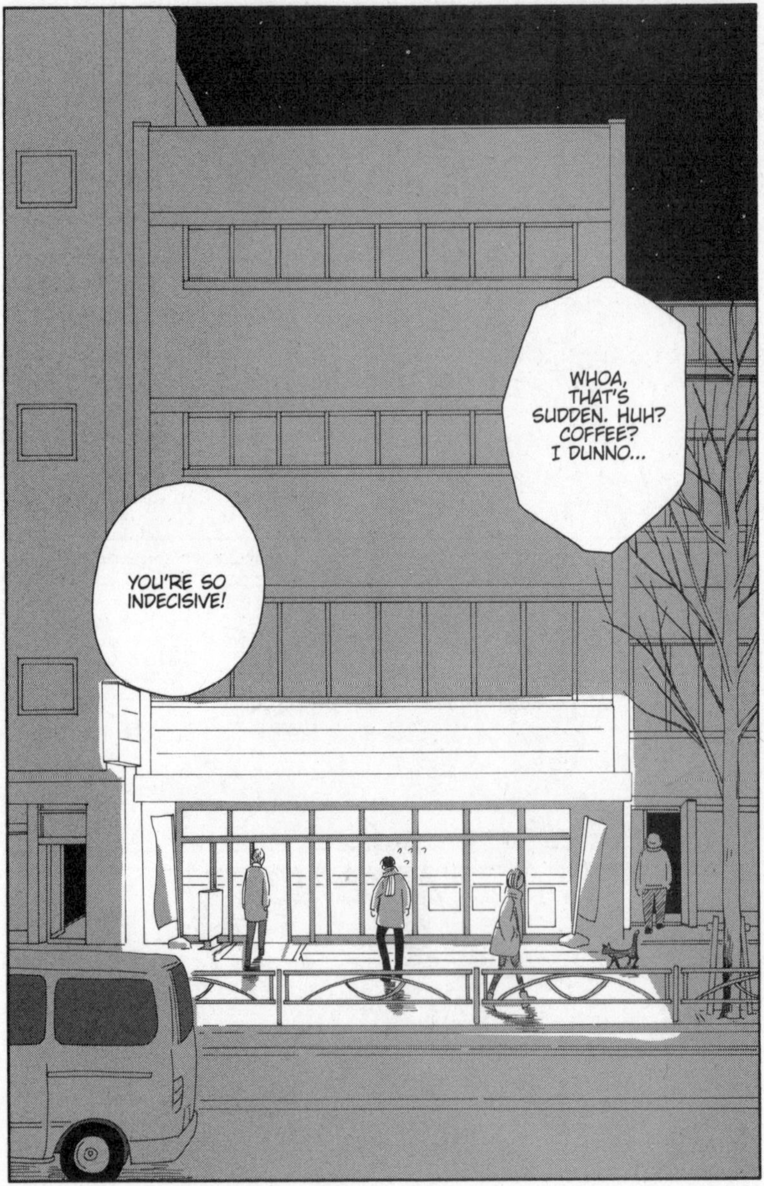
WHOA, THAT'S SUDDEN. HUH? COFFEE? I DUNNO...
YOU'RE SO INDECISIVE!

Episode 3
Three-Shift Kokura

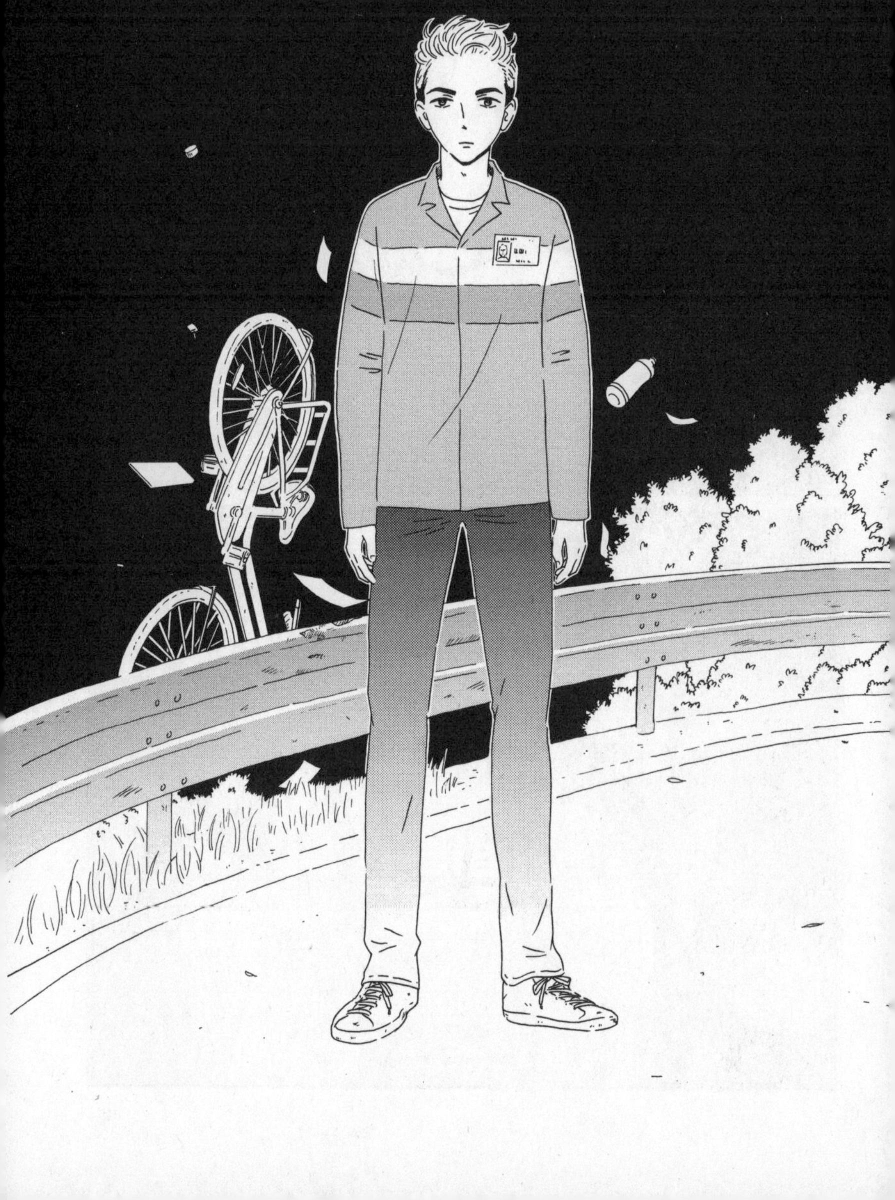

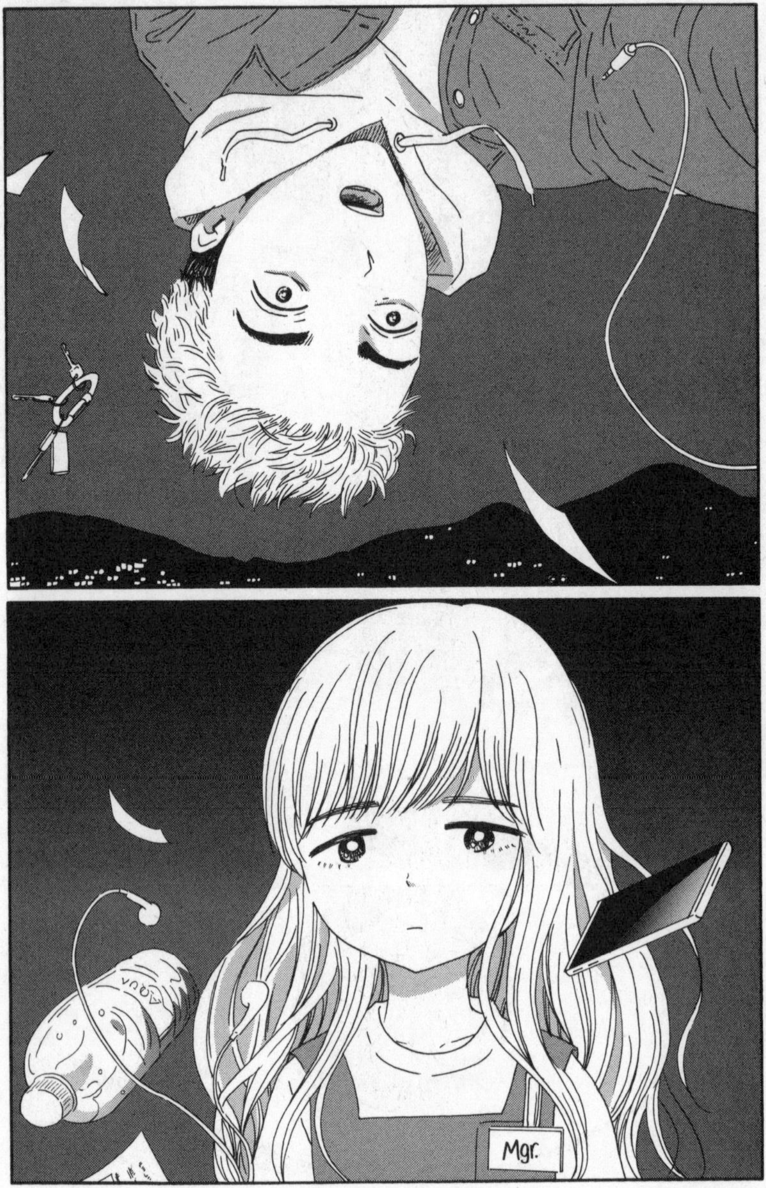
AQUA
Mgr.

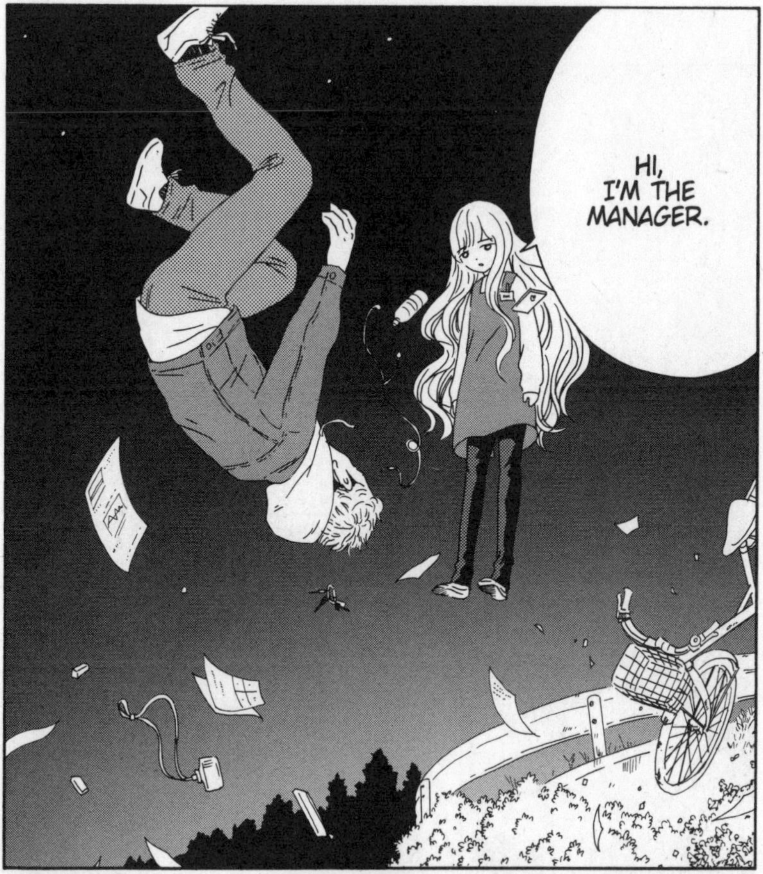
HI, I'M THE MANAGER.
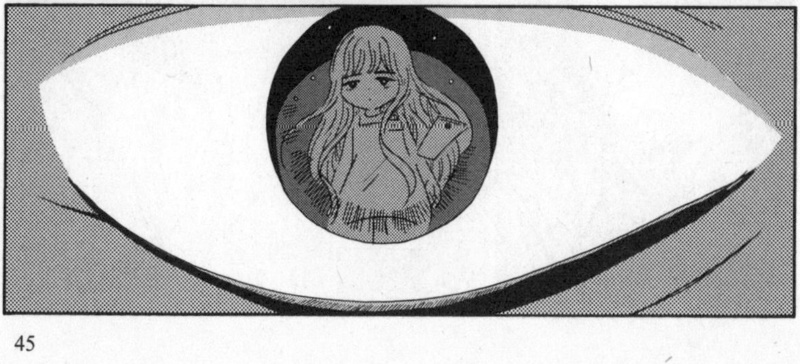

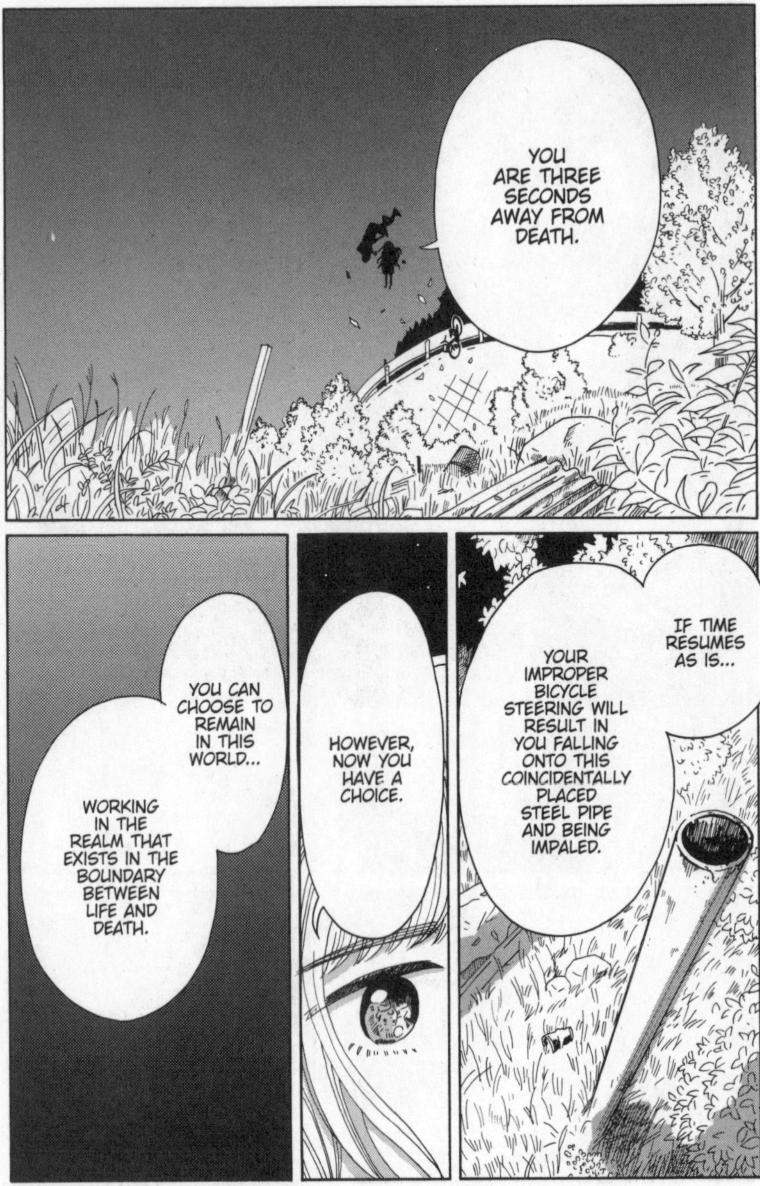
YOU ARE THREE SECONDS AWAY FROM DEATH.
IF TIME RESUMES AS IS...
YOUR IMPROPER BICYCLE STEERING WILL RESULT IN YOU FALLING ONTO THIS COINCIDENTALLY PLACED STEEL PIPE AND BEING IMPALED.
HOWEVER, NOW YOU HAVE A CHOICE.
YOU CAN CHOOSE TO REMAIN IN THIS WORLD...
WORKING IN THE REALM THAT EXISTS IN THE BOUNDARY BETWEEN LIFE AND DEATH.

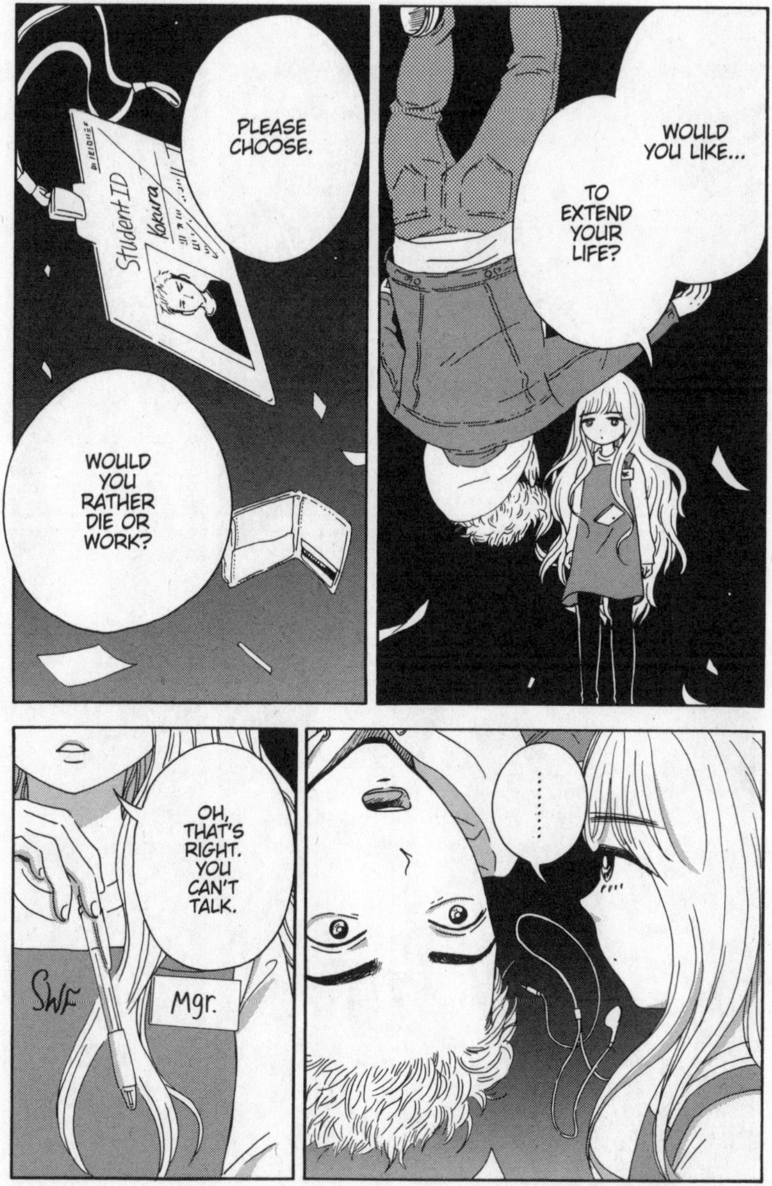
WOULD YOU LIKE...
TO EXTEND YOUR LIFE?
PLEASE CHOOSE.
Student ID
Kokura
WOULD YOU RATHER DIE OR WORK?
......
OH, THAT'S RIGHT. YOU CAN'T TALK.
SWF
Mgr.

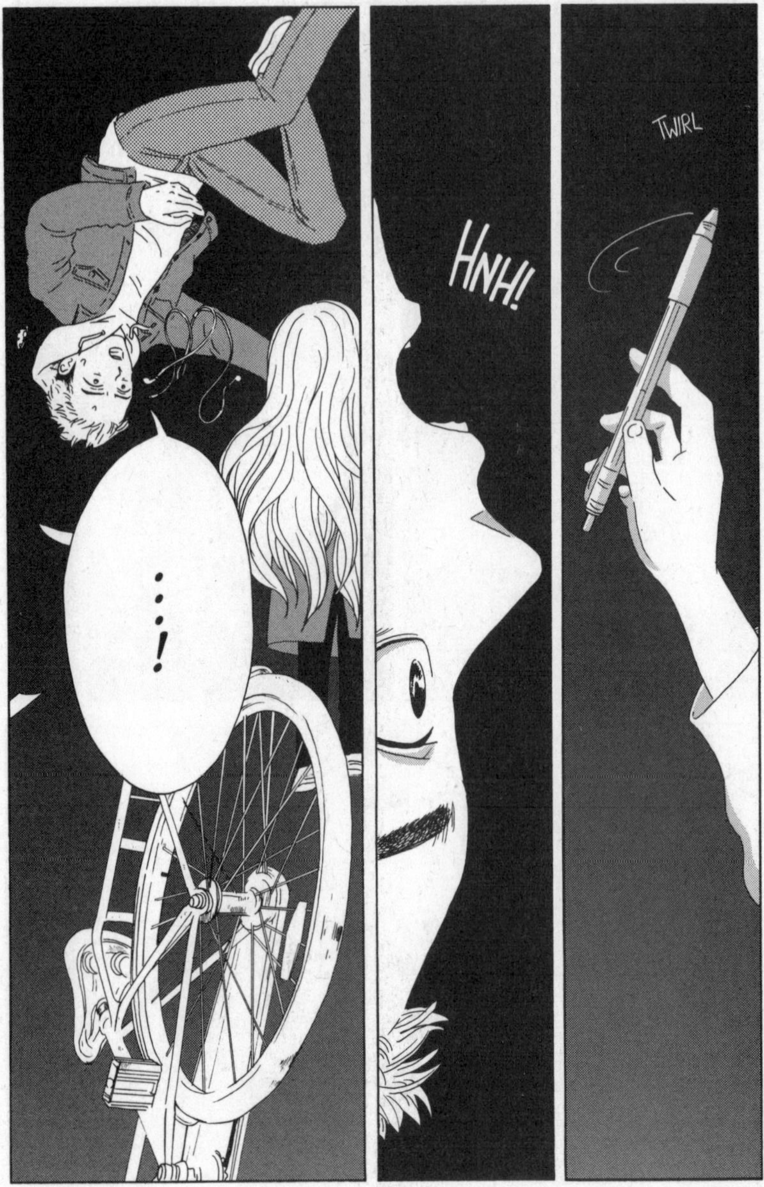
TWIRL
HNH!
...!

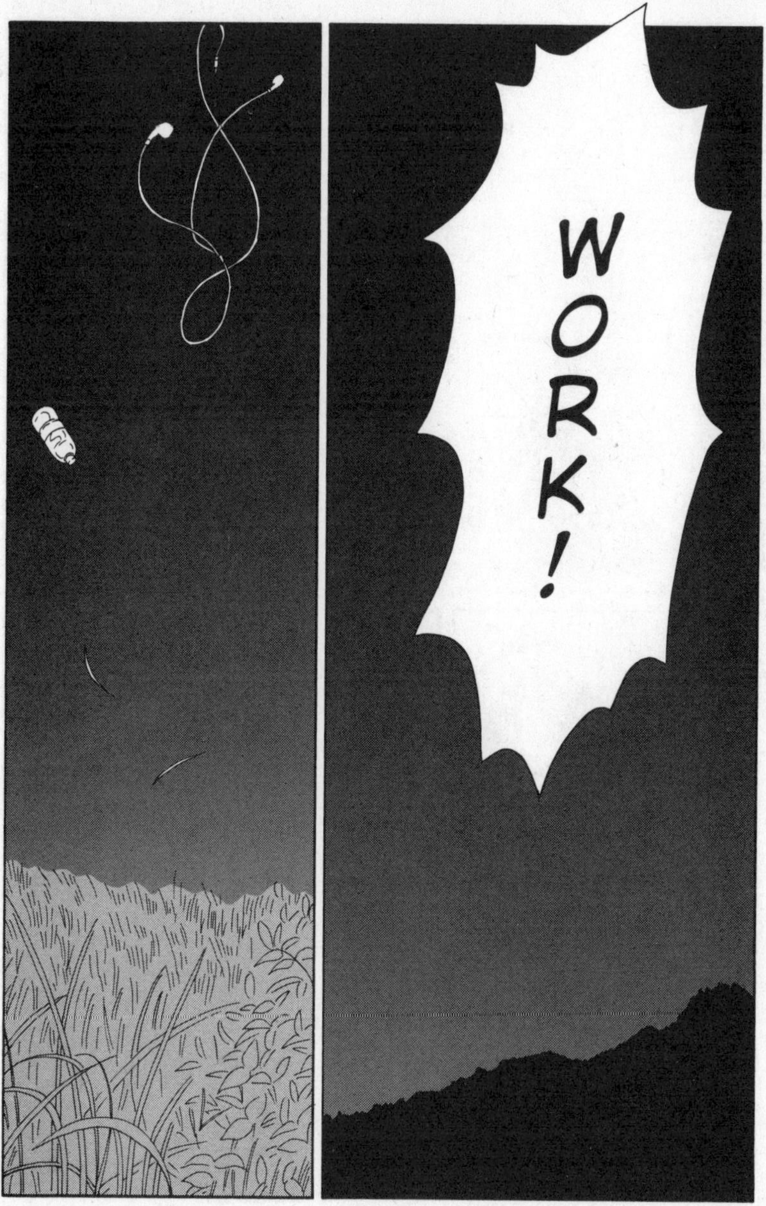
WORK!

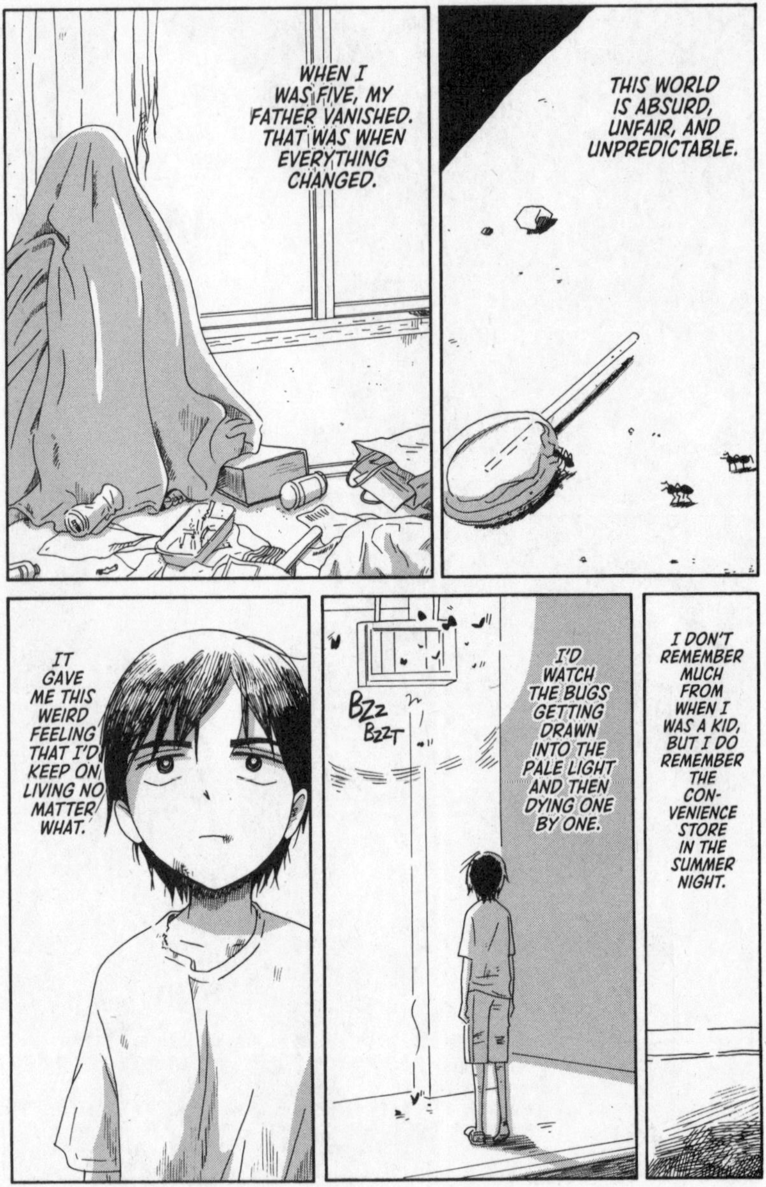
THIS WORLD IS ABSURD, UNFAIR, AND UNPREDICTABLE.
WHEN I WAS FIVE, MY FATHER VANISHED. THAT WAS WHEN EVERYTHING CHANGED.
I DON'T REMEMBER MUCH FROM WHEN I WAS A KID, BUT I DO REMEMBER THE CON-VENIENCE STORE IN THE SUMMER NIGHT.
I'D WATCH THE BUGS GETTING DRAWN INTO THE PALE LIGHT AND THEN DYING ONE BY ONE.
BZZ BZZT
IT GAVE ME THIS WEIRD FEELING THAT I'D KEEP ON LIVING NO MATTER WHAT.

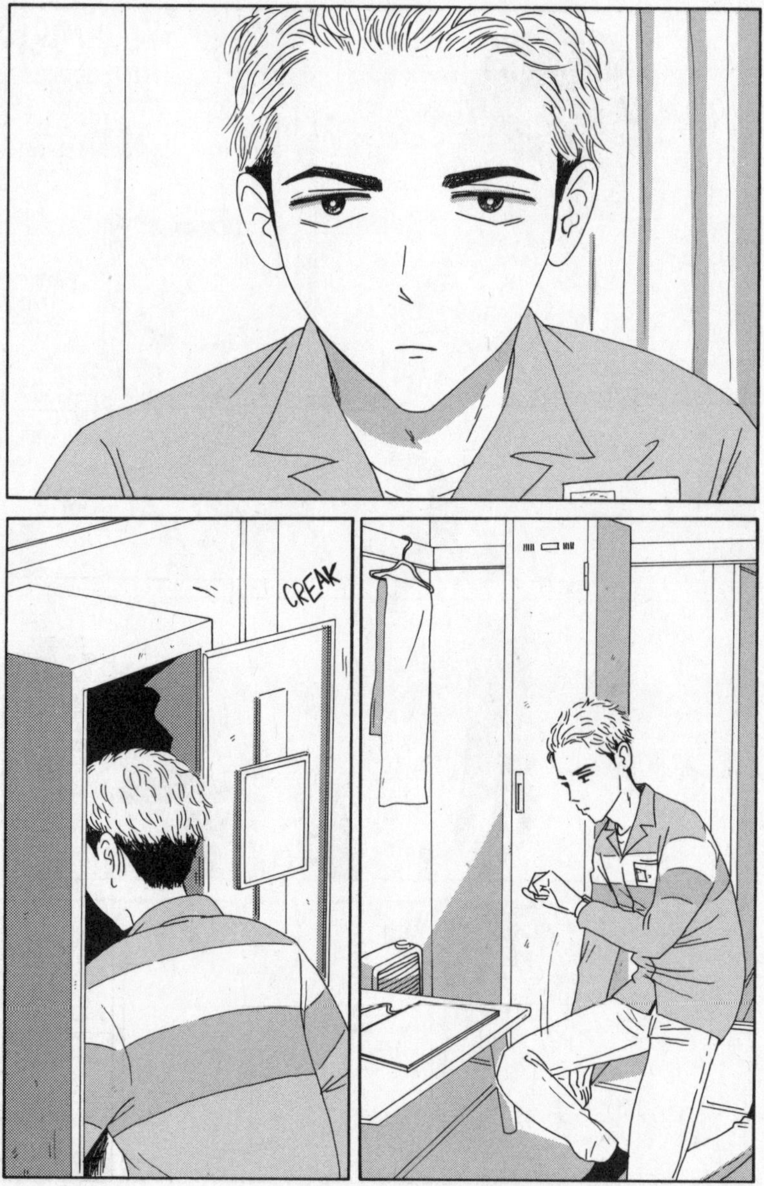
CREAK

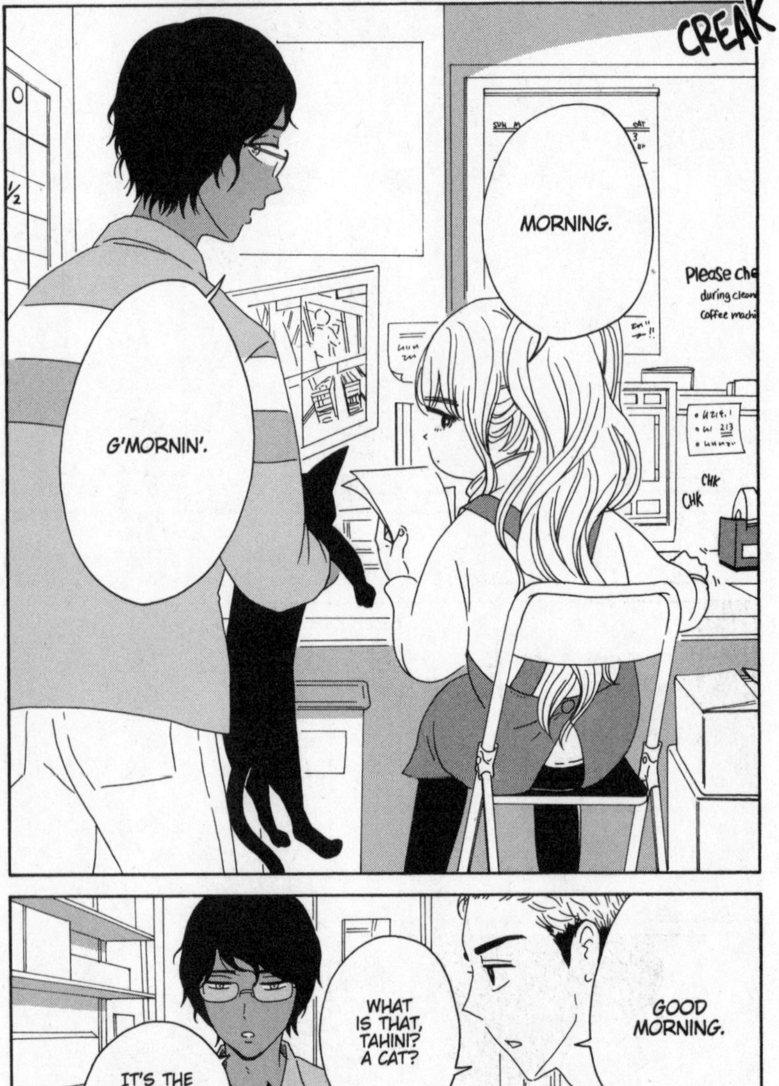
CREAK
MORNING.
CHK CHK
G'MORNIN'.
GOOD MORNING.
WHAT IS THAT, TAHINI? A CAT?
IT'S THE DARKNESS I CAUGHT THE OTHER DAY.

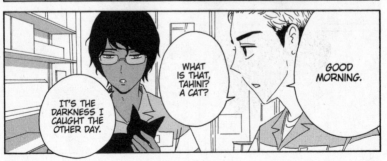

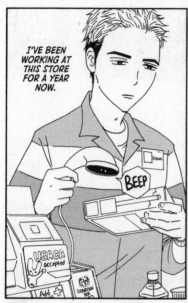

I'VE BEEN WORKING AT THIS STORE FOR A YEAR NOW.
Kokura
BEEP
USACA accepted
DONATION BOX
WHEN I STARTED, I WAS TERRIFIED THAT IT MIGHT BE SOME REALLY SCREWED UP KIND OF JOB...
oden
WELCOME.
BUT ACTUALLY IT'S JUST A NORMAL CONVENIENCE STORE, ASIDE FROM ONE OR TWO FUNNY THINGS.
Would you like chop-sticks?
Kokura
ONE IS THAT THE MANAGER AND THE NEW GUY, TAHINI, AREN'T HUMAN.
Thank you.

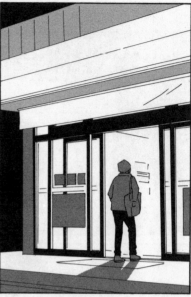

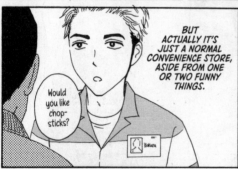

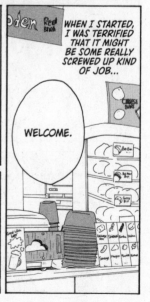

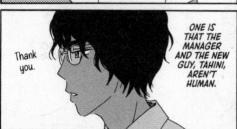

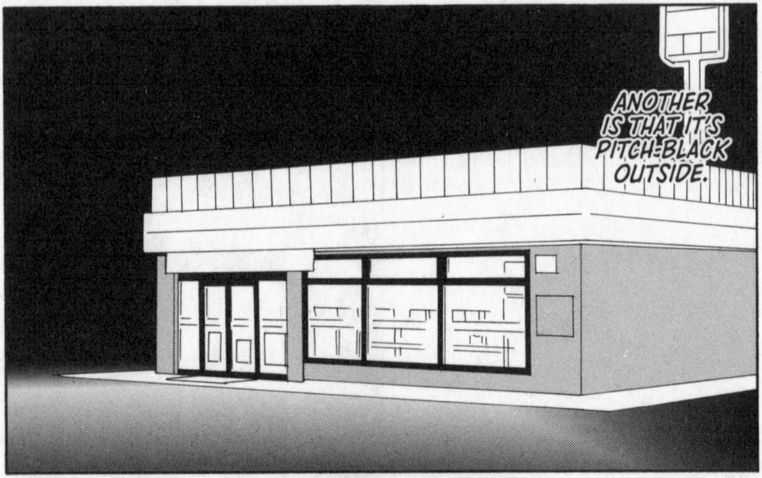
ANOTHER IS THAT IT'S PITCH-BLACK OUTSIDE.
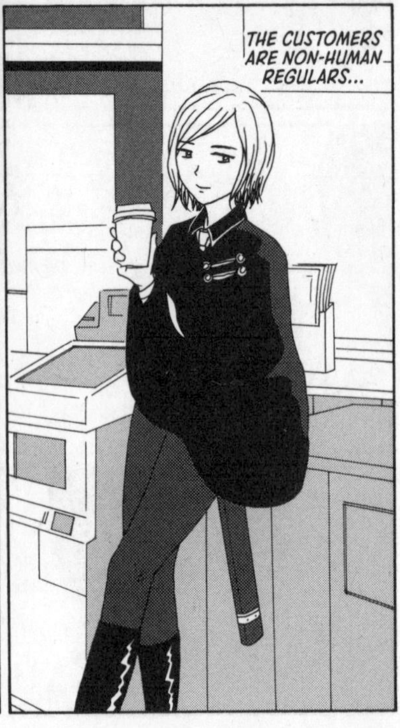
THE CUSTOMERS ARE NON-HUMAN REGULARS...
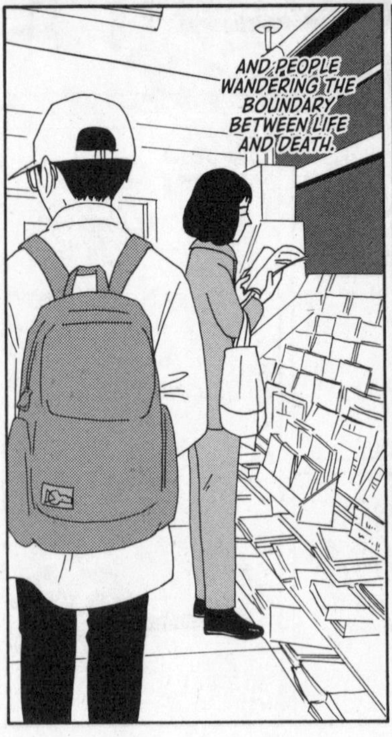
AND PEOPLE WANDERING THE BOUNDARY BETWEEN LIFE AND DEATH.

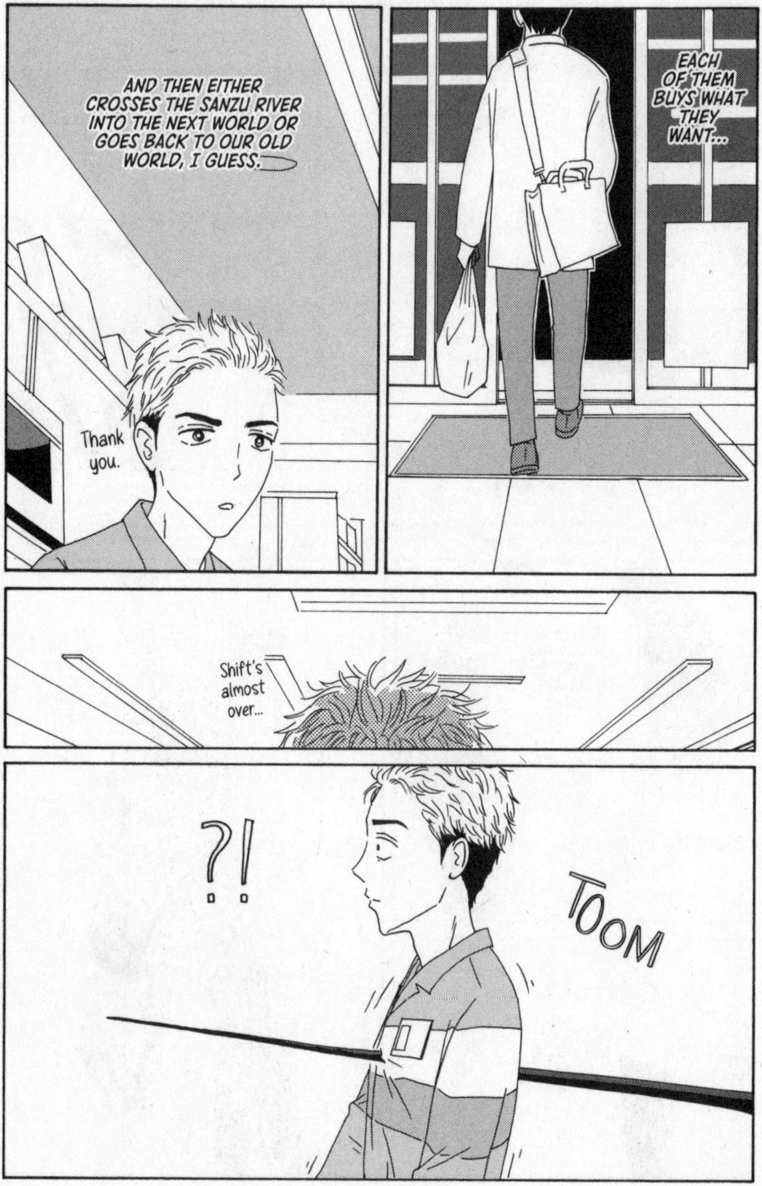
EACH OF THEM BUYS WHAT THEY WANT...
AND THEN EITHER CROSSES THE SANZU RIVER INTO THE NEXT WORLD OR GOES BACK TO OUR OLD WORLD, I GUESS.
Thank you.
Shift's almost over...
?!
TOOM

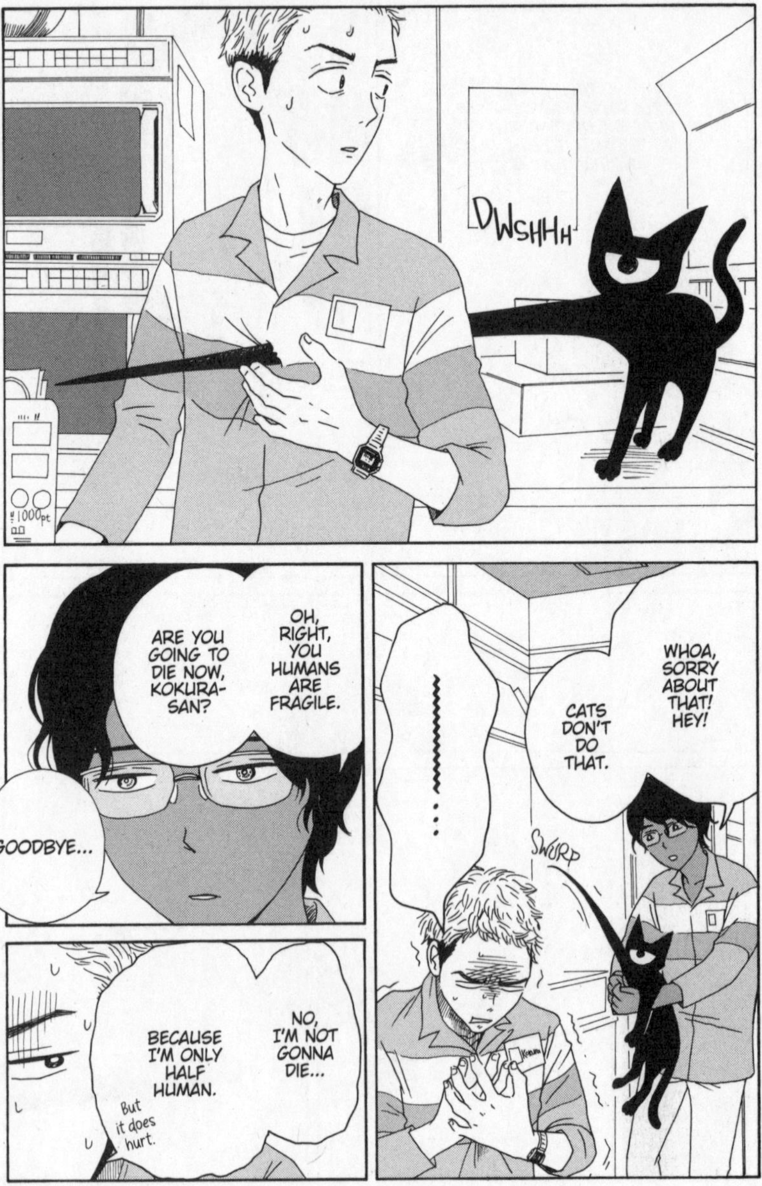
DWSHHH
WHOA, SORRY ABOUT THAT! HEY!
CATS DON'T DO THAT.
......
SWURP
OH, RIGHT, YOU HUMANS ARE FRAGILE.
ARE YOU GOING TO DIE NOW, KOKURA-SAN?
GOODBYE...
NO, I'M NOT GONNA DIE...
BECAUSE I'M ONLY HALF HUMAN.
But it does hurt.

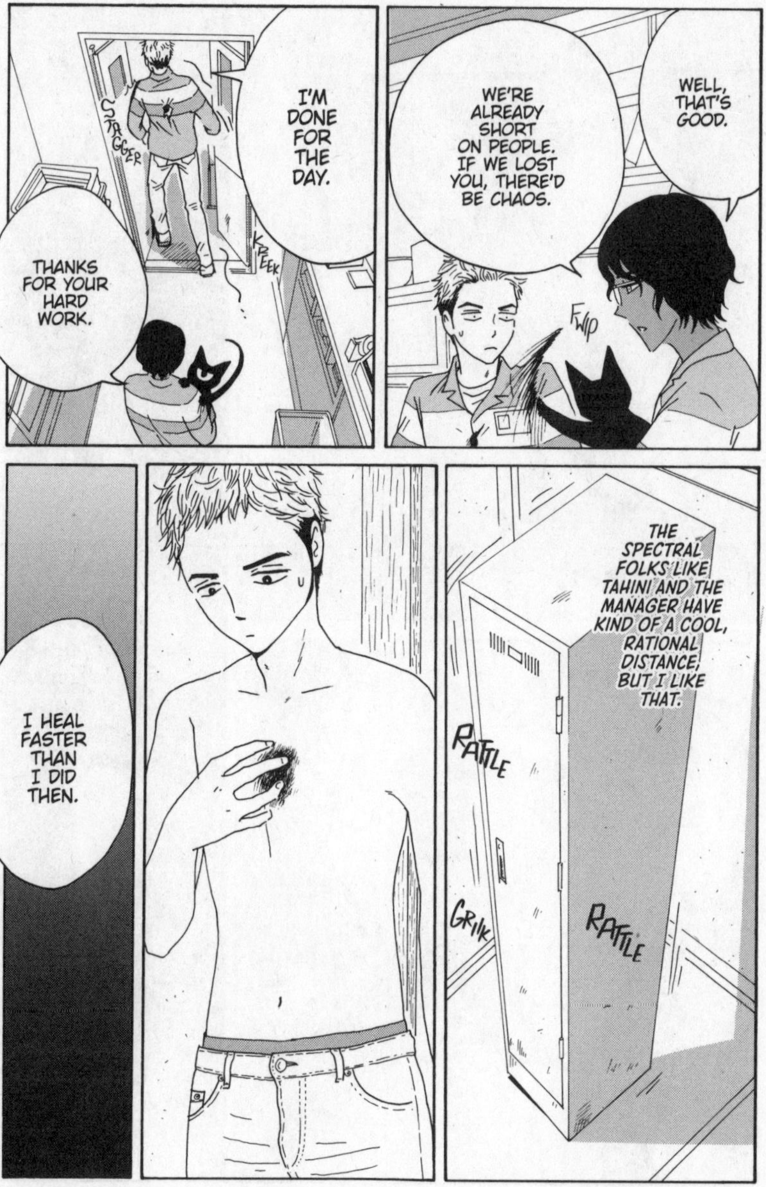
WELL, THAT'S GOOD.
WE'RE ALREADY SHORT ON PEOPLE. IF WE LOST YOU, THERE'D BE CHAOS.
FWIP
I'M DONE FOR THE DAY.
STAGGER
KREEEK
THANKS FOR YOUR HARD WORK.
THE SPECTRAL FOLKS LIKE TAHINI AND THE MANAGER HAVE KIND OF A COOL, RATIONAL DISTANCE, BUT I LIKE THAT.
RATTLE
GRIK
RATTLE
I HEAL FASTER THAN I DID THEN.

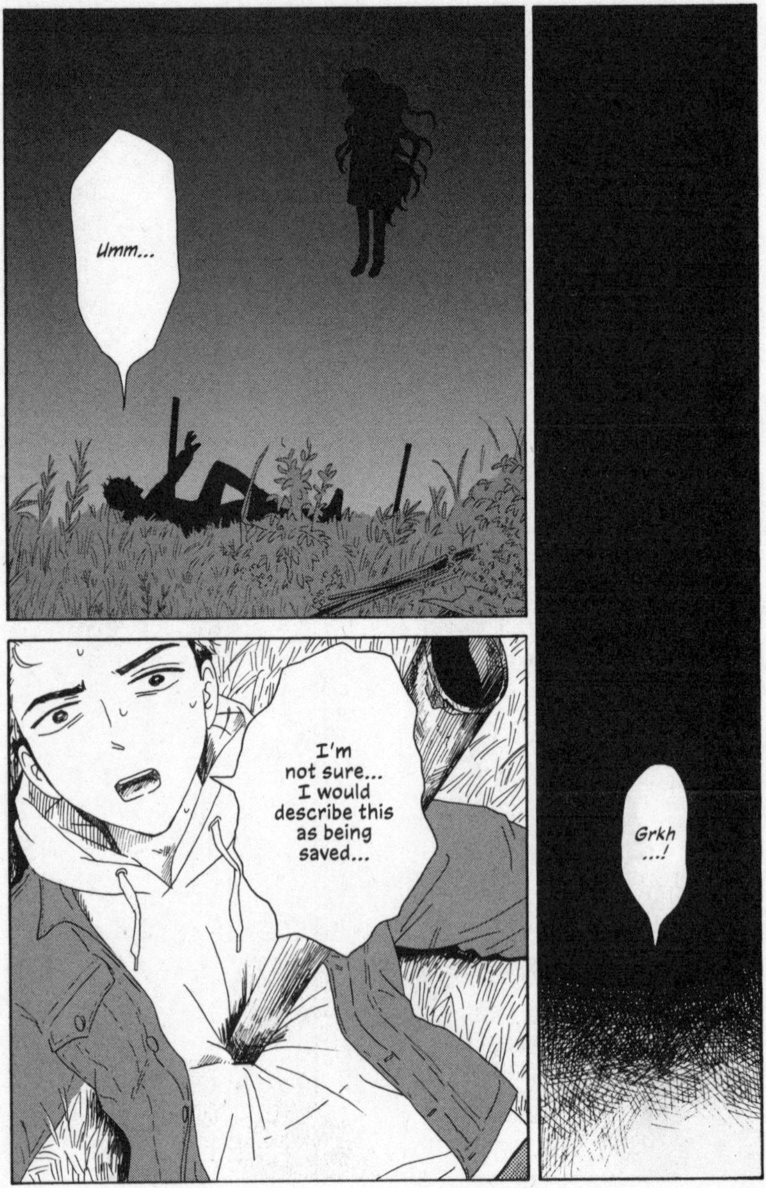
Grkh ...!
Umm...
I'm not sure... I would describe this as being saved...

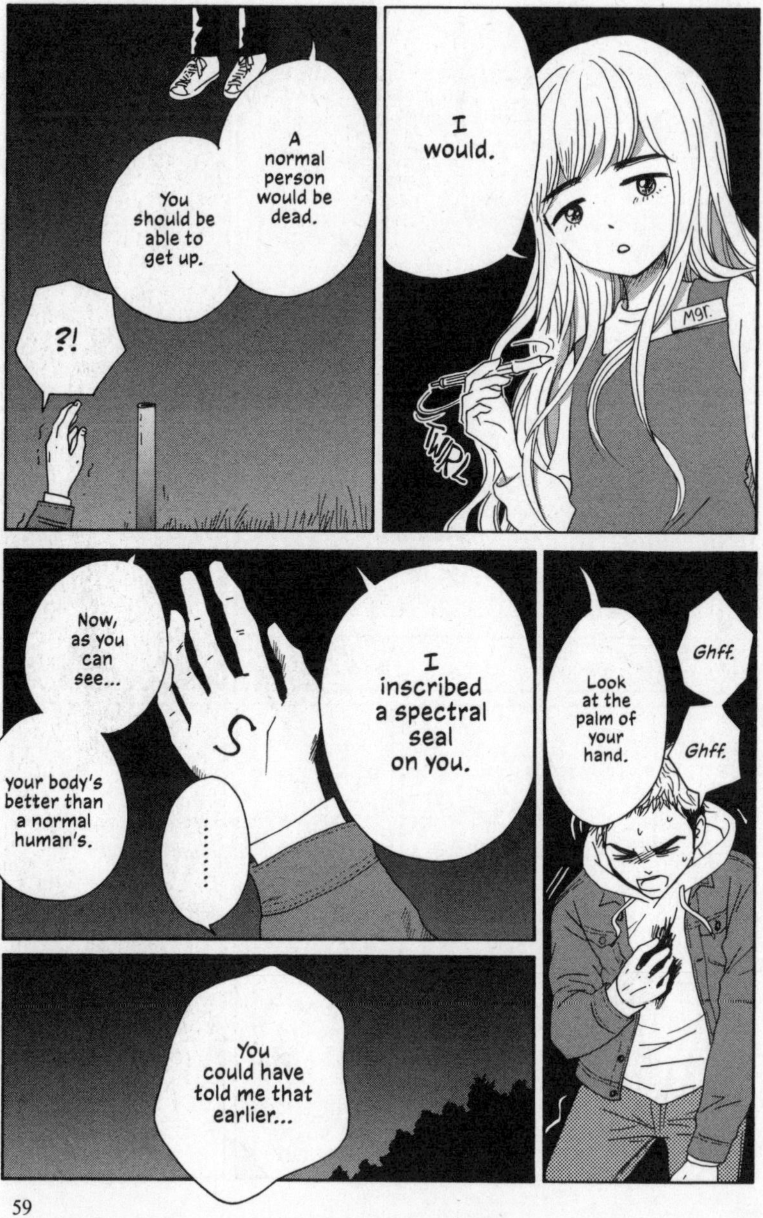

I would.
Mgr.
TWIRL
A normal person would be dead.
You should be able to get up.
?!
Ghff.
Ghff.
Look at the palm of your hand.
I inscribed a spectral seal on you.
Now, as you can see...
your body's better than a normal human's.
....
You could have told me that earlier...

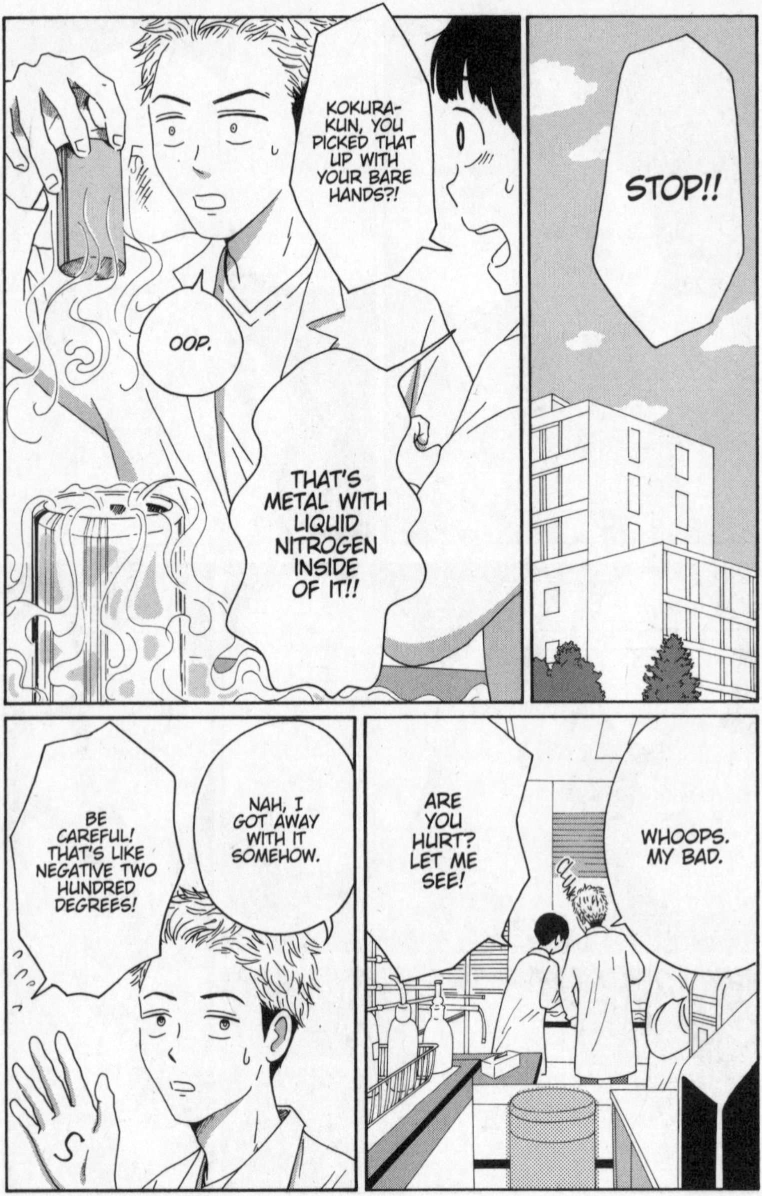
STOP!!
KOKURA-KUN, YOU PICKED THAT UP WITH YOUR BARE HANDS?!
OOP.
THAT'S METAL WITH LIQUID NITROGEN INSIDE OF IT!!
WHOOPS. MY BAD.
ARE YOU HURT? LET ME SEE!
NAH, I GOT AWAY WITH IT SOMEHOW.
BE CAREFUL! THAT'S LIKE NEGATIVE TWO HUNDRED DEGREES!

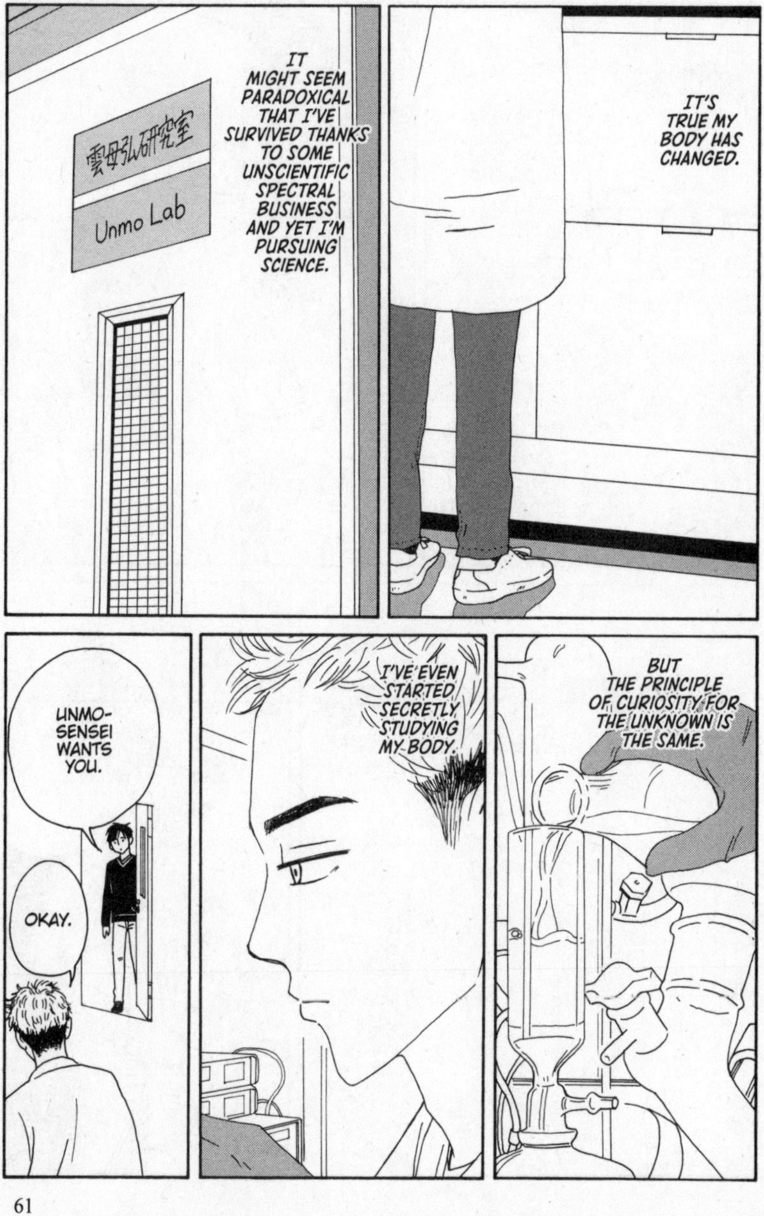
IT'S TRUE MY BODY HAS CHANGED.
IT MIGHT SEEM PARADOXICAL THAT I'VE SURVIVED THANKS TO SOME UNSCIENTIFIC SPECTRAL BUSINESS AND YET I'M PURSUING SCIENCE.
雲母弘研究室
Unmo Lab
BUT THE PRINCIPLE OF CURIOSITY FOR THE UNKNOWN IS THE SAME.
I'VE EVEN STARTED SECRETLY STUDYING MY BODY.
UNMO-SENSEI WANTS YOU.
OKAY.

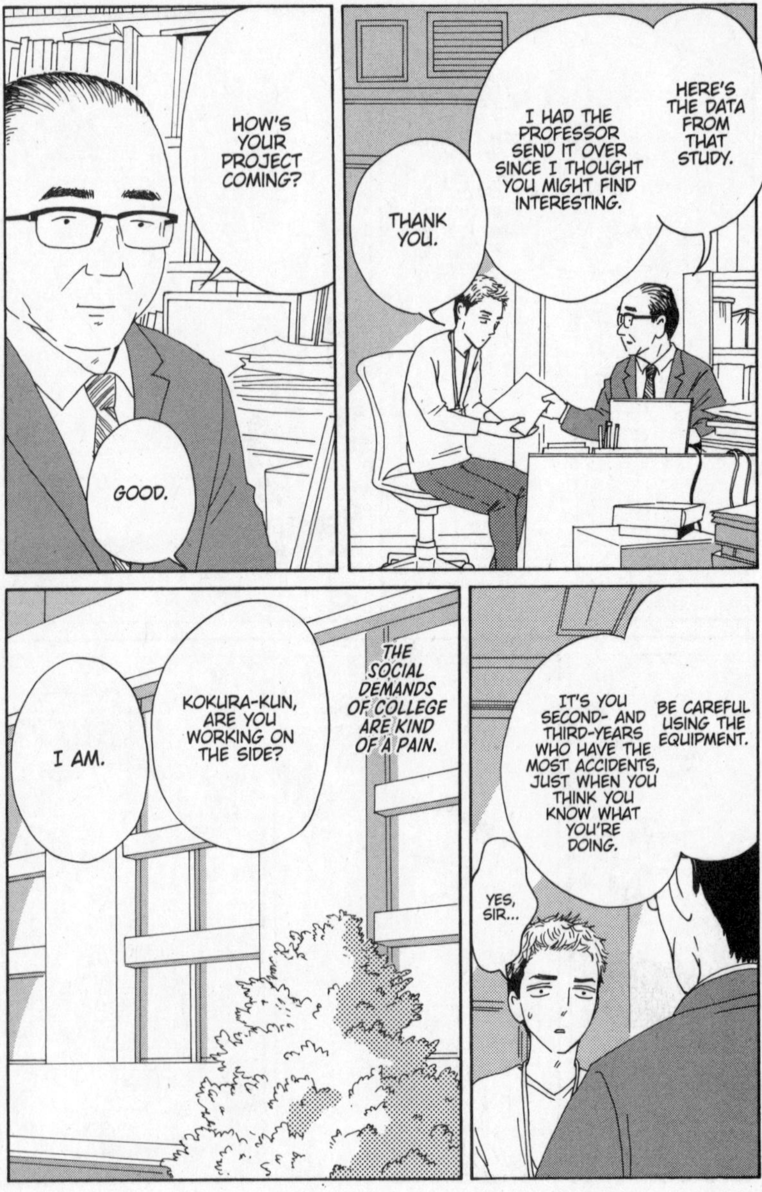
HERE'S THE DATA FROM THAT STUDY.
I HAD THE PROFESSOR SEND IT OVER SINCE I THOUGHT YOU MIGHT FIND INTERESTING.
THANK YOU.
HOW'S YOUR PROJECT COMING?
GOOD.
BE CAREFUL USING THE EQUIPMENT.
IT'S YOU SECOND- AND THIRD-YEARS WHO HAVE THE MOST ACCIDENTS, JUST WHEN YOU THINK YOU KNOW WHAT YOU'RE DOING.
YES, SIR...
THE SOCIAL DEMANDS OF COLLEGE ARE KIND OF A PAIN.
KOKURA-KUN, ARE YOU WORKING ON THE SIDE?
I AM.

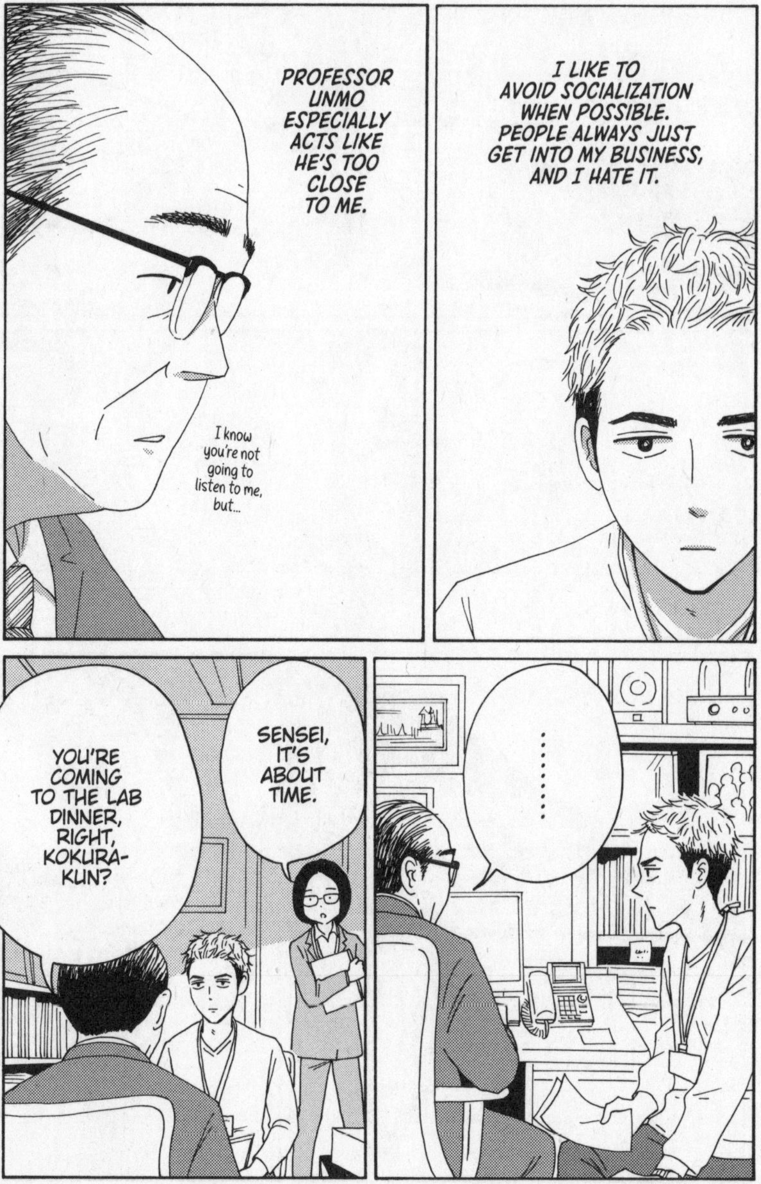
I LIKE TO AVOID SOCIALIZATION WHEN POSSIBLE. PEOPLE ALWAYS JUST GET INTO MY BUSINESS, AND I HATE IT.
PROFESSOR UNMO ESPECIALLY ACTS LIKE HE'S TOO CLOSE TO ME.
I know you're not going to listen to me, but...
......
SENSEI, IT'S ABOUT TIME.
YOU'RE COMING TO THE LAB DINNER, RIGHT, KOKURA-KUN?

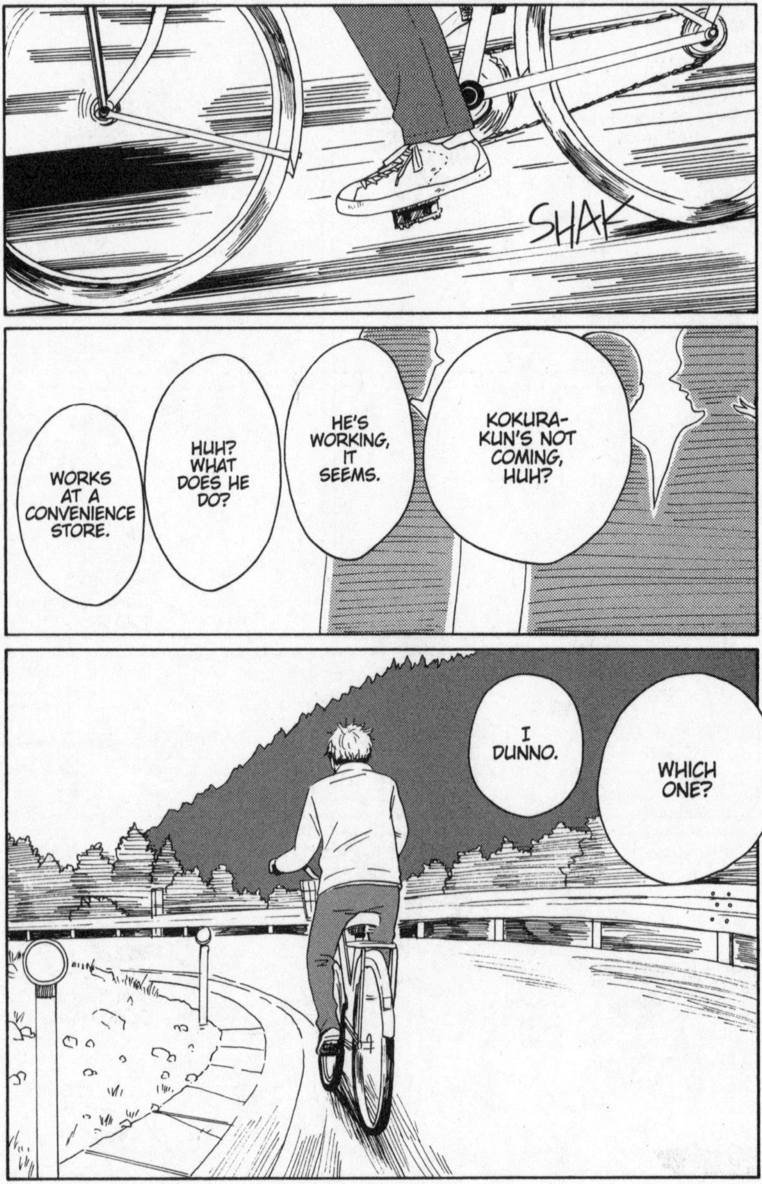
SHAK
KOKURA-KUN'S NOT COMING, HUH?
HE'S WORKING, IT SEEMS.
HUH? WHAT DOES HE DO?
WORKS AT A CONVENIENCE STORE.
WHICH ONE?
I DUNNO.

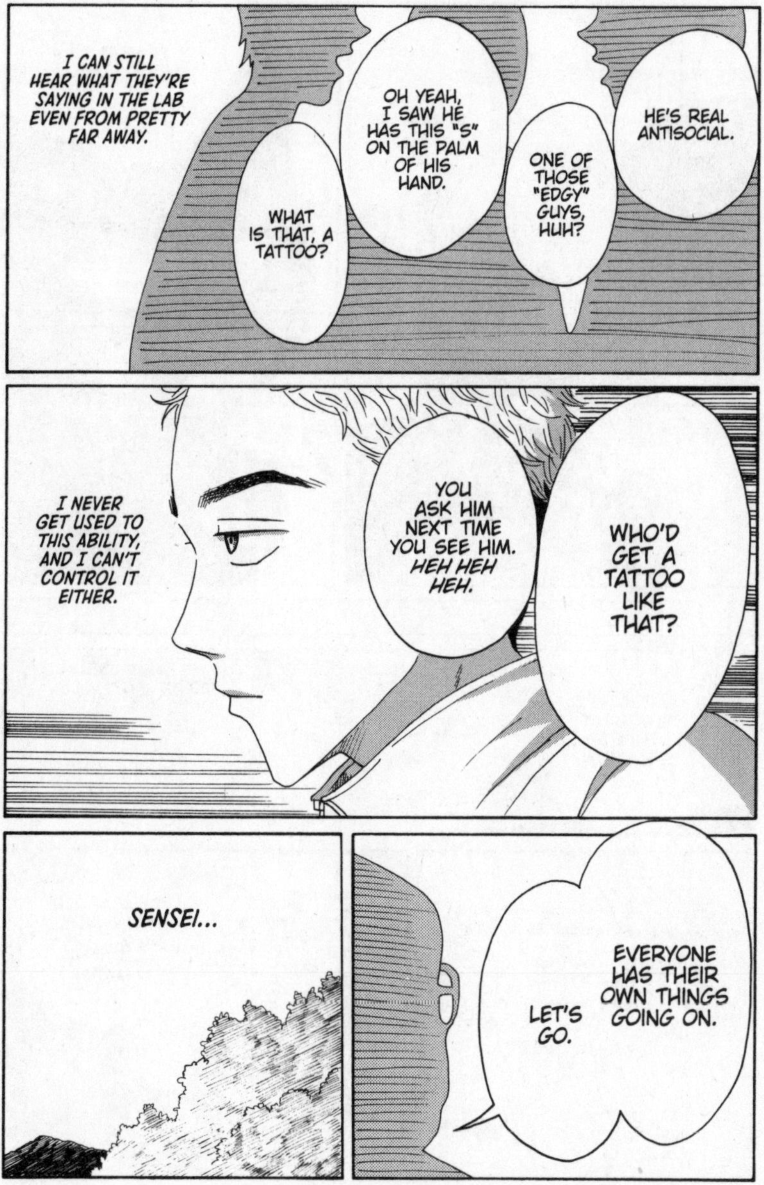
HE'S REAL ANTISOCIAL.
ONE OF THOSE "EDGY" GUYS, HUH?
OH YEAH, I SAW HE HAS THIS "S" ON THE PALM OF HIS HAND.
WHAT IS THAT, A TATTOO?
I CAN STILL HEAR WHAT THEY'RE SAYING IN THE LAB EVEN FROM PRETTY FAR AWAY.
WHO'D GET A TATTOO LIKE THAT?
YOU ASK HIM NEXT TIME YOU SEE HIM. *HEH HEH HEH.*
I NEVER GET USED TO THIS ABILITY, AND I CAN'T CONTROL IT EITHER.
EVERYONE HAS THEIR OWN THINGS GOING ON.
LET'S GO.
SENSEI...

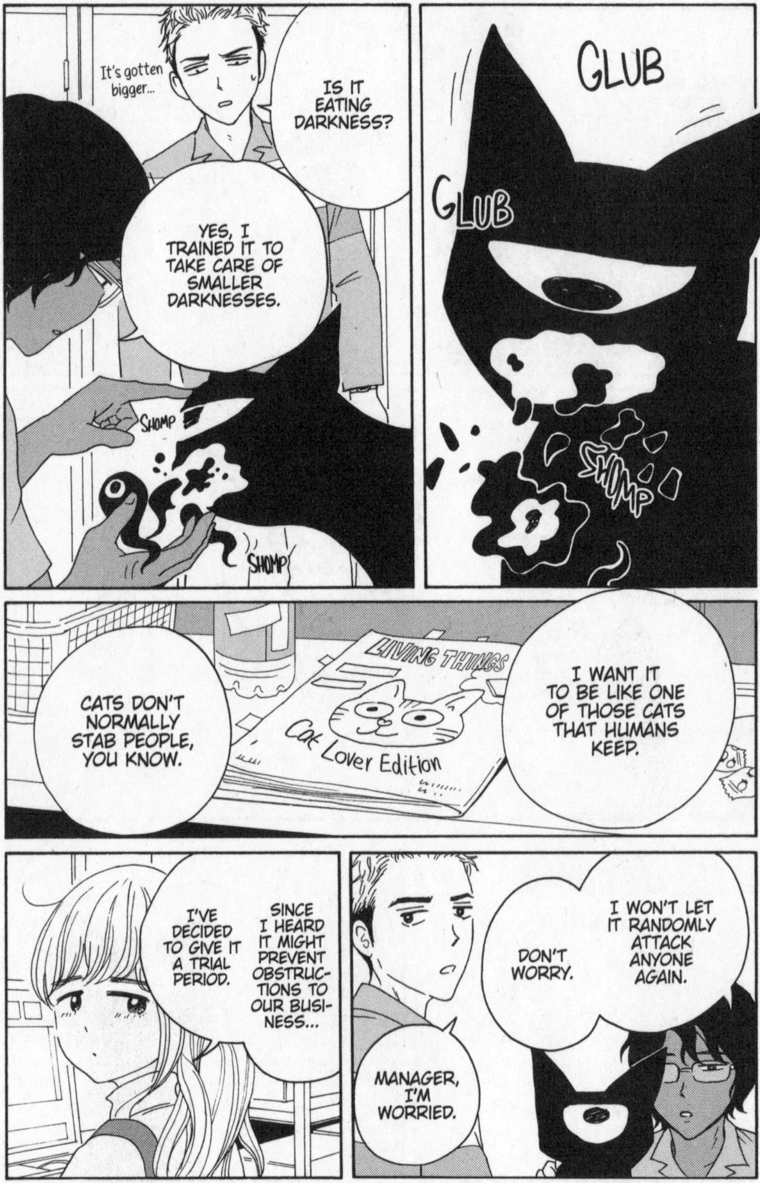
GLUB
GLUB
SHOMP
IS IT EATING DARKNESS?
It's gotten bigger...
YES, I TRAINED IT TO TAKE CARE OF SMALLER DARKNESSES.
SHOMP
SHOMP
I WANT IT TO BE LIKE ONE OF THOSE CATS THAT HUMANS KEEP.
LIVING THINGS
Cat Lover Edition
CATS DON'T NORMALLY STAB PEOPLE, YOU KNOW.
DON'T WORRY.
I WON'T LET IT RANDOMLY ATTACK ANYONE AGAIN.
MANAGER, I'M WORRIED.
SINCE I HEARD IT MIGHT PREVENT OBSTRUCTIONS TO OUR BUSINESS...
I'VE DECIDED TO GIVE IT A TRIAL PERIOD.

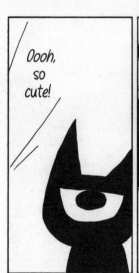

Oooh, so cute!
IS THAT YOUR MASCOT?
NO, IT'S A CAT.
IT LIKES CREAM DORAYAKI.
EEEEK!♡
OM
VWRSH...
DING-DONG

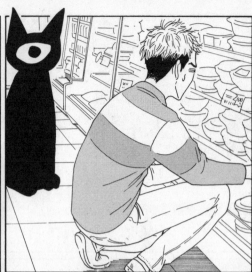

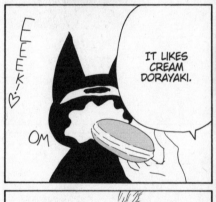

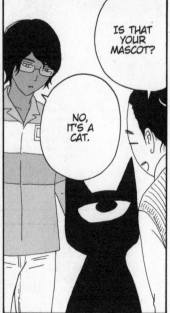

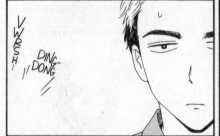

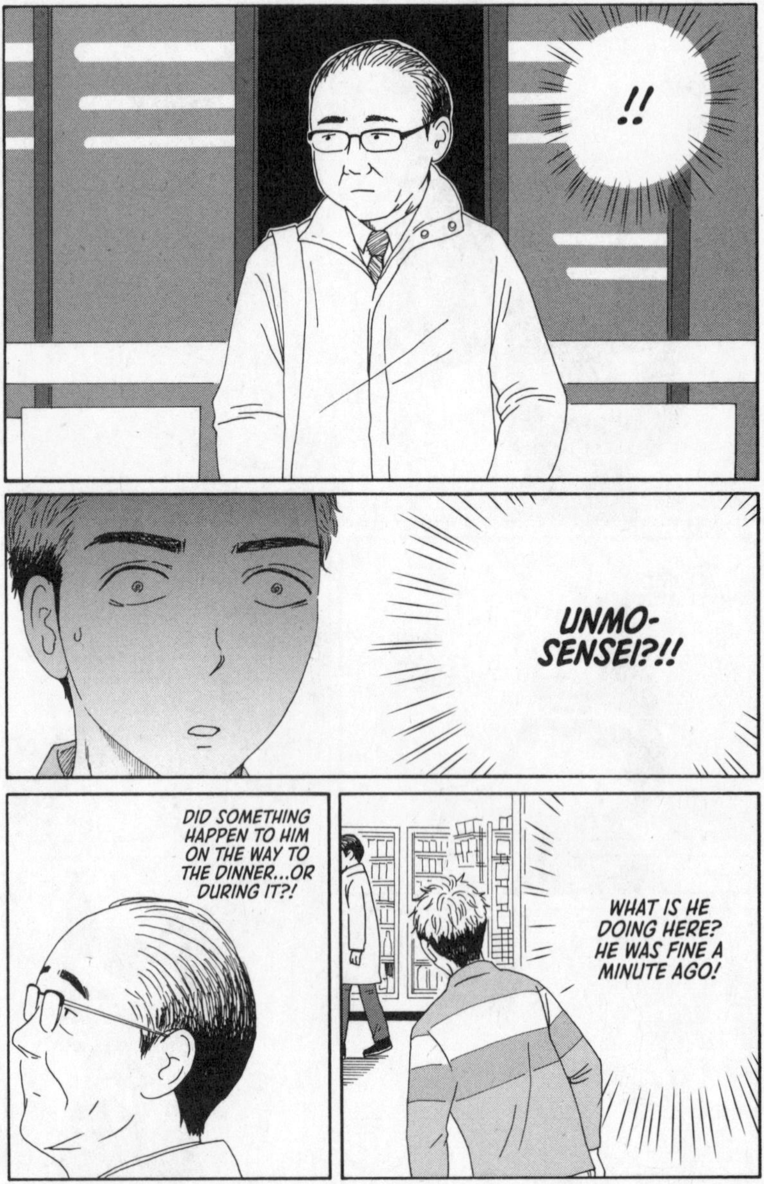
!!
UNMO-SENSEI?!!
WHAT IS HE DOING HERE? HE WAS FINE A MINUTE AGO!
DID SOMETHING HAPPEN TO HIM ON THE WAY TO THE DINNER...OR DURING IT?!

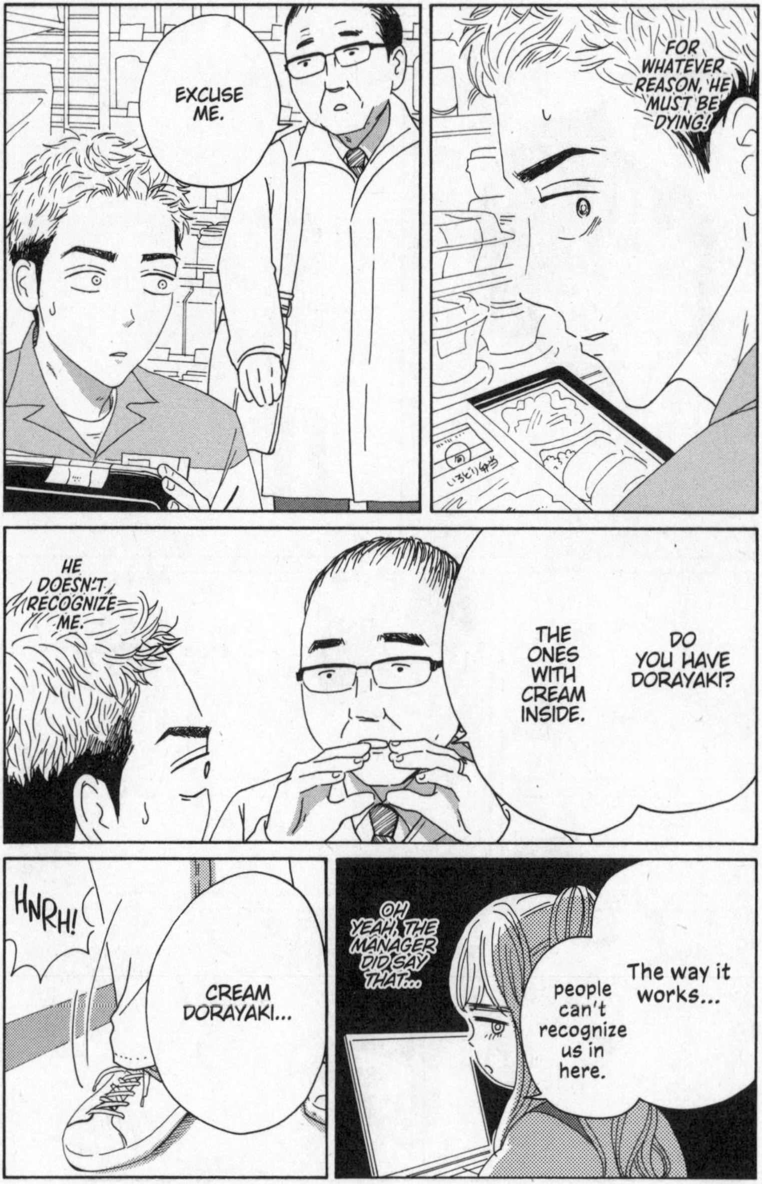
FOR WHATEVER REASON, HE MUST BE DYING!
EXCUSE ME.
DO YOU HAVE DORAYAKI?
THE ONES WITH CREAM INSIDE.
HE DOESN'T RECOGNIZE ME.
The way it works...
people can't recognize us in here.
OH YEAH, THE MANAGER DID SAY THAT...
CREAM DORAYAKI...
HNRH!

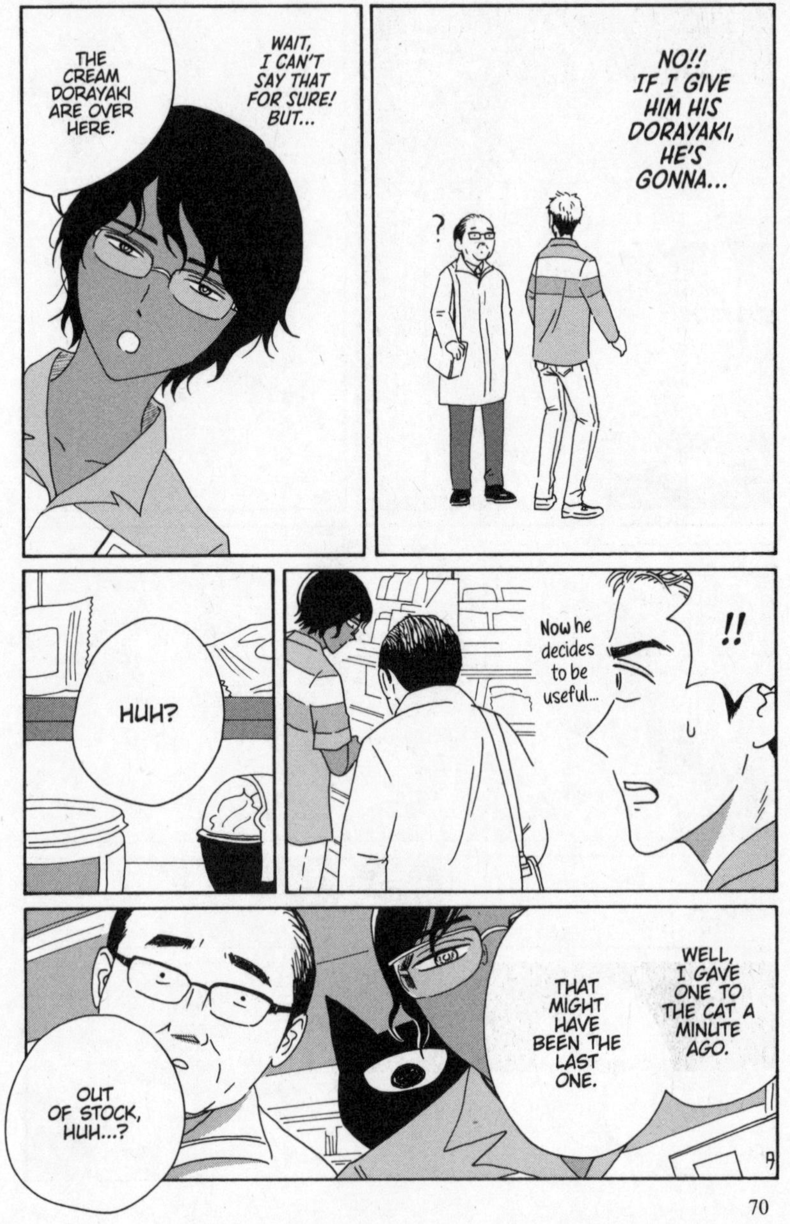
NO!! IF I GIVE HIM HIS DORAYAKI, HE'S GONNA...
WAIT, I CAN'T SAY THAT FOR SURE! BUT...
THE CREAM DORAYAKI ARE OVER HERE.
!!
Now he decides to be useful...
HUH?
WELL, I GAVE ONE TO THE CAT A MINUTE AGO.
THAT MIGHT HAVE BEEN THE LAST ONE.
OUT OF STOCK, HUH...?

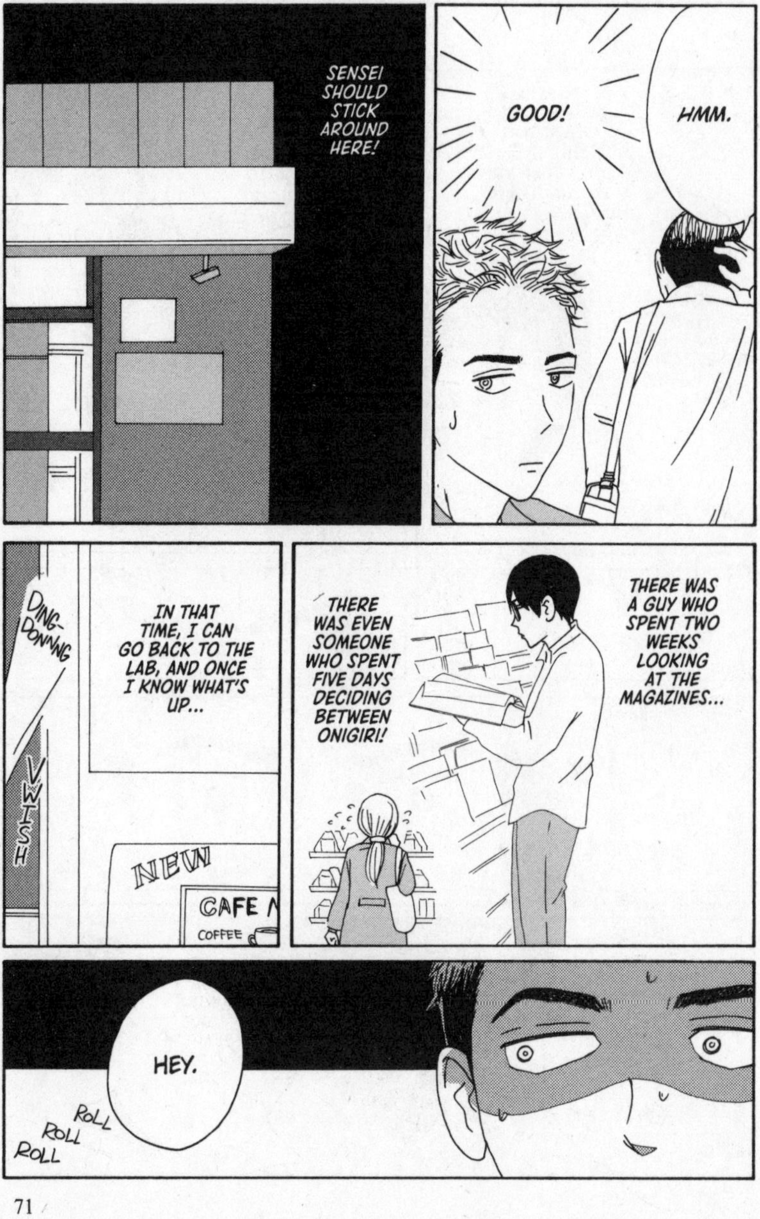
HMM.
GOOD!
SENSEI SHOULD STICK AROUND HERE!
THERE WAS A GUY WHO SPENT TWO WEEKS LOOKING AT THE MAGAZINES...
THERE WAS EVEN SOMEONE WHO SPENT FIVE DAYS DECIDING BETWEEN ONIGIRI!
DING-DONNNG
IN THAT TIME, I CAN GO BACK TO THE LAB, AND ONCE I KNOW WHAT'S UP...
VWISH
NEW
CAFE
COFFEE
HEY.
ROLL ROLL ROLL

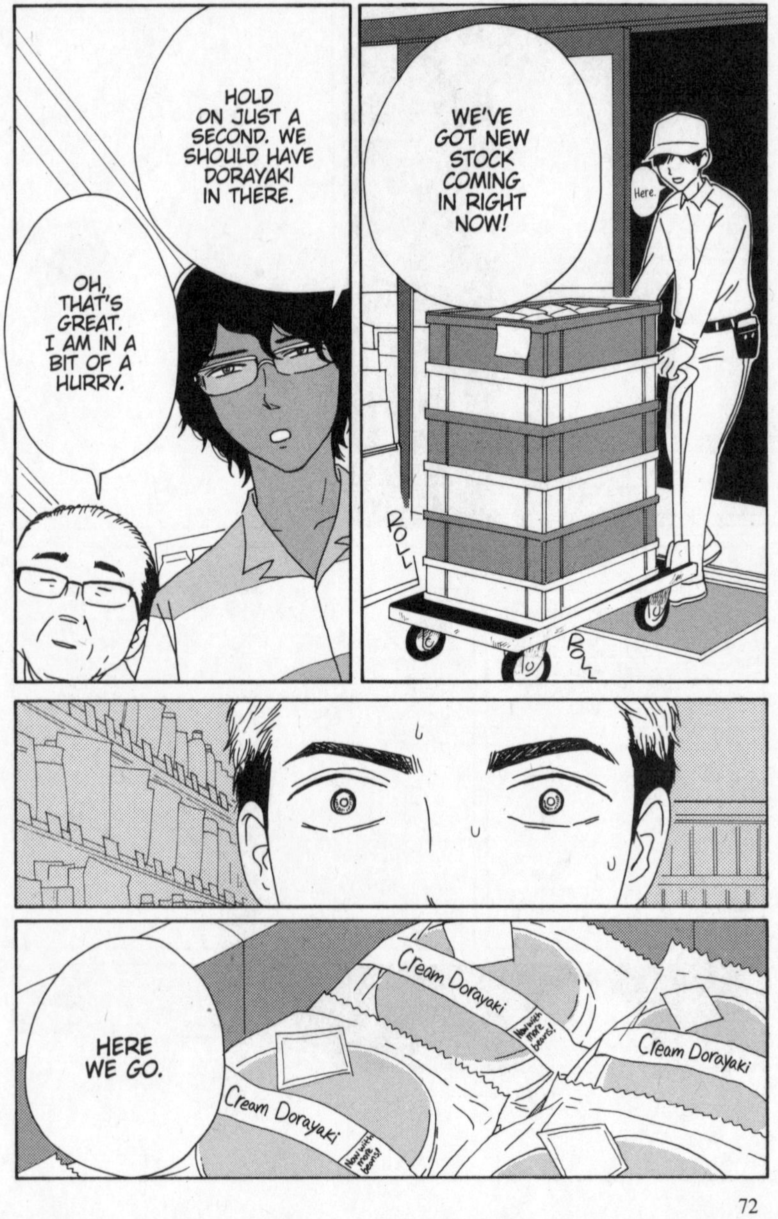
WE'VE GOT NEW STOCK COMING IN RIGHT NOW!
Here.
ROLL
ROLL
HOLD ON JUST A SECOND. WE SHOULD HAVE DORAYAKI IN THERE.
OH, THAT'S GREAT. I AM IN A BIT OF A HURRY.
HERE WE GO.
Cream Dorayaki
Now with more beans!
Cream Dorayaki
Cream Dorayaki
Now with more beans!

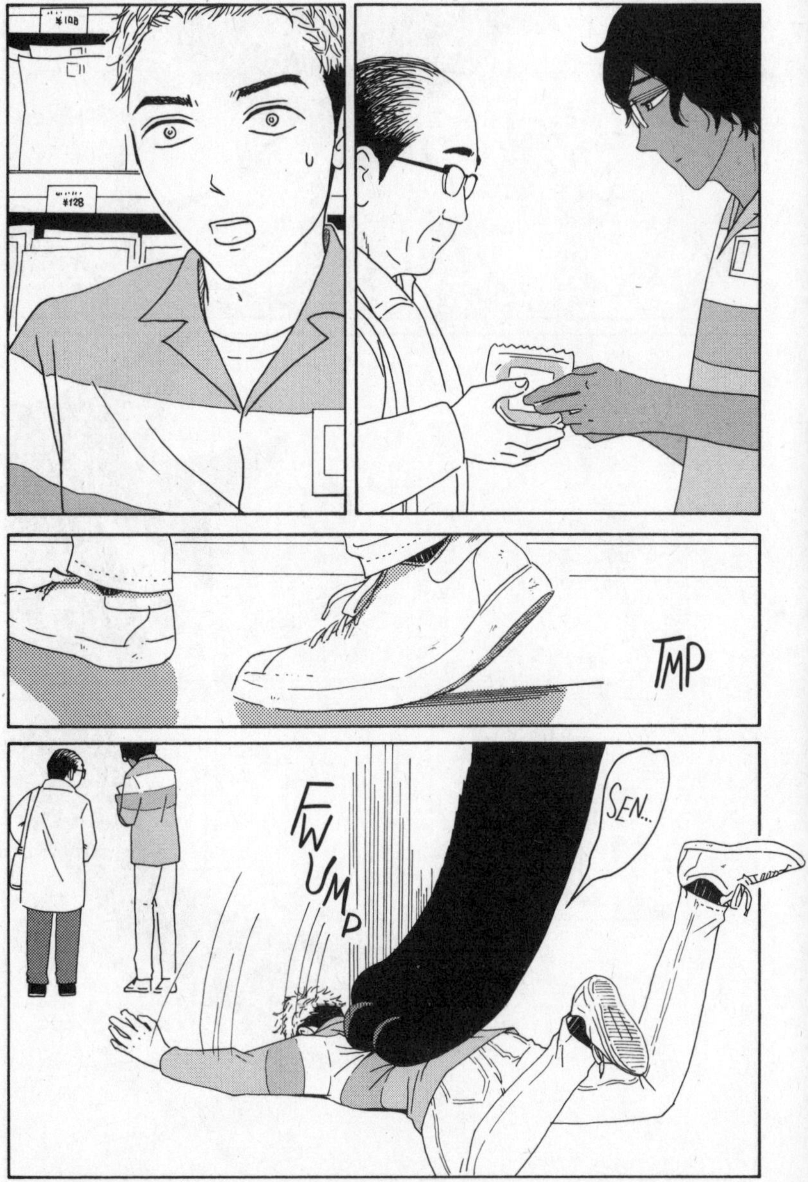
¥128
TMP
SEN...
FWUMP

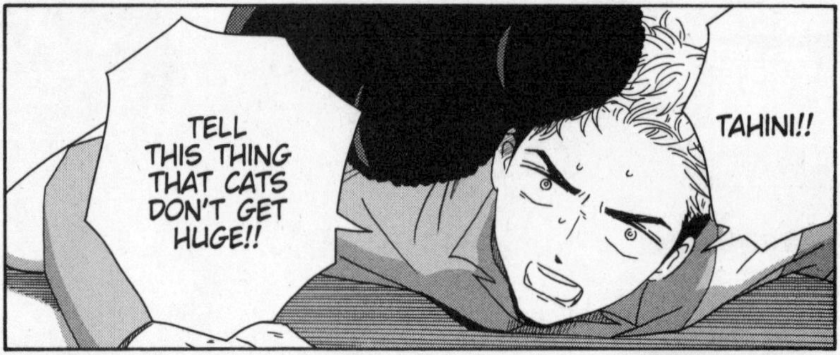
TAHINI!!
TELL THIS THING THAT CATS DON'T GET HUGE!!

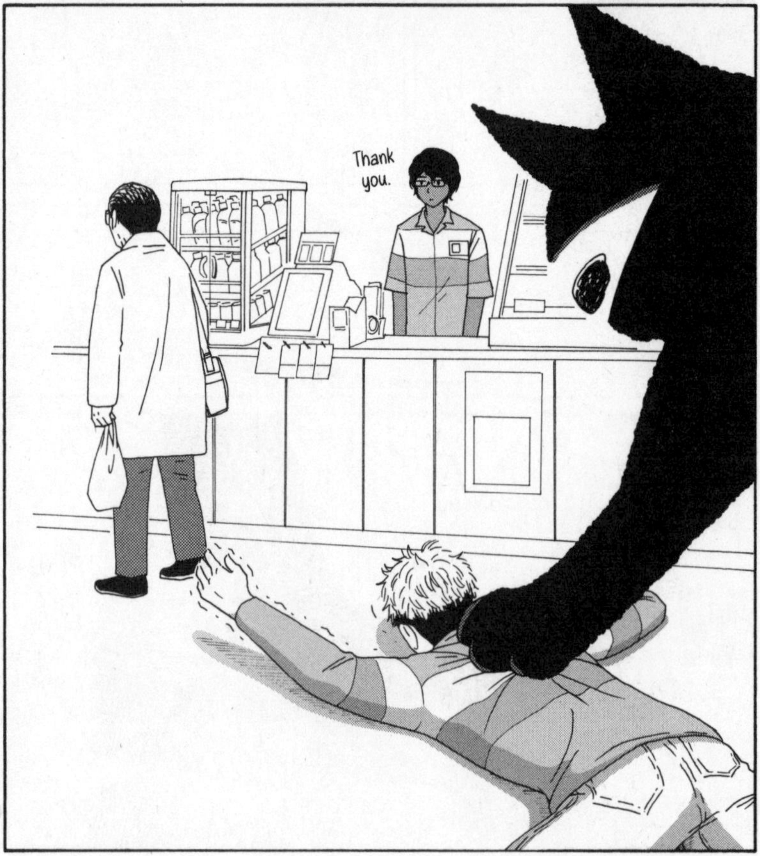
Thank you.

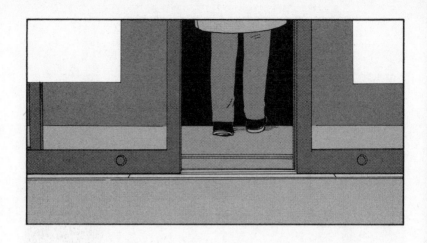

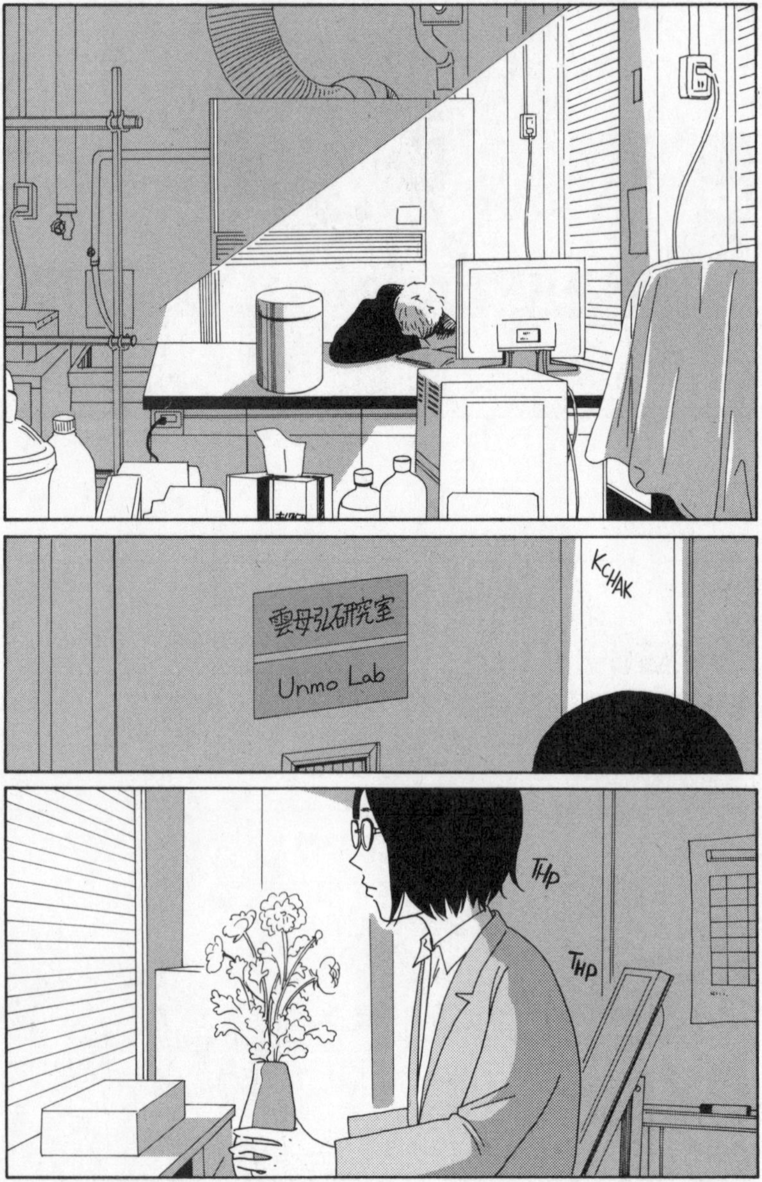
KCHAK
雲母弘研究室
Unmo Lab
THP
THP

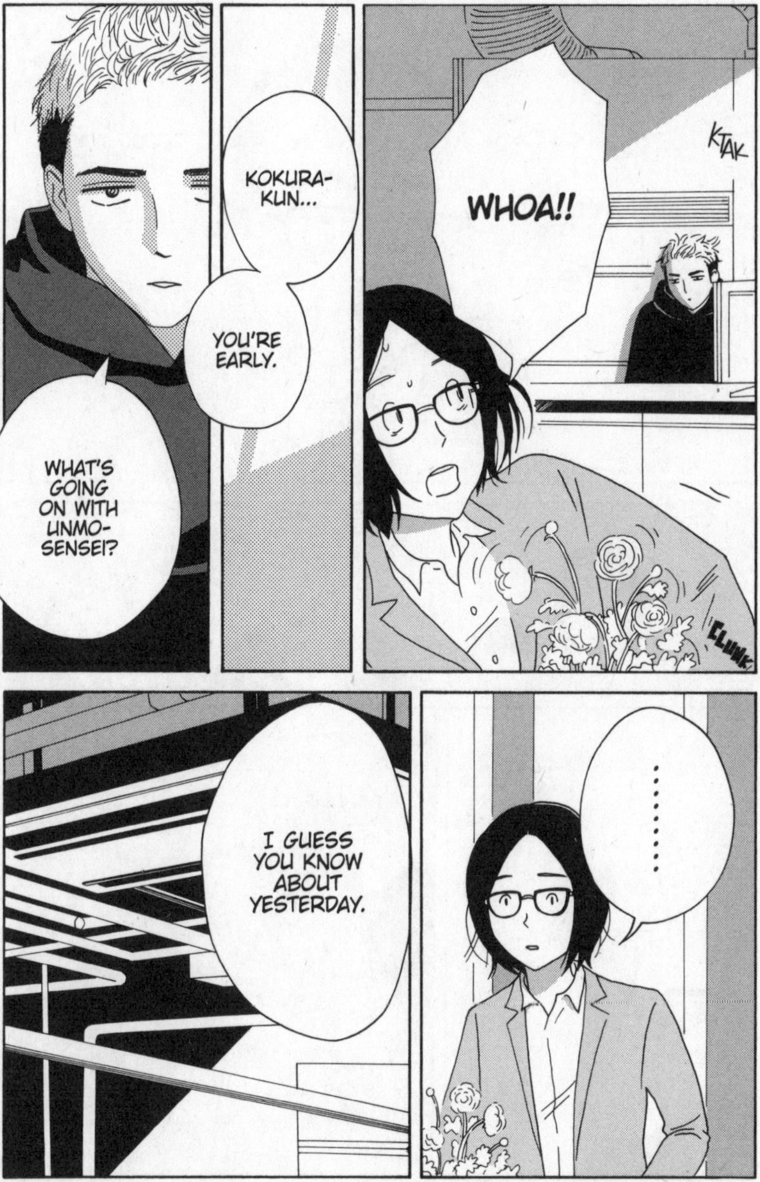
KTAK
WHOA!!
CLUNK
KOKURA-KUN...
YOU'RE EARLY.
WHAT'S GOING ON WITH UNMO-SENSEI?
......
I GUESS YOU KNOW ABOUT YESTERDAY.

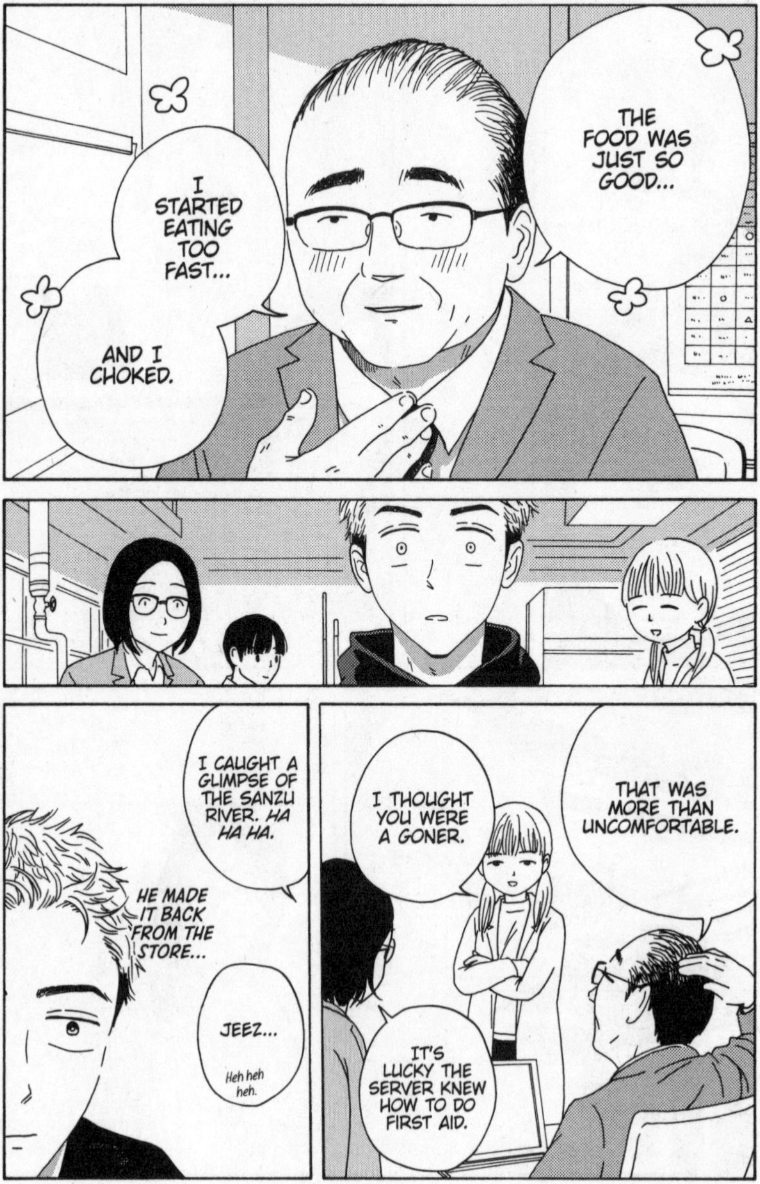
THE FOOD WAS JUST SO GOOD...
I STARTED EATING TOO FAST...
AND I CHOKED.
THAT WAS MORE THAN UNCOMFORTABLE.
I THOUGHT YOU WERE A GONER.
IT'S LUCKY THE SERVER KNEW HOW TO DO FIRST AID.
I CAUGHT A GLIMPSE OF THE SANZU RIVER. HA HA HA.
HE MADE IT BACK FROM THE STORE...
JEEZ...
Heh heh heh.

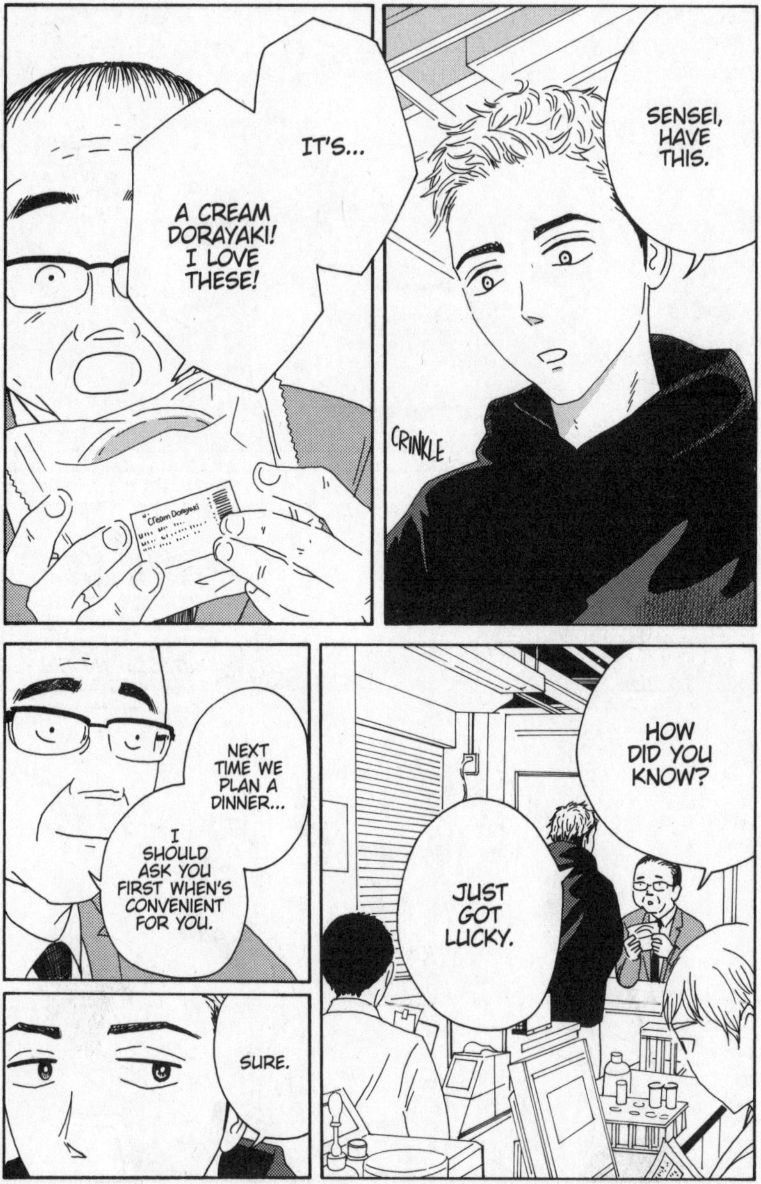
SENSEI, HAVE THIS.
CRINKLE
IT'S...
A CREAM DORAYAKI! I LOVE THESE!
Cream Dorayaki
HOW DID YOU KNOW?
JUST GOT LUCKY.
NEXT TIME WE PLAN A DINNER...
I SHOULD ASK YOU FIRST WHEN'S CONVENIENT FOR YOU.
SURE.

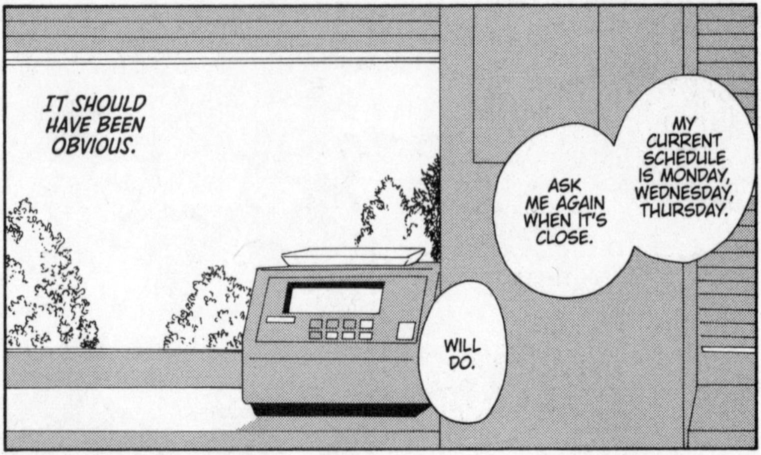
MY CURRENT SCHEDULE IS MONDAY, WEDNESDAY, THURSDAY.
ASK ME AGAIN WHEN IT'S CLOSE.
WILL DO.
IT SHOULD HAVE BEEN OBVIOUS.

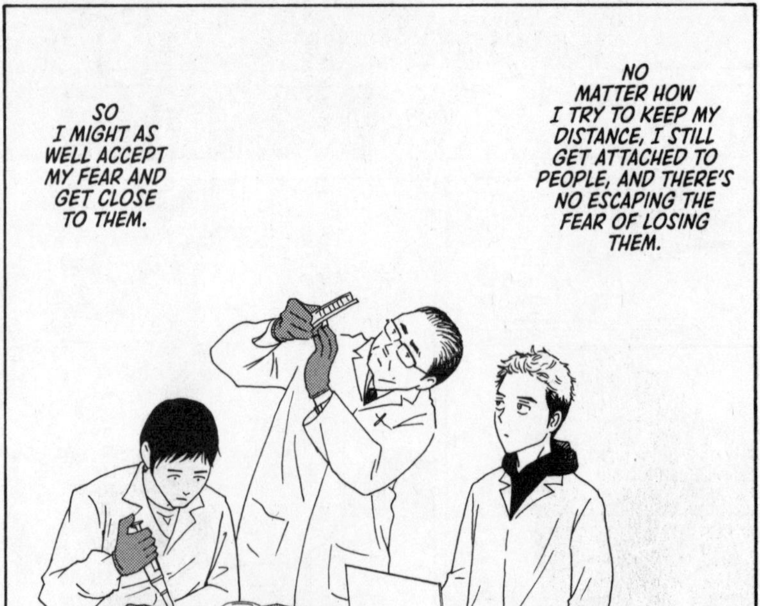
NO MATTER HOW I TRY TO KEEP MY DISTANCE, I STILL GET ATTACHED TO PEOPLE, AND THERE'S NO ESCAPING THE FEAR OF LOSING THEM.
SO I MIGHT AS WELL ACCEPT MY FEAR AND GET CLOSE TO THEM.

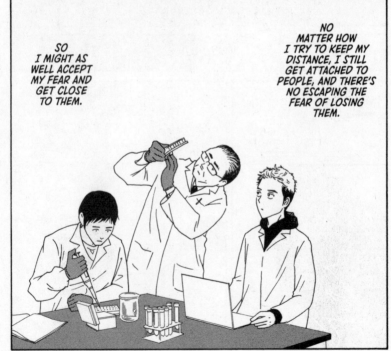

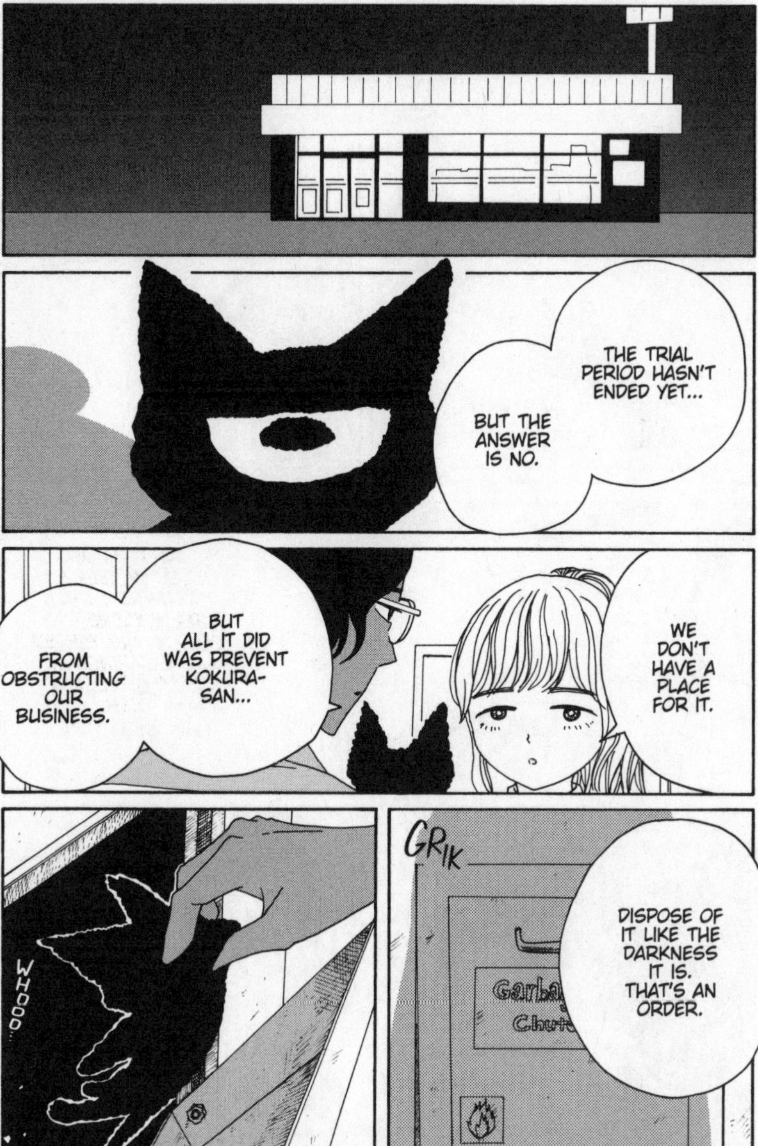
THE TRIAL PERIOD HASN'T ENDED YET...
BUT THE ANSWER IS NO.
WE DON'T HAVE A PLACE FOR IT.
BUT ALL IT DID WAS PREVENT KOKURA-SAN...
FROM OBSTRUCTING OUR BUSINESS.
GRIK
DISPOSE OF IT LIKE THE DARKNESS IT IS. THAT'S AN ORDER.
WHOOO...

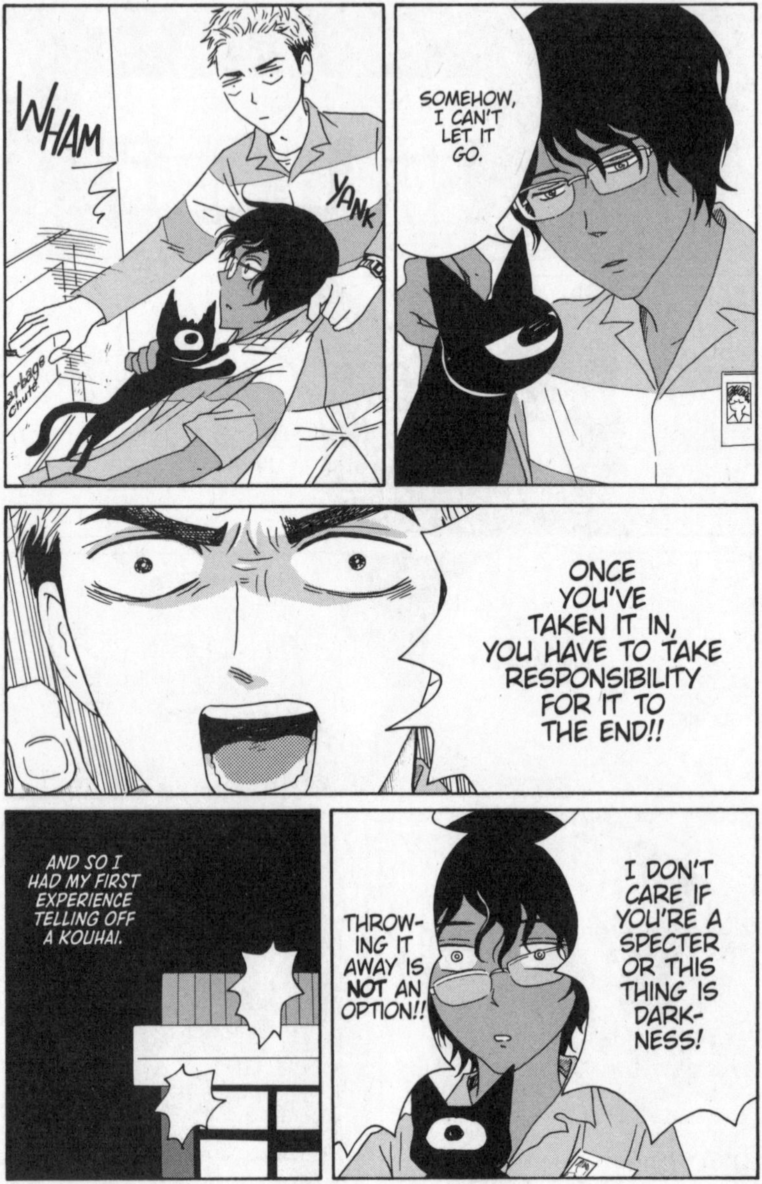
SOMEHOW, I CAN'T LET IT GO.
WHAM
YANK
Garbage Chute
ONCE YOU'VE TAKEN IT IN, YOU HAVE TO TAKE RESPONSIBILITY FOR IT TO THE END!!
I DON'T CARE IF YOU'RE A SPECTER OR THIS THING IS DARK-NESS!
THROW-ING IT AWAY IS NOT AN OPTION!!
AND SO I HAD MY FIRST EXPERIENCE TELLING OFF A KOUHAI.

Episode 4
Tahini and Humans

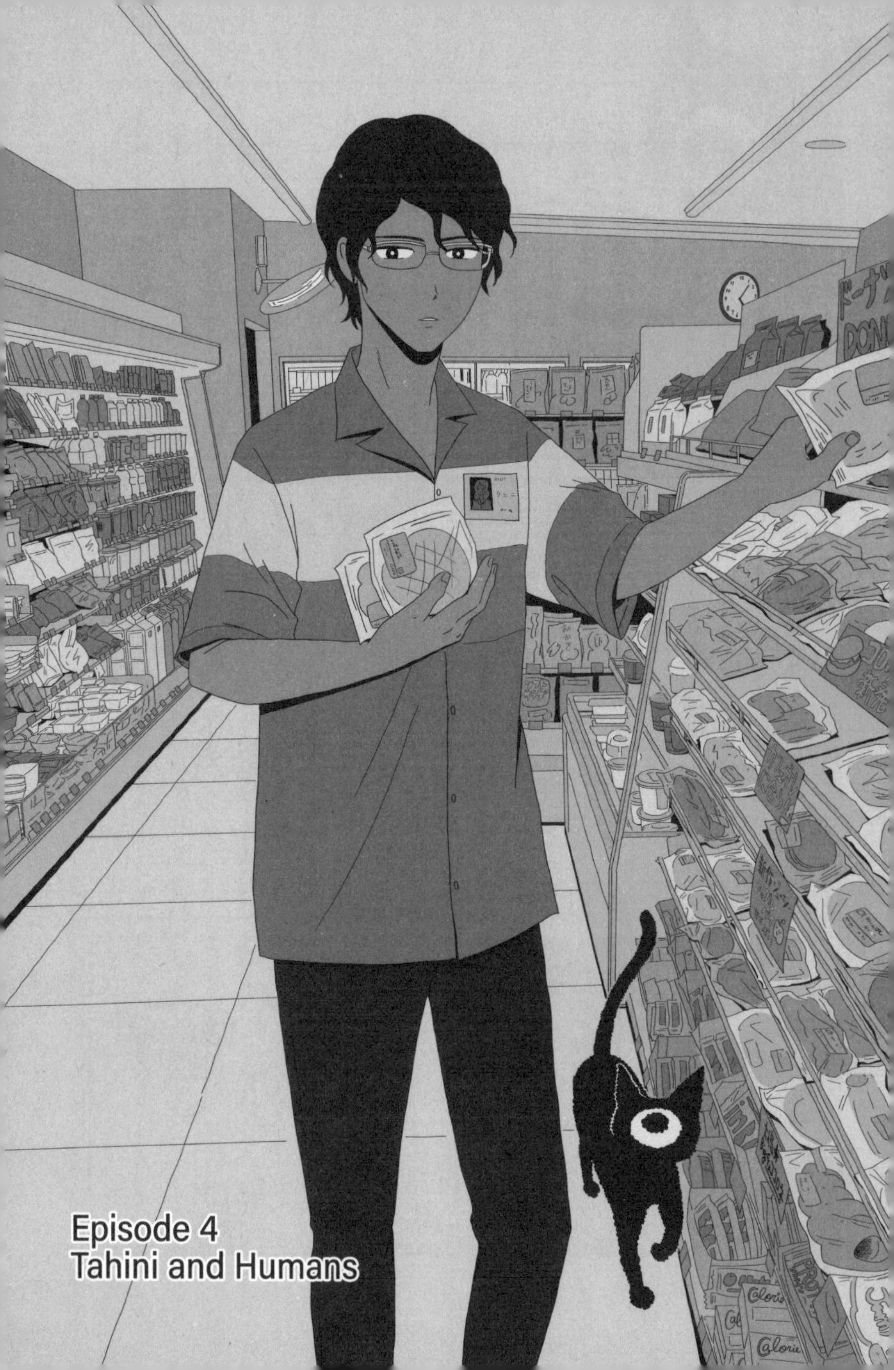

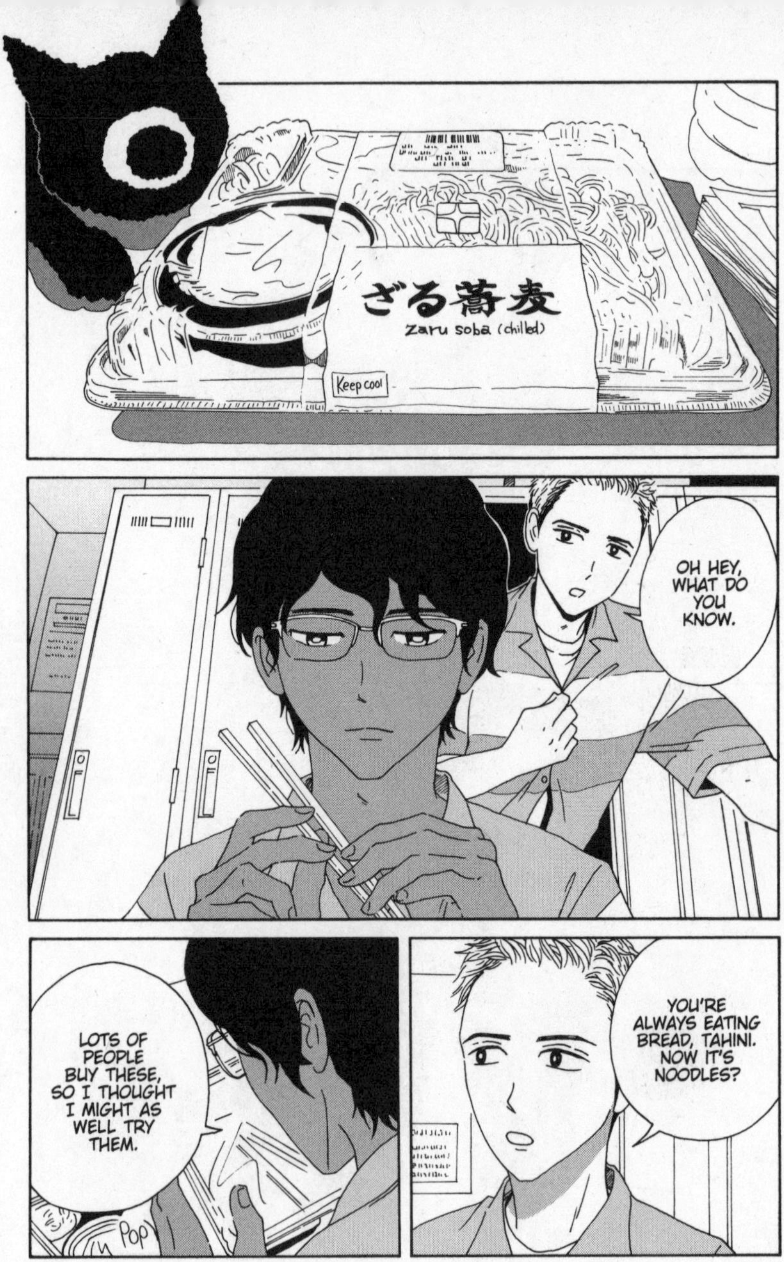
ざる蕎麦
Zaru soba (chilled)
Keep cool
OH HEY, WHAT DO YOU KNOW.
YOU'RE ALWAYS EATING BREAD, TAHINI. NOW IT'S NOODLES?
LOTS OF PEOPLE BUY THESE, SO I THOUGHT I MIGHT AS WELL TRY THEM.
Pop

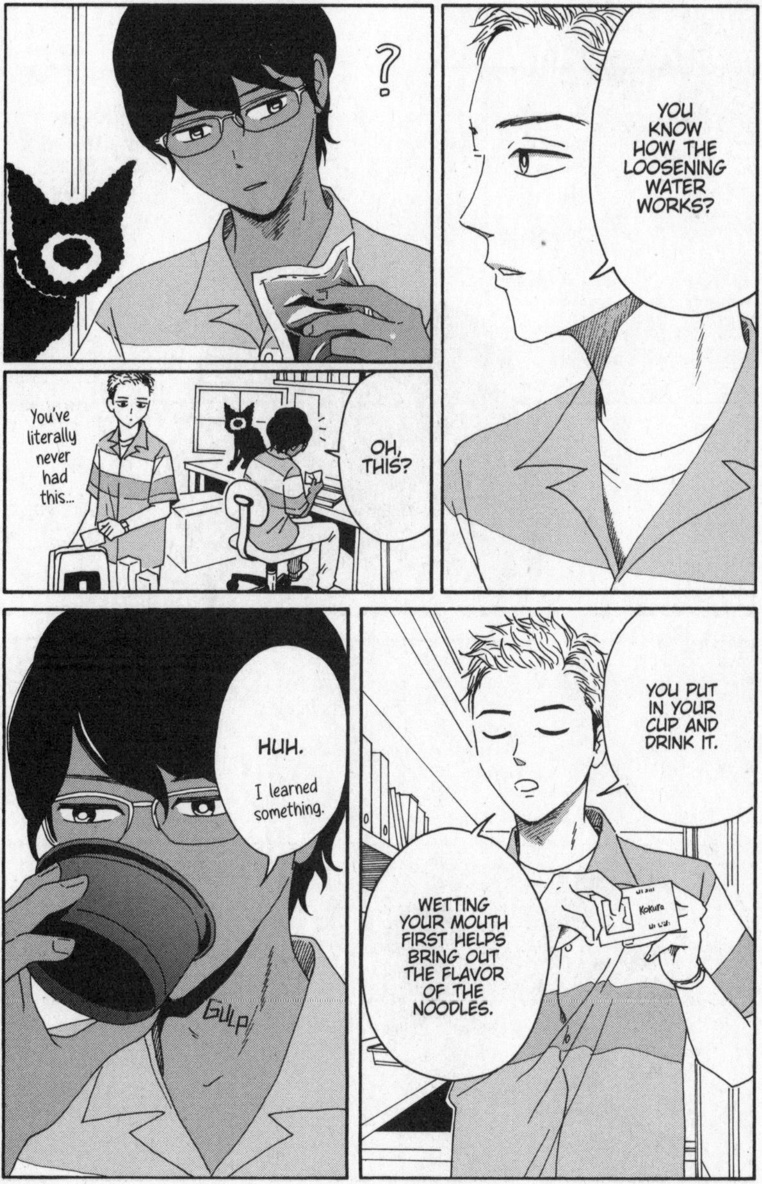
YOU KNOW HOW THE LOOSENING WATER WORKS?
?
OH, THIS?
You've literally never had this...
YOU PUT IN YOUR CUP AND DRINK IT.
WETTING YOUR MOUTH FIRST HELPS BRING OUT THE FLAVOR OF THE NOODLES.
Kokura
HUH.
I learned something.
GULP

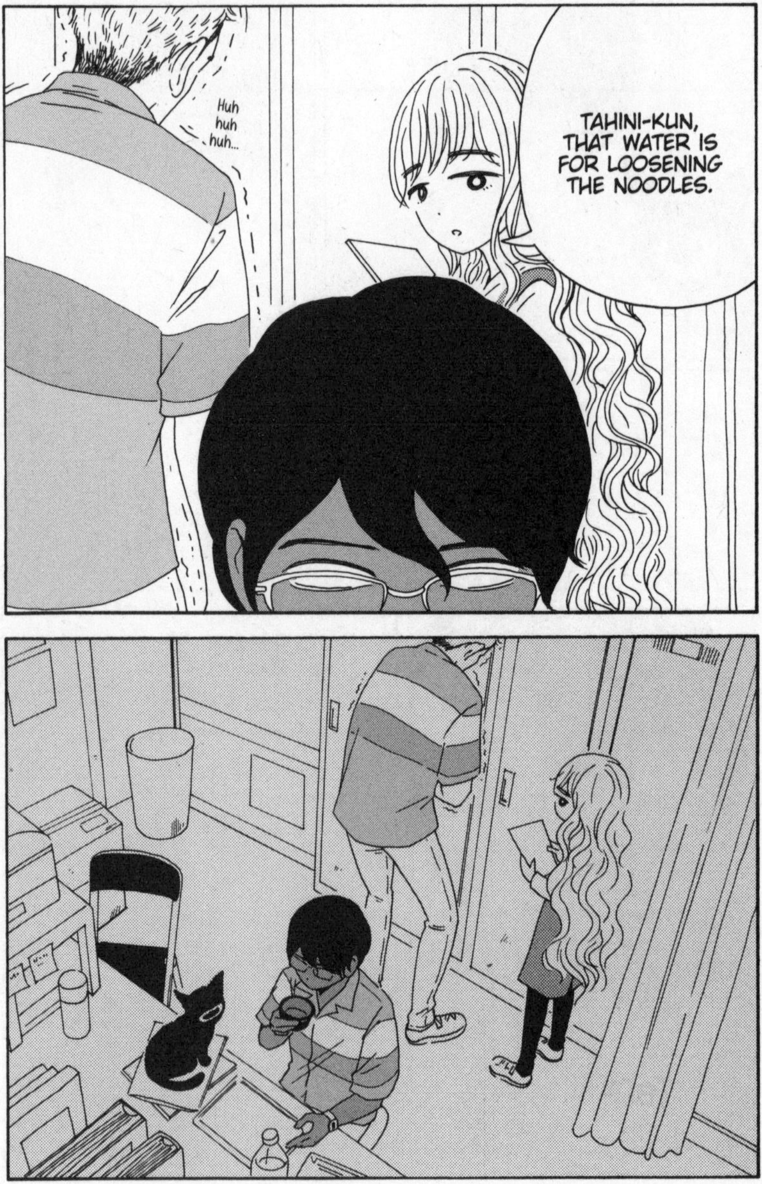
TAHINI-KUN, THAT WATER IS FOR LOOSENING THE NOODLES.
Huh huh huh...

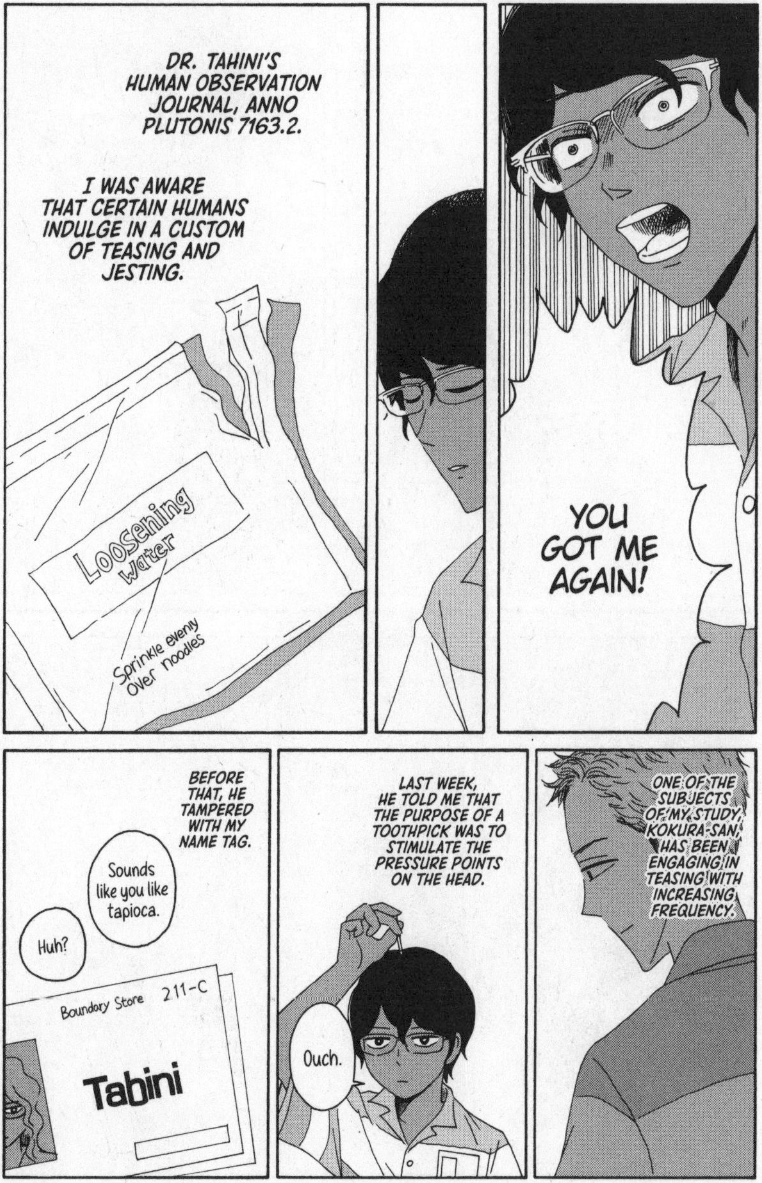
YOU GOT ME AGAIN!
DR. TAHINI'S HUMAN OBSERVATION JOURNAL, ANNO PLUTONIS 7163.2.
I WAS AWARE THAT CERTAIN HUMANS INDULGE IN A CUSTOM OF TEASING AND JESTING.
Loosening water
Sprinkle evenly over noodles
ONE OF THE SUBJECTS OF MY STUDY, KOKURA-SAN, HAS BEEN ENGAGING IN TEASING WITH INCREASING FREQUENCY.
LAST WEEK, HE TOLD ME THAT THE PURPOSE OF A TOOTHPICK WAS TO STIMULATE THE PRESSURE POINTS ON THE HEAD.
Ouch.
BEFORE THAT, HE TAMPERED WITH MY NAME TAG.
Sounds like you like tapioca.
Huh?
Boundary Store 211-C
Tabini

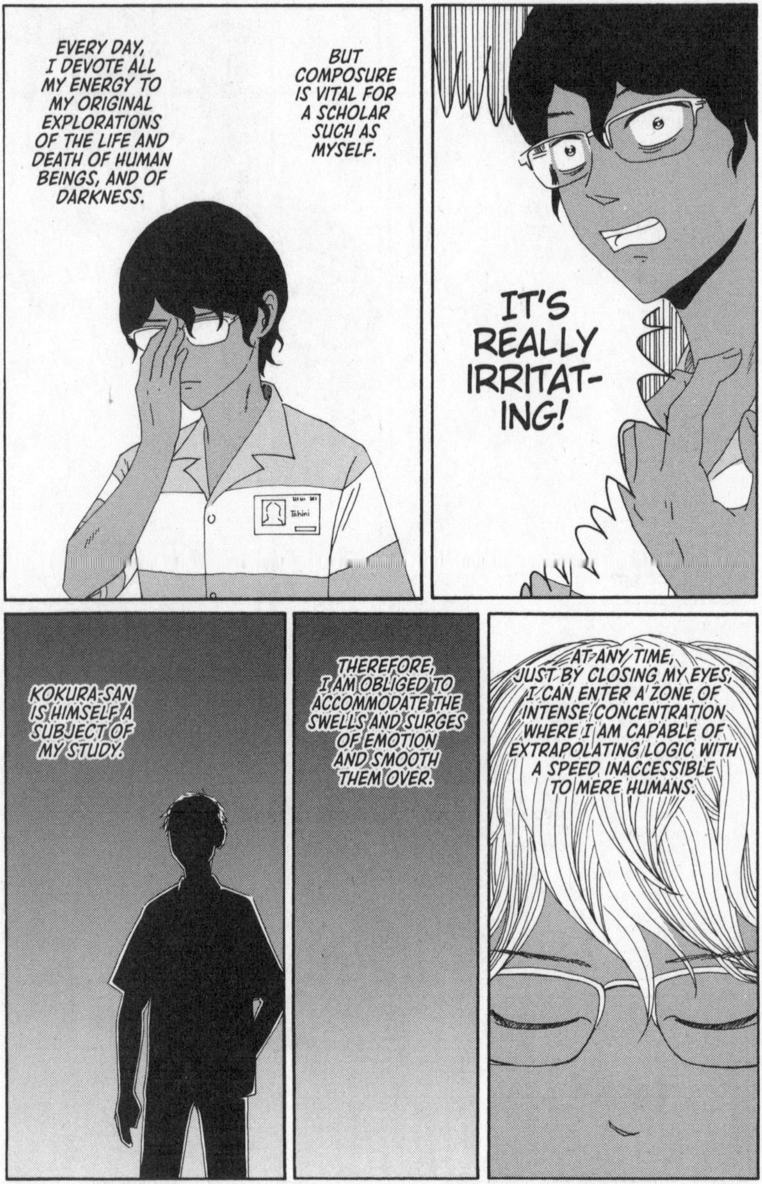
EVERY DAY, I DEVOTE ALL MY ENERGY TO MY ORIGINAL EXPLORATIONS OF THE LIFE AND DEATH OF HUMAN BEINGS, AND OF DARKNESS.
BUT COMPOSURE IS VITAL FOR A SCHOLAR SUCH AS MYSELF.
Tahini
IT'S REALLY IRRITAT-ING!
KOKURA-SAN IS HIMSELF A SUBJECT OF MY STUDY.
THEREFORE, I AM OBLIGED TO ACCOMMODATE THE SWELLS AND SURGES OF EMOTION AND SMOOTH THEM OVER.
AT ANY TIME, JUST BY CLOSING MY EYES, I CAN ENTER A ZONE OF INTENSE CONCENTRATION WHERE I AM CAPABLE OF EXTRAPOLATING LOGIC WITH A SPEED INACCESSIBLE TO MERE HUMANS.

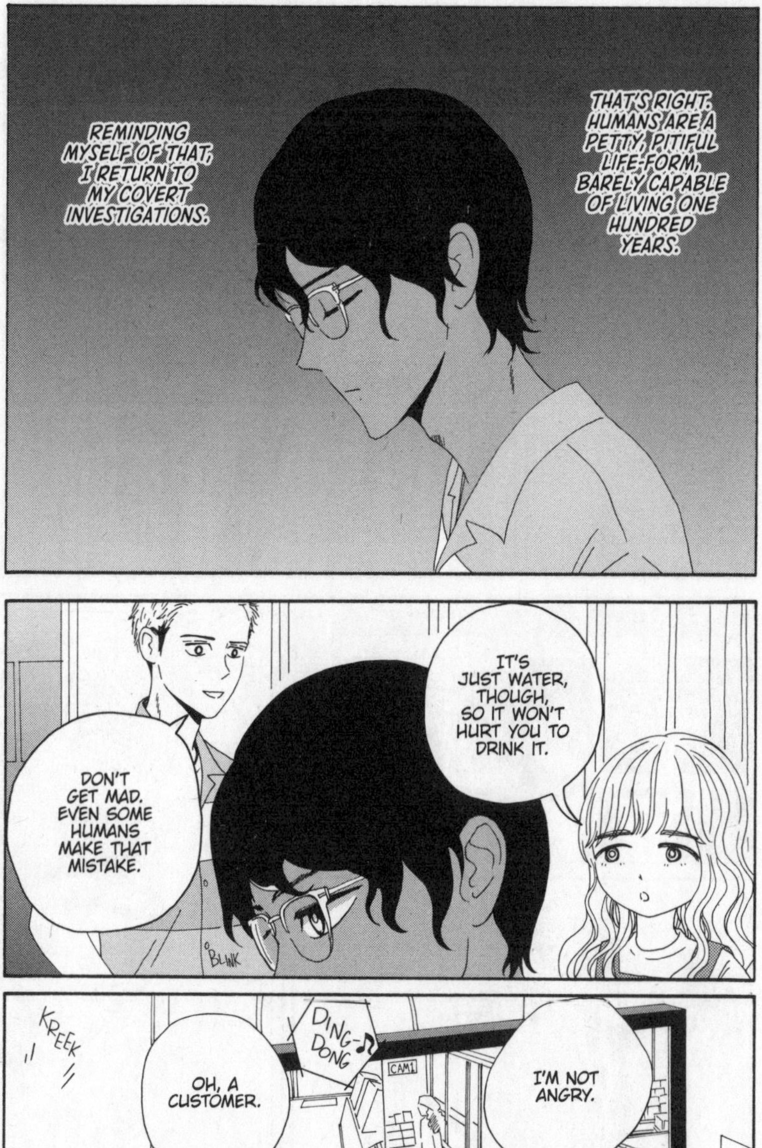
THAT'S RIGHT. HUMANS ARE A PETTY, PITIFUL LIFE-FORM, BARELY CAPABLE OF LIVING ONE HUNDRED YEARS.
REMINDING MYSELF OF THAT, I RETURN TO MY COVERT INVESTIGATIONS.
IT'S JUST WATER, THOUGH, SO IT WON'T HURT YOU TO DRINK IT.
DON'T GET MAD. EVEN SOME HUMANS MAKE THAT MISTAKE.
BLINK
I'M NOT ANGRY.
CAM1
CAM4
DING-DONG♪
OH, A CUSTOMER.
KREEK

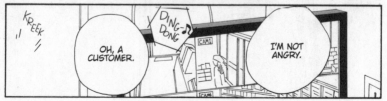

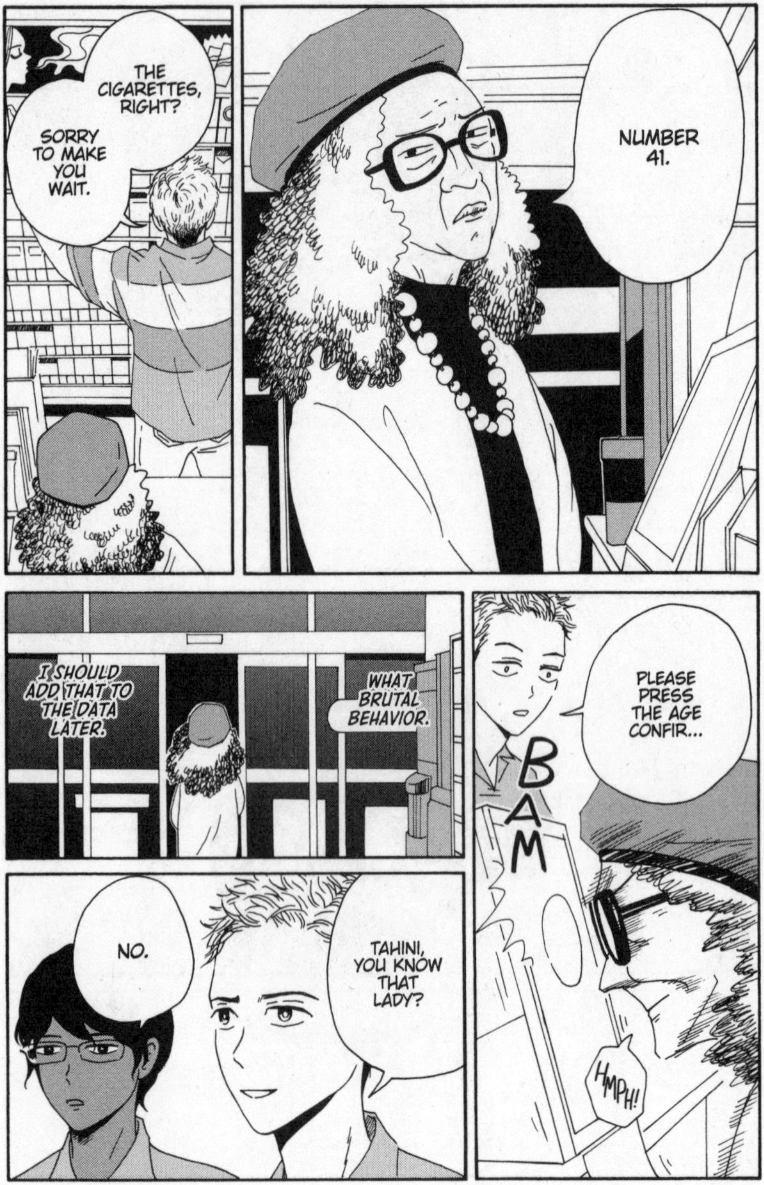
NUMBER 41.
THE CIGARETTES, RIGHT?
SORRY TO MAKE YOU WAIT.
PLEASE PRESS THE AGE CONFIR...
BAM
HMPH!
WHAT BRUTAL BEHAVIOR.
I SHOULD ADD THAT TO THE DATA LATER.
TAHINI, YOU KNOW THAT LADY?
NO.

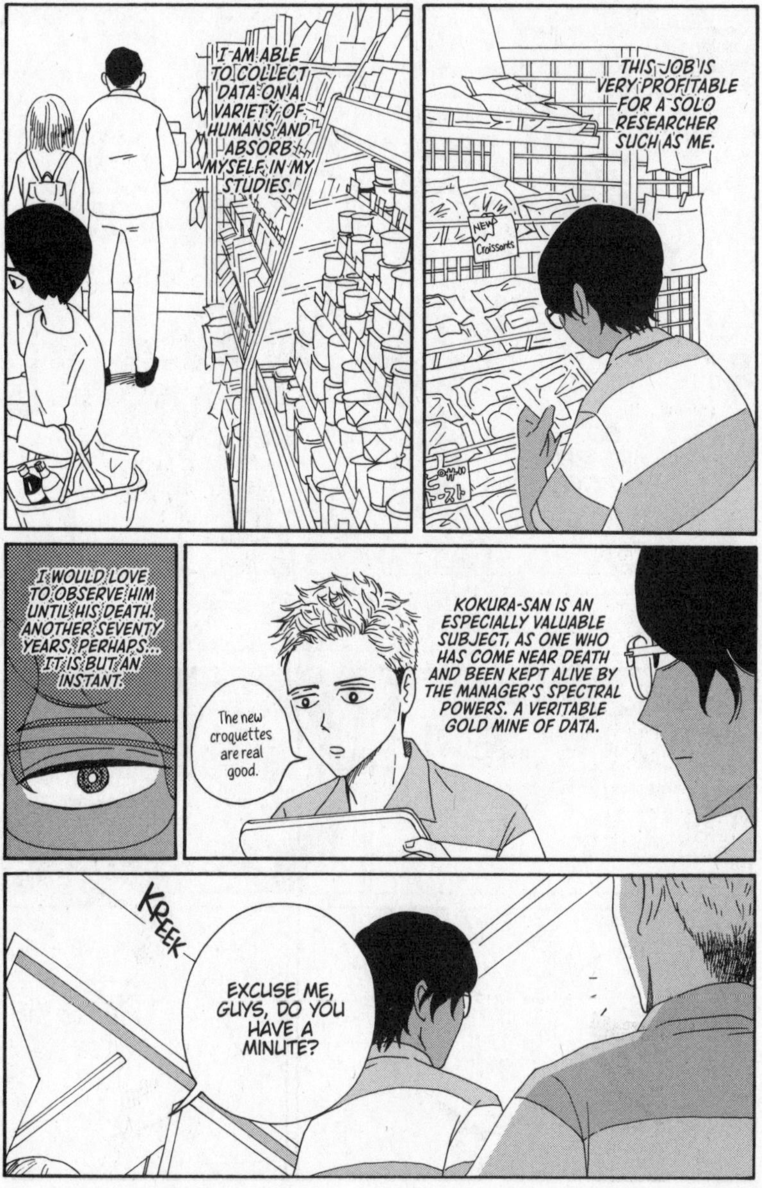
THIS JOB IS VERY PROFITABLE FOR A SOLO RESEARCHER SUCH AS ME.
NEW
Croissants
I AM ABLE TO COLLECT DATA ON A VARIETY OF HUMANS AND ABSORB MYSELF IN MY STUDIES.
KOKURA-SAN IS AN ESPECIALLY VALUABLE SUBJECT, AS ONE WHO HAS COME NEAR DEATH AND BEEN KEPT ALIVE BY THE MANAGER'S SPECTRAL POWERS. A VERITABLE GOLD MINE OF DATA.
The new croquettes are real good.
I WOULD LOVE TO OBSERVE HIM UNTIL HIS DEATH. ANOTHER SEVENTY YEARS, PERHAPS... IT IS BUT AN INSTANT.
KREEK
EXCUSE ME, GUYS, DO YOU HAVE A MINUTE?

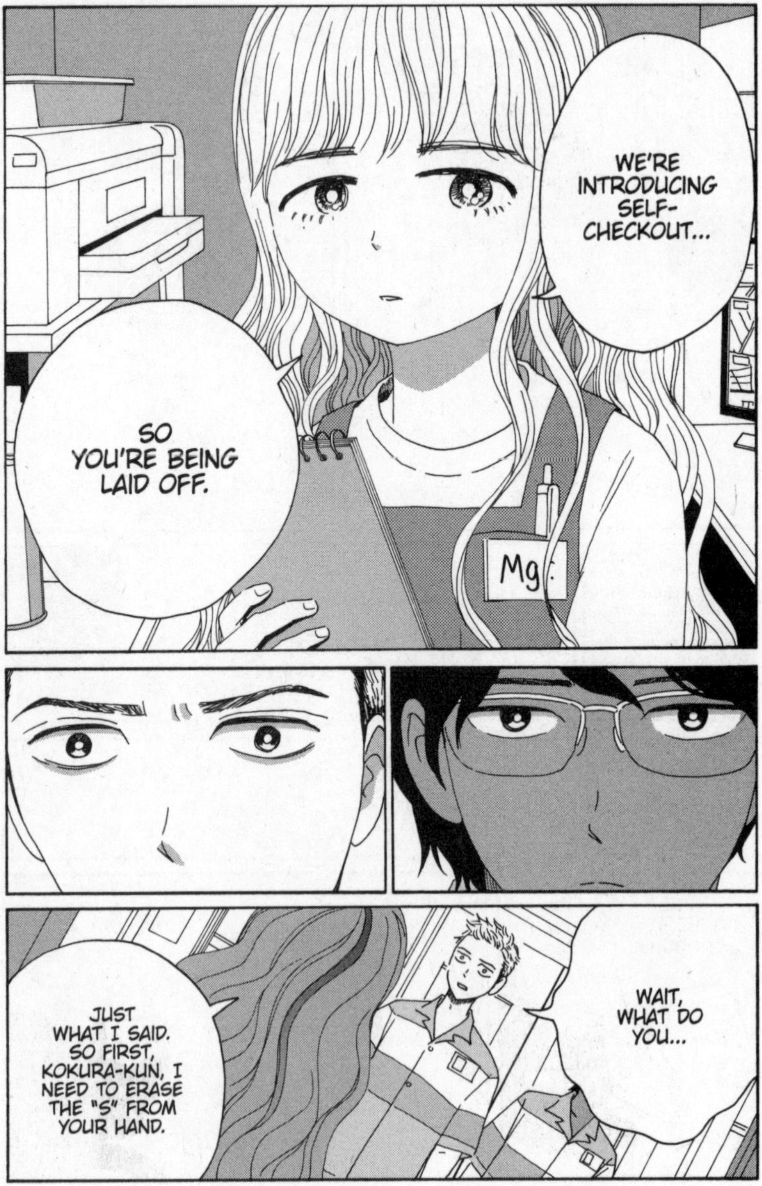
WE'RE INTRODUCING SELF-CHECKOUT...
SO YOU'RE BEING LAID OFF.
WAIT, WHAT DO YOU...
JUST WHAT I SAID. SO FIRST, KOKURA-KUN, I NEED TO ERASE THE "S" FROM YOUR HAND.

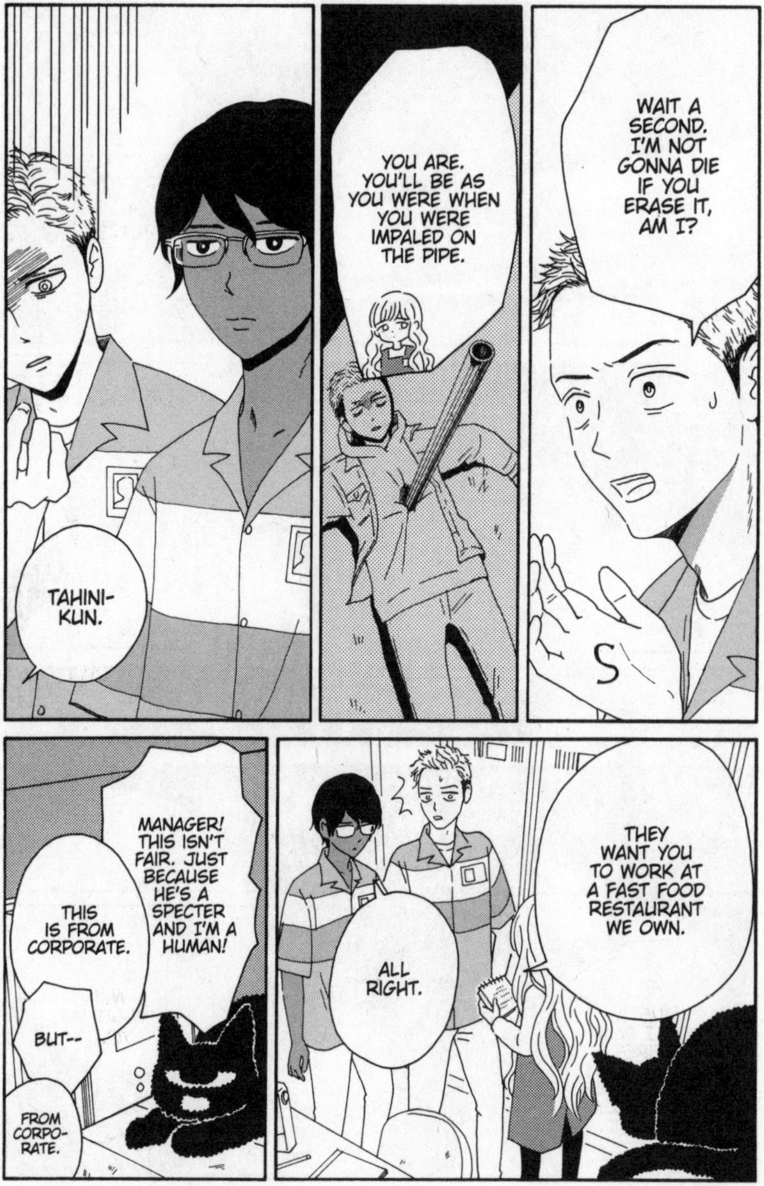

WAIT A SECOND. I'M NOT GONNA DIE IF YOU ERASE IT, AM I?
YOU ARE. YOU'LL BE AS YOU WERE WHEN YOU WERE IMPALED ON THE PIPE.
TAHINI-KUN.
THEY WANT YOU TO WORK AT A FAST FOOD RESTAURANT WE OWN.
ALL RIGHT.
MANAGER! THIS ISN'T FAIR. JUST BECAUSE HE'S A SPECTER AND I'M A HUMAN!
THIS IS FROM CORPORATE.
BUT--
FROM CORPO-RATE.

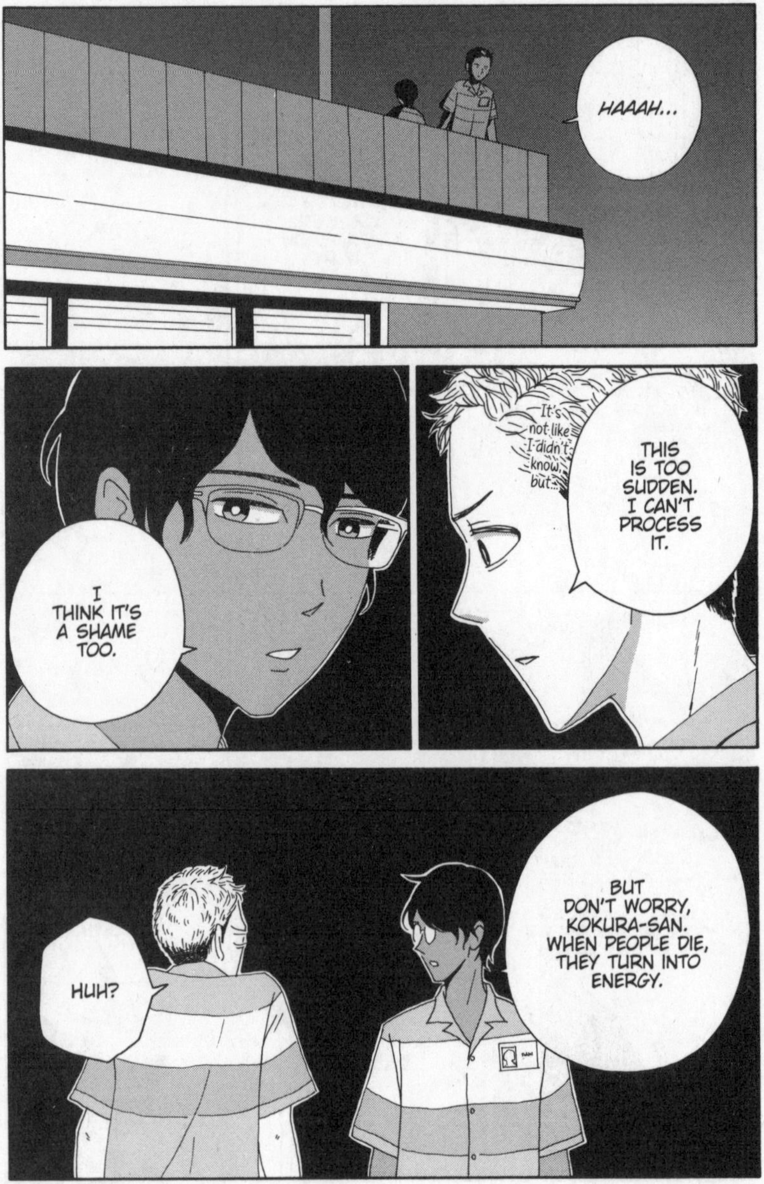
HAAAH...
THIS IS TOO SUDDEN. I CAN'T PROCESS IT.
It's not like I didn't know, but...
I THINK IT'S A SHAME TOO.
BUT DON'T WORRY, KOKURA-SAN. WHEN PEOPLE DIE, THEY TURN INTO ENERGY.
HUH?

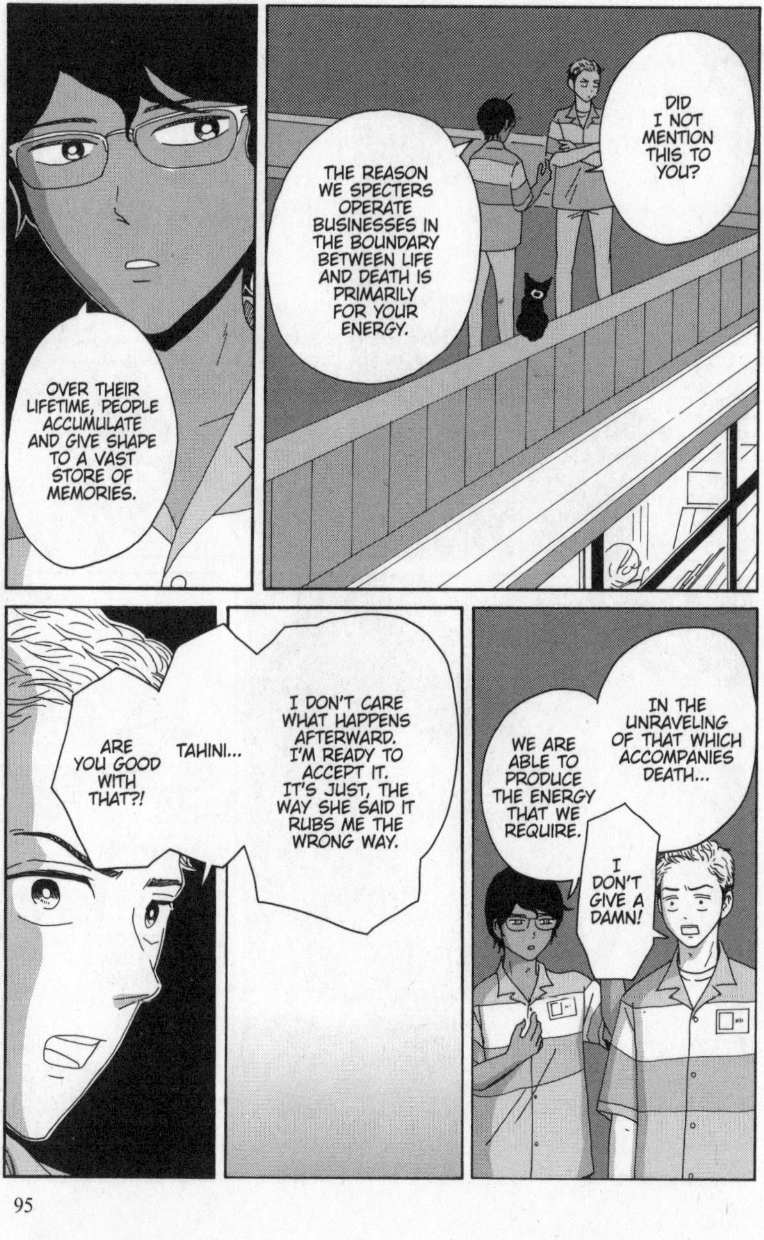
DID I NOT MENTION THIS TO YOU?
THE REASON WE SPECTERS OPERATE BUSINESSES IN THE BOUNDARY BETWEEN LIFE AND DEATH IS PRIMARILY FOR YOUR ENERGY.
OVER THEIR LIFETIME, PEOPLE ACCUMULATE AND GIVE SHAPE TO A VAST STORE OF MEMORIES.
IN THE UNRAVELING OF THAT WHICH ACCOMPANIES DEATH...
WE ARE ABLE TO PRODUCE THE ENERGY THAT WE REQUIRE.
I DON'T GIVE A DAMN!
I DON'T CARE WHAT HAPPENS AFTERWARD. I'M READY TO ACCEPT IT. IT'S JUST, THE WAY SHE SAID IT RUBS ME THE WRONG WAY.
TAHINI...
ARE YOU GOOD WITH THAT?!

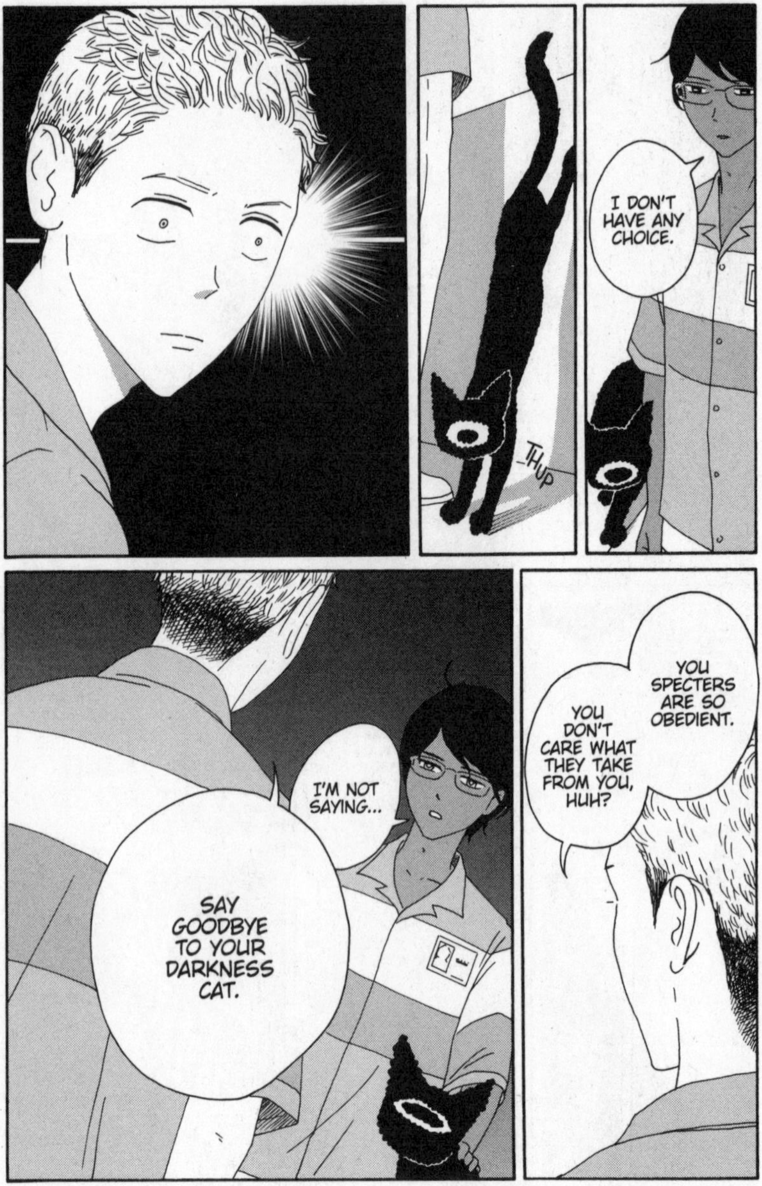
I DON'T HAVE ANY CHOICE.
THUP
YOU SPECTERS ARE SO OBEDIENT.
YOU DON'T CARE WHAT THEY TAKE FROM YOU, HUH?
I'M NOT SAYING...
SAY GOODBYE TO YOUR DARKNESS CAT.

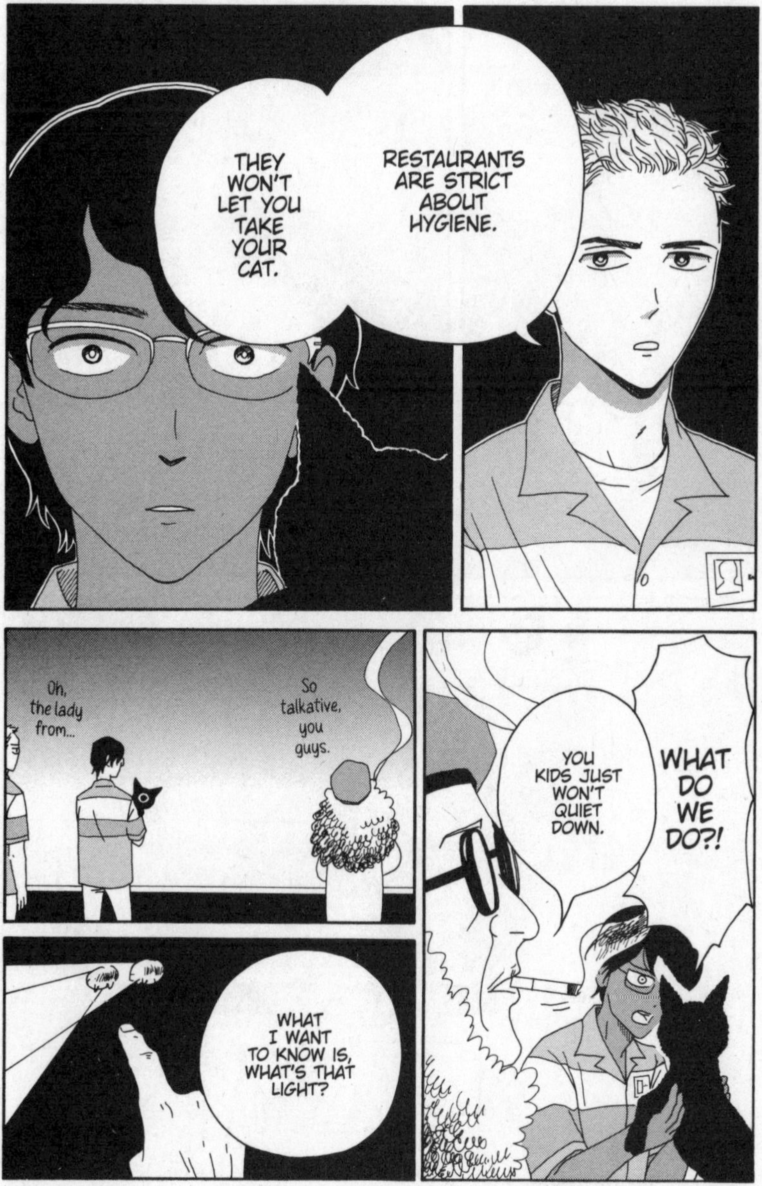
RESTAURANTS ARE STRICT ABOUT HYGIENE.
THEY WON'T LET YOU TAKE YOUR CAT.
WHAT DO WE DO?!
YOU KIDS JUST WON'T QUIET DOWN.
So talkative, you guys.
Oh, the lady from...
WHAT I WANT TO KNOW IS, WHAT'S THAT LIGHT?

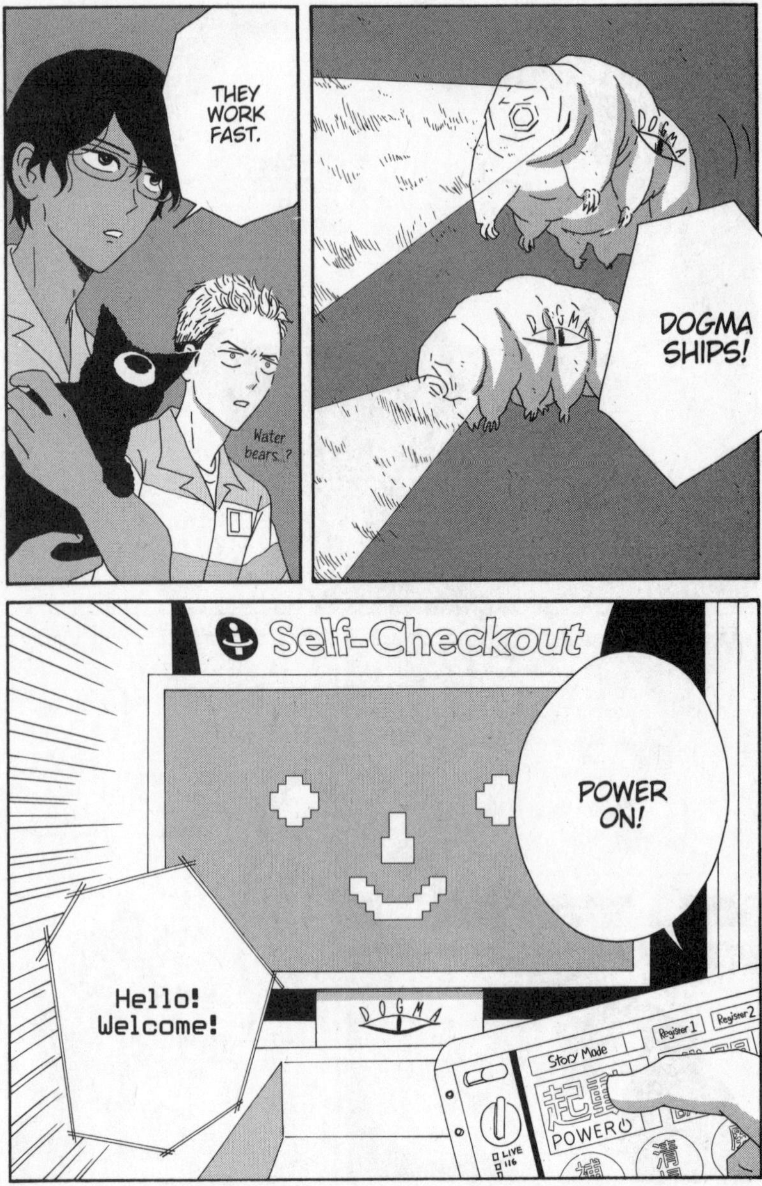
DOGMA
DOGMA
DOGMA SHIPS!
THEY WORK FAST.
Water bears...?
Self-Checkout
POWER ON!
Hello! Welcome!
DOGMA
Register 1
Register 2
Story Mode
POWER

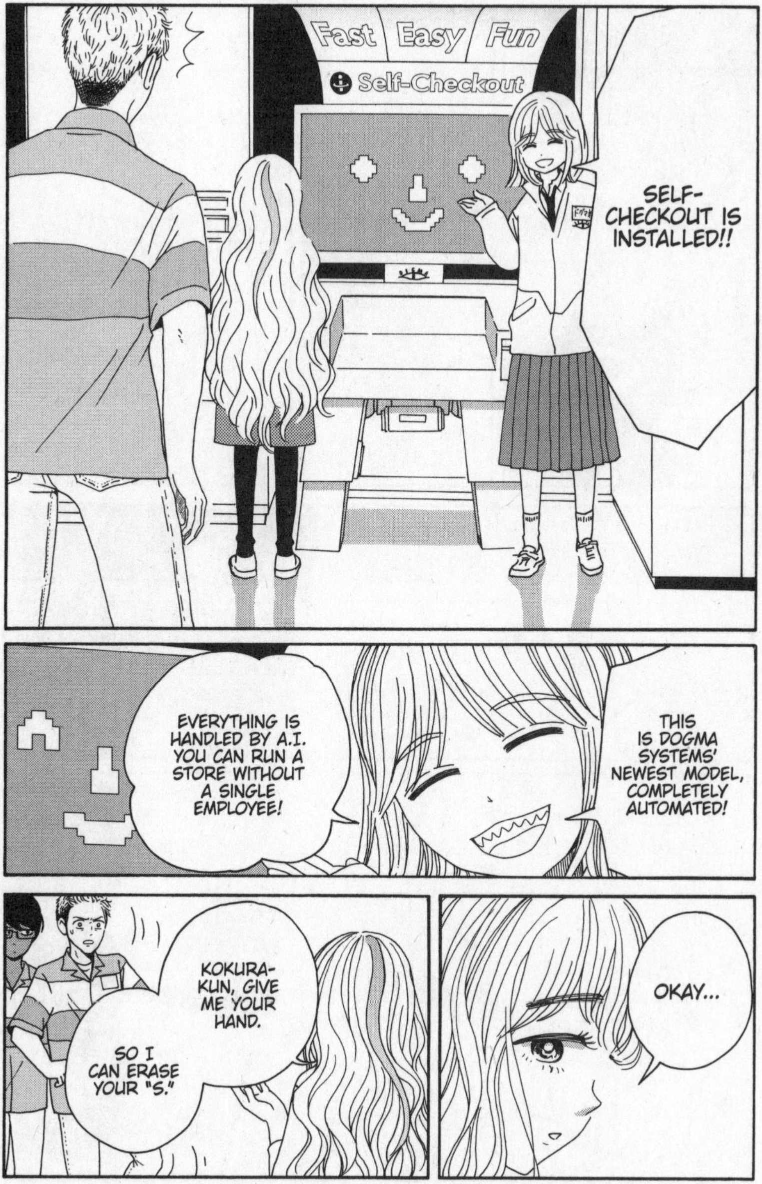

Fast Easy Fun
Self-Checkout
SELF-CHECKOUT IS INSTALLED!!
THIS IS DOGMA SYSTEMS' NEWEST MODEL, COMPLETELY AUTOMATED!
EVERYTHING IS HANDLED BY A.I. YOU CAN RUN A STORE WITHOUT A SINGLE EMPLOYEE!
OKAY...
KOKURA-KUN, GIVE ME YOUR HAND.
SO I CAN ERASE YOUR "S."

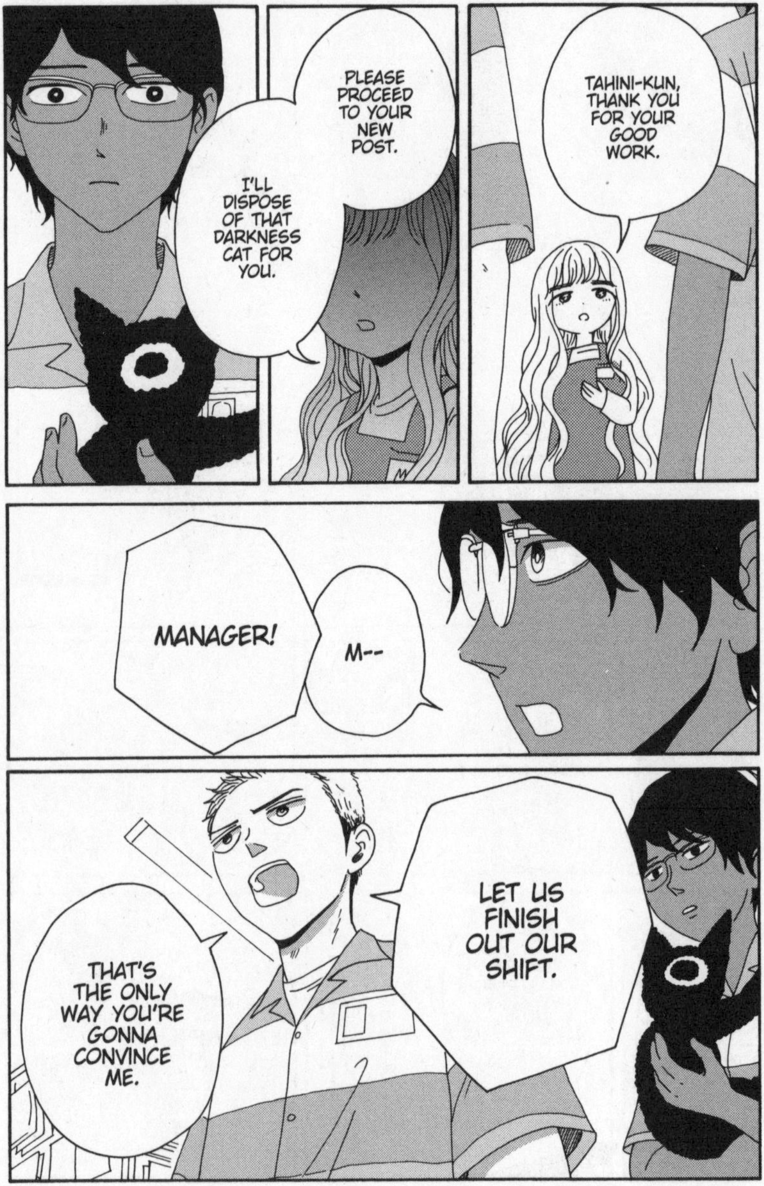
TAHINI-KUN, THANK YOU FOR YOUR GOOD WORK.
PLEASE PROCEED TO YOUR NEW POST.
I'LL DISPOSE OF THAT DARKNESS CAT FOR YOU.
M--
MANAGER!
LET US FINISH OUT OUR SHIFT.
THAT'S THE ONLY WAY YOU'RE GONNA CONVINCE ME.

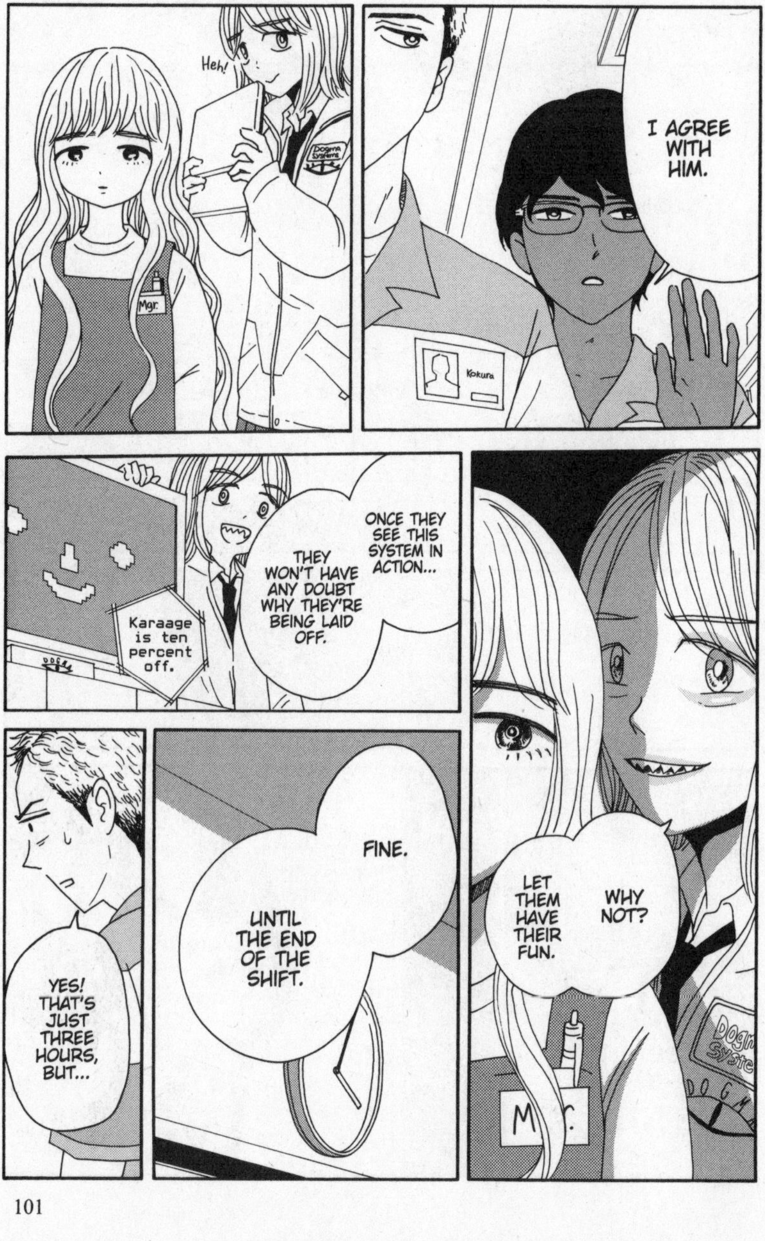
I AGREE WITH HIM.
Kokura
Heh!
Dogma Systems
Mgr.
WHY NOT?
LET THEM HAVE THEIR FUN.
Mgr.
ONCE THEY SEE THIS SYSTEM IN ACTION...
THEY WON'T HAVE ANY DOUBT WHY THEY'RE BEING LAID OFF.
Karaage is ten percent off.
FINE.
UNTIL THE END OF THE SHIFT.
YES! THAT'S JUST THREE HOURS, BUT...

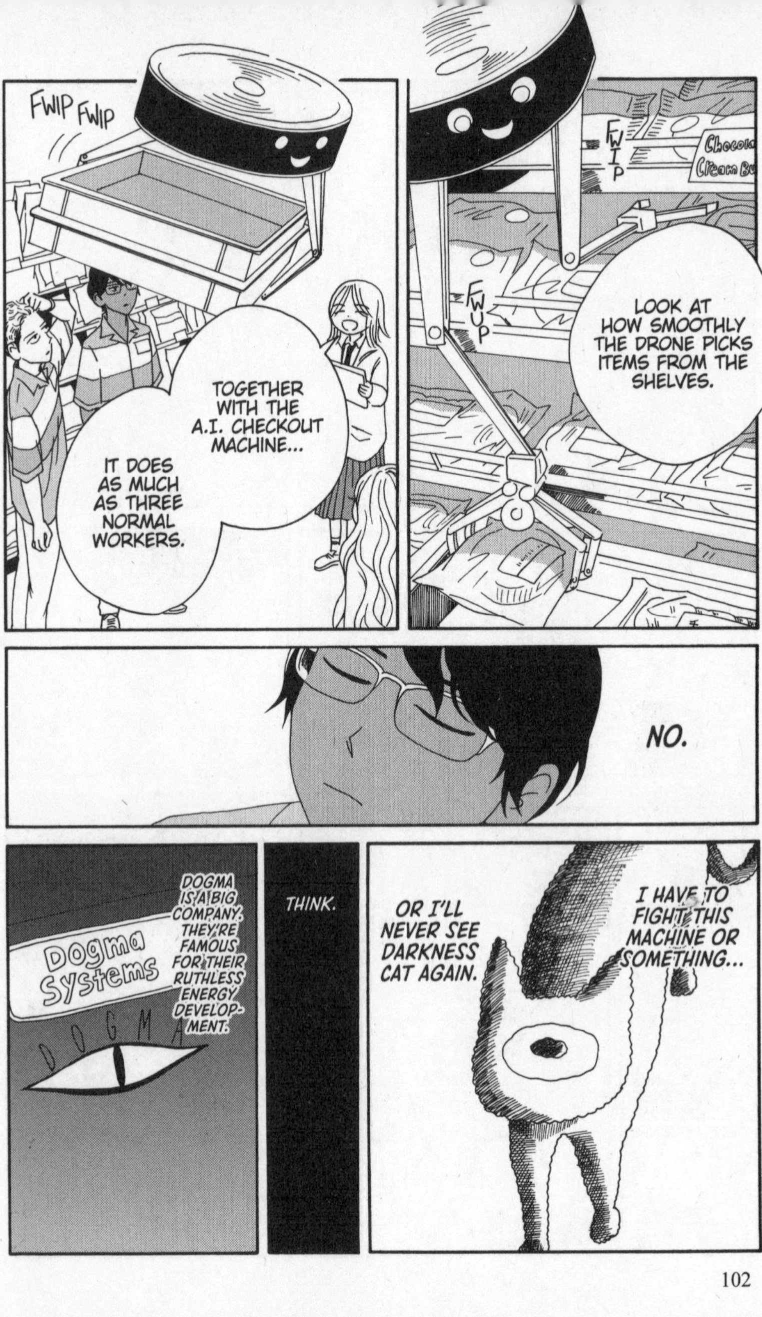
FWIP
FWUP
LOOK AT HOW SMOOTHLY THE DRONE PICKS ITEMS FROM THE SHELVES.
FWIP FWIP
TOGETHER WITH THE A.I. CHECKOUT MACHINE...
IT DOES AS MUCH AS THREE NORMAL WORKERS.
NO.
I HAVE TO FIGHT THIS MACHINE OR SOMETHING...
OR I'LL NEVER SEE DARKNESS CAT AGAIN.
THINK.
DOGMA IS A BIG COMPANY. THEY'RE FAMOUS FOR THEIR RUTHLESS ENERGY DEVELOPMENT.
Dogma Systems
DOGMA

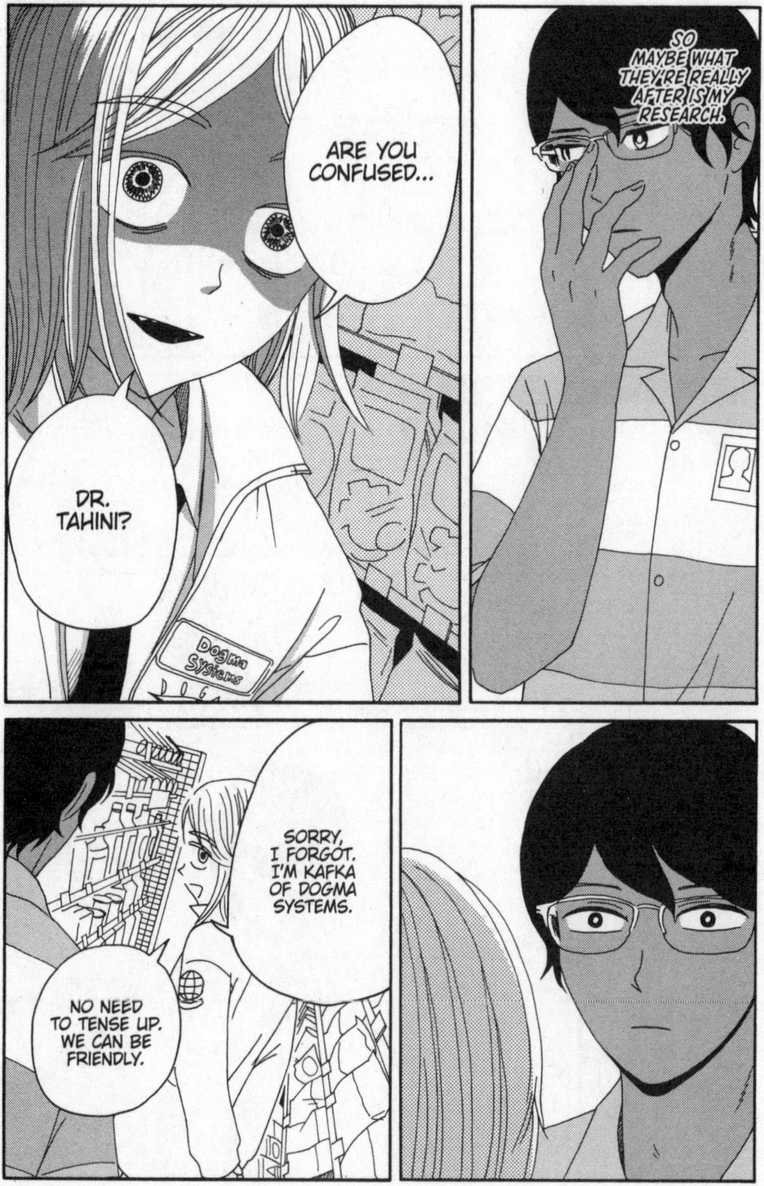
SO MAYBE WHAT THEY'RE REALLY AFTER IS MY RESEARCH.
ARE YOU CONFUSED...
DR. TAHINI?
Dogma Systems
SORRY, I FORGOT. I'M KAFKA OF DOGMA SYSTEMS.
NO NEED TO TENSE UP. WE CAN BE FRIENDLY.

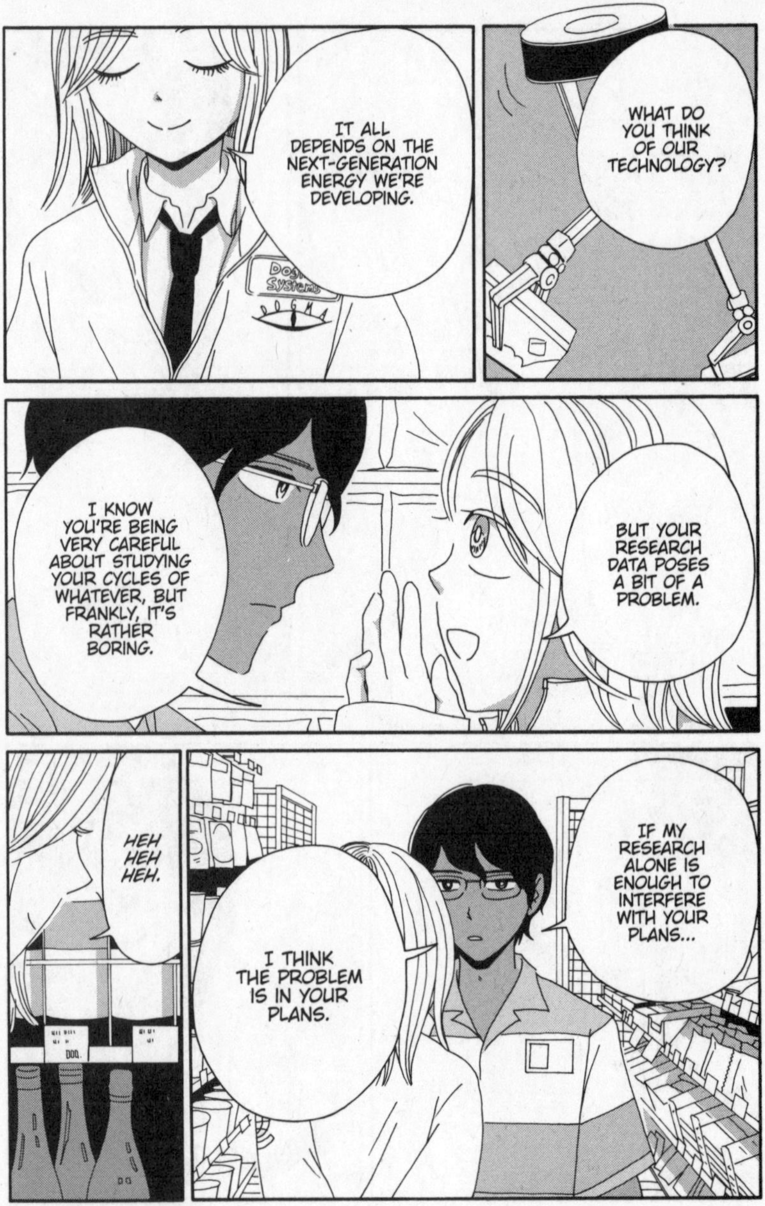
WHAT DO YOU THINK OF OUR TECHNOLOGY?
IT ALL DEPENDS ON THE NEXT-GENERATION ENERGY WE'RE DEVELOPING.
Dogma Systems
DOGMA
BUT YOUR RESEARCH DATA POSES A BIT OF A PROBLEM.
I KNOW YOU'RE BEING VERY CAREFUL ABOUT STUDYING YOUR CYCLES OF WHATEVER, BUT FRANKLY, IT'S RATHER BORING.
IF MY RESEARCH ALONE IS ENOUGH TO INTERFERE WITH YOUR PLANS...
I THINK THE PROBLEM IS IN YOUR PLANS.
HEH HEH HEH.

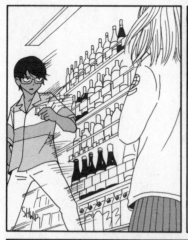

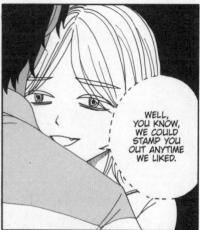

WELL, YOU KNOW, WE COULD STAMP YOU OUT ANYTIME WE LIKED.
SHWIP
OH, DON'T MAKE A SCENE IN THE MIDDLE OF THE STORE.
CAM4
ANYWAY, IF YOUR PLAN IS TO HOLD ON TO YOUR DATA AND CONTINUE YOUR RESEARCH...
WE HAVE OUR OWN THOUGHTS ABOUT THAT.
SQUEAK
I SUGGEST YOU WATCH OUR MACHINE A LITTLE LONGER AND THINK IT OVER.
DING-DONG
OH! A CUSTOMER!

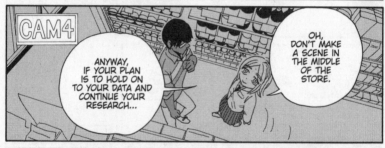

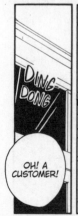

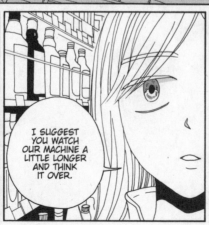

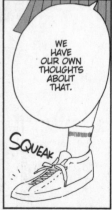

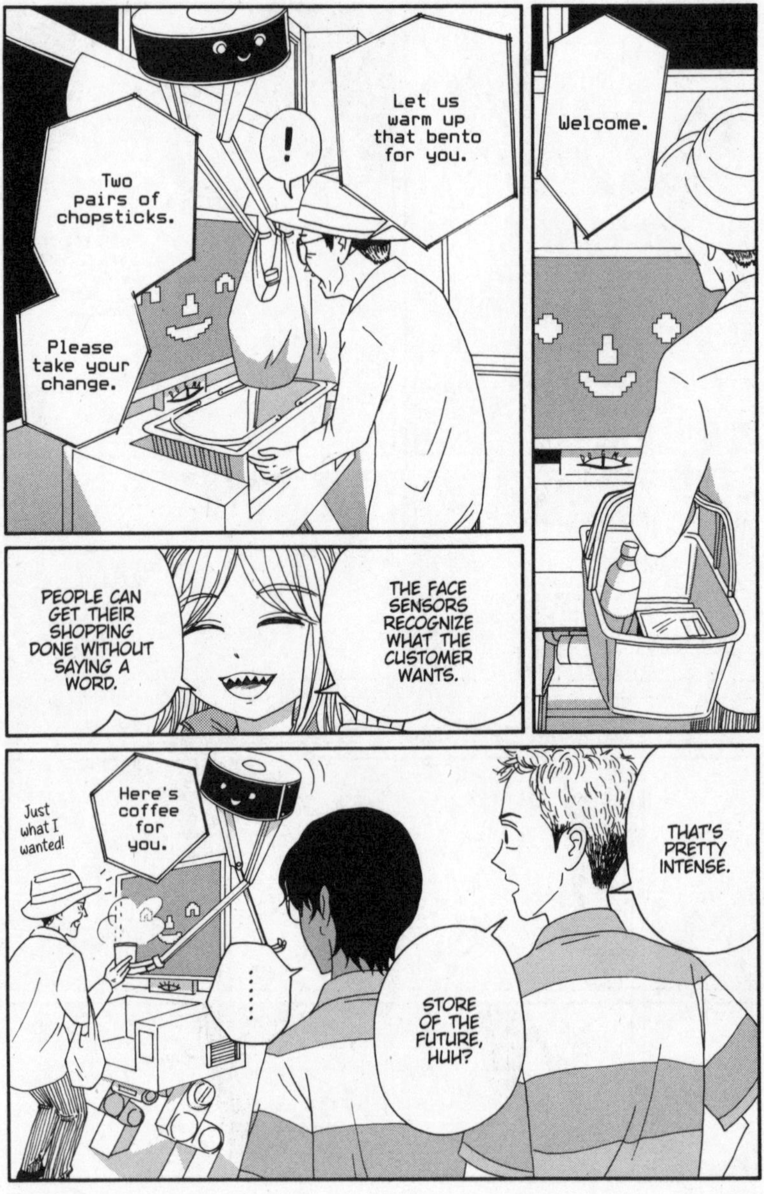
Welcome.
Let us warm up that bento for you.
!
Two pairs of chopsticks.
Please take your change.
THE FACE SENSORS RECOGNIZE WHAT THE CUSTOMER WANTS.
PEOPLE CAN GET THEIR SHOPPING DONE WITHOUT SAYING A WORD.
THAT'S PRETTY INTENSE.
Here's coffee for you.
Just what I wanted!
......
STORE OF THE FUTURE, HUH?

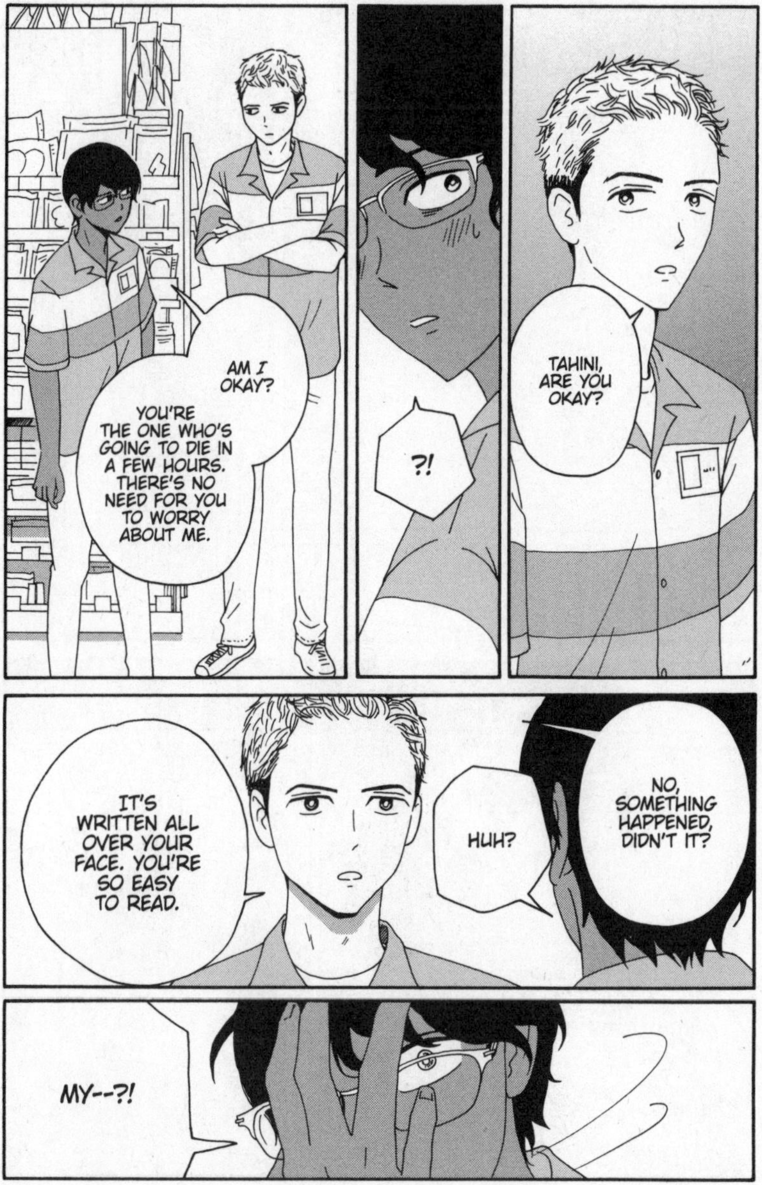
TAHINI, ARE YOU OKAY?
?!
AM I OKAY?
YOU'RE THE ONE WHO'S GOING TO DIE IN A FEW HOURS. THERE'S NO NEED FOR YOU TO WORRY ABOUT ME.
NO, SOMETHING HAPPENED, DIDN'T IT?
HUH?
IT'S WRITTEN ALL OVER YOUR FACE. YOU'RE SO EASY TO READ.
MY--?!

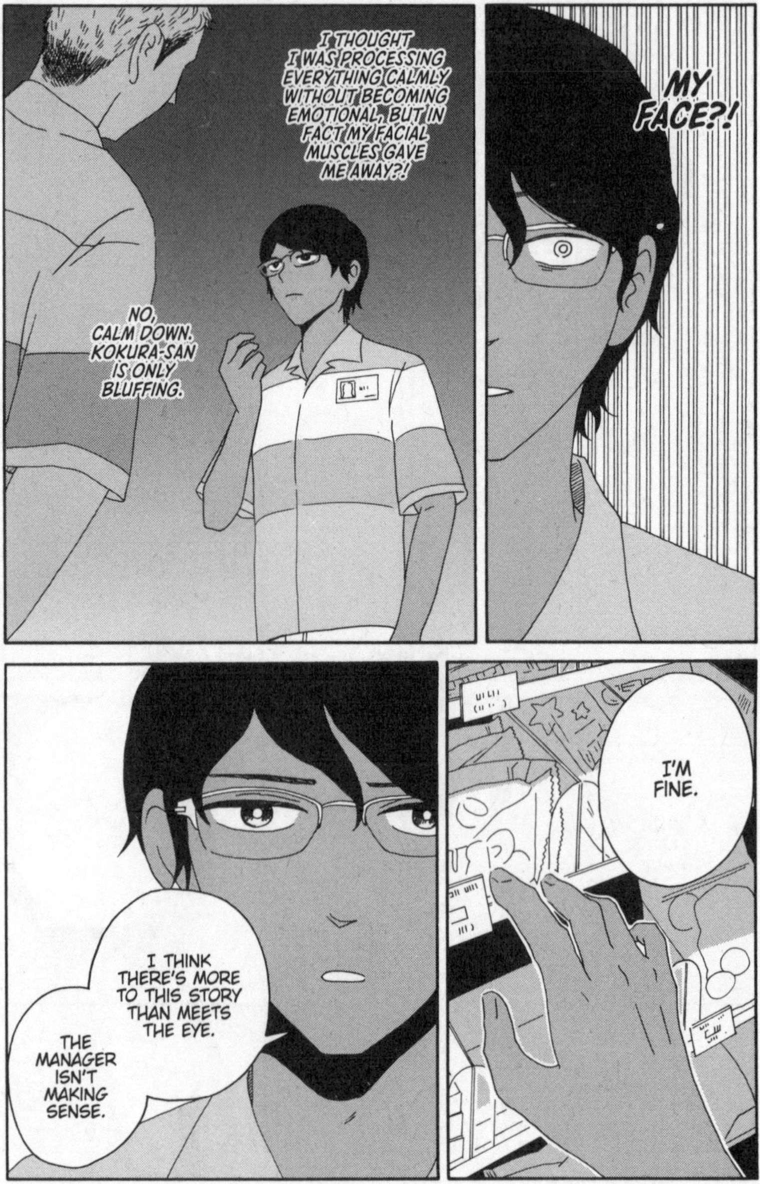
MY FACE?!
I THOUGHT I WAS PROCESSING EVERYTHING CALMLY WITHOUT BECOMING EMOTIONAL, BUT IN FACT MY FACIAL MUSCLES GAVE ME AWAY?!
NO, CALM DOWN. KOKURA-SAN IS ONLY BLUFFING.
I'M FINE.
I THINK THERE'S MORE TO THIS STORY THAN MEETS THE EYE.
THE MANAGER ISN'T MAKING SENSE.

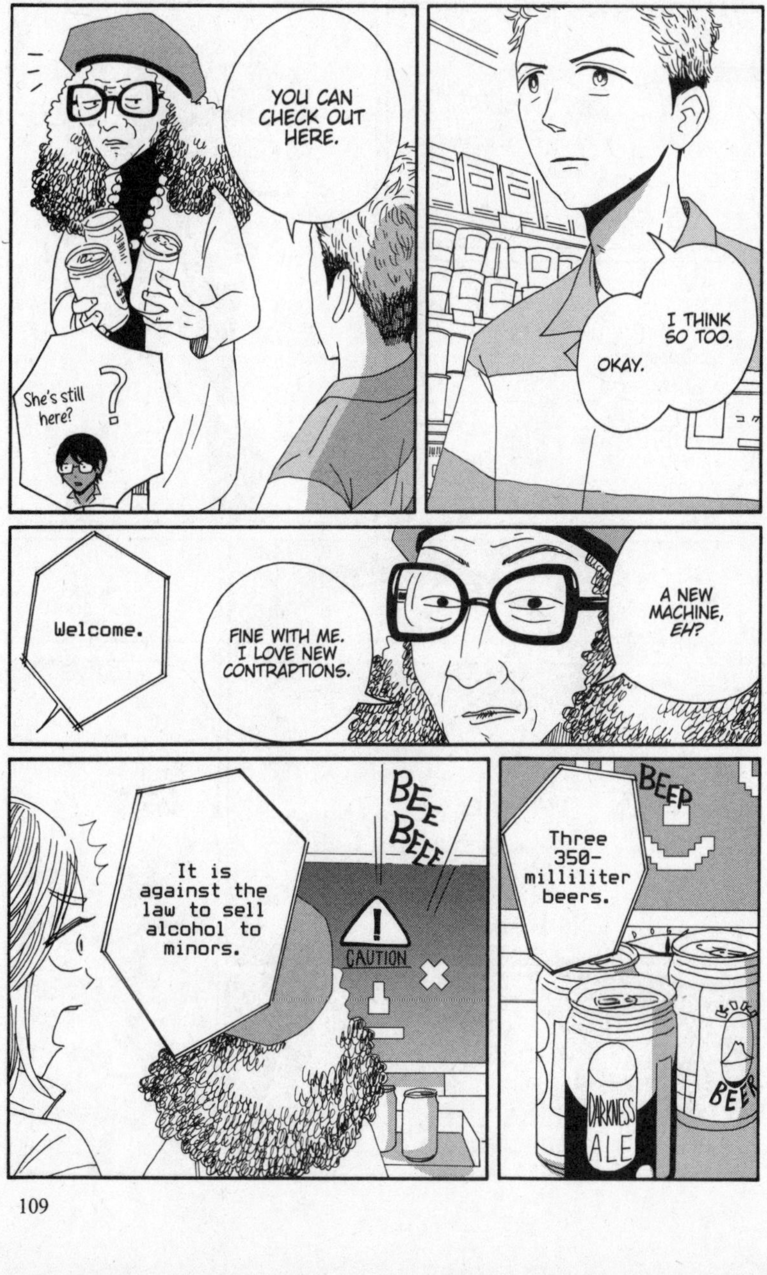
I THINK SO TOO.
OKAY.
YOU CAN CHECK OUT HERE.
She's still here?
A NEW MACHINE, EH?
FINE WITH ME. I LOVE NEW CONTRAPTIONS.
Welcome.
BEEP
Three 350-milliliter beers.
DARKNESS ALE
BEER
BEE BEEE
CAUTION
It is against the law to sell alcohol to minors.

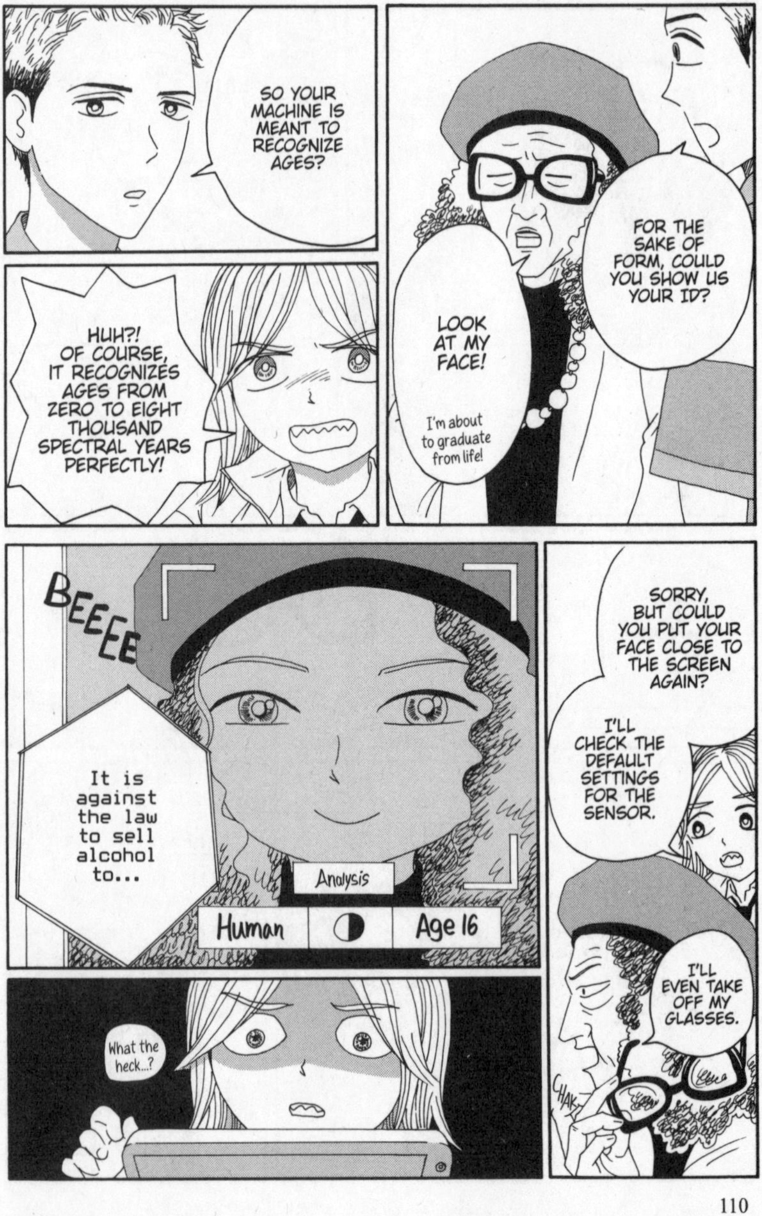

FOR THE SAKE OF FORM, COULD YOU SHOW US YOUR ID?
LOOK AT MY FACE!
I'm about to graduate from life!
SO YOUR MACHINE IS MEANT TO RECOGNIZE AGES?
HUH?! OF COURSE, IT RECOGNIZES AGES FROM ZERO TO EIGHT THOUSAND SPECTRAL YEARS PERFECTLY!
SORRY, BUT COULD YOU PUT YOUR FACE CLOSE TO THE SCREEN AGAIN?
I'LL CHECK THE DEFAULT SETTINGS FOR THE SENSOR.
I'LL EVEN TAKE OFF MY GLASSES.
CHAK
BEEEE
It is against the law to sell alcohol to...
Analysis
Human
Age 16
What the heck...?

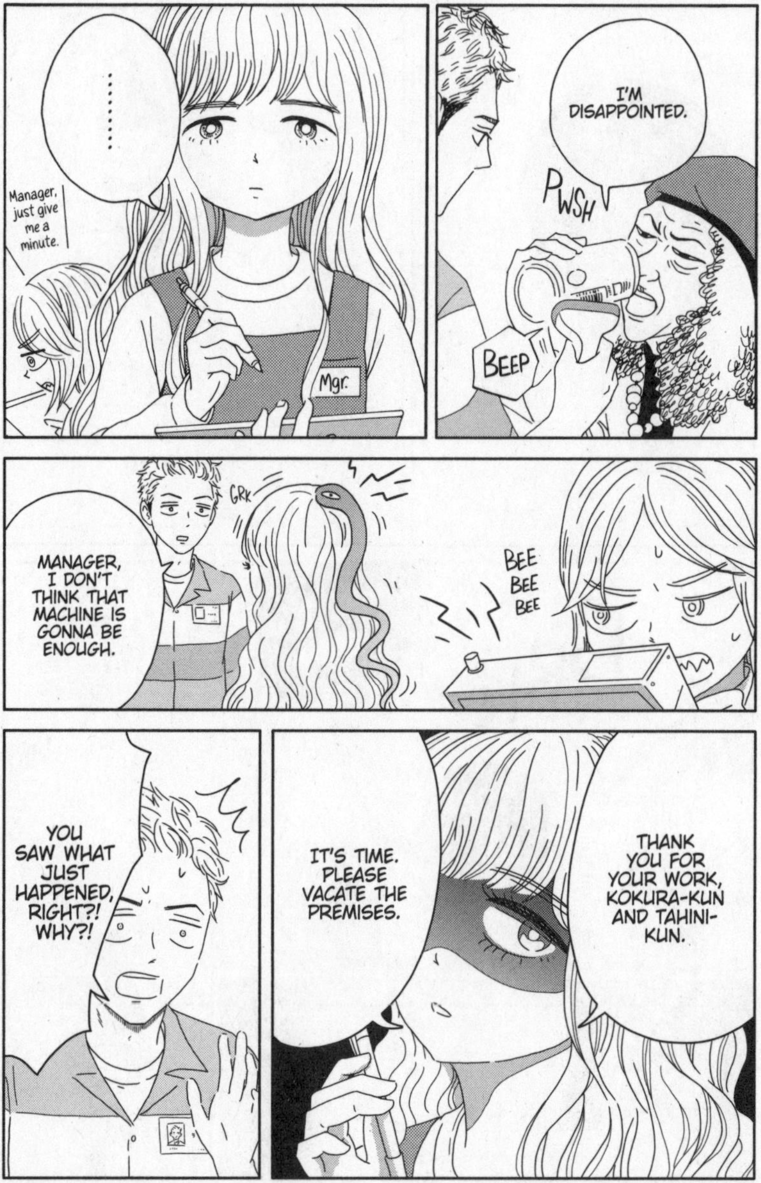
I'M DISAPPOINTED.
PWSH
BEEP
......
Manager, just give me a minute.
BEE BEE BEE
GRK
MANAGER, I DON'T THINK THAT MACHINE IS GONNA BE ENOUGH.
THANK YOU FOR YOUR WORK, KOKURA-KUN AND TAHINI-KUN.
IT'S TIME. PLEASE VACATE THE PREMISES.
YOU SAW WHAT JUST HAPPENED, RIGHT?! WHY?!

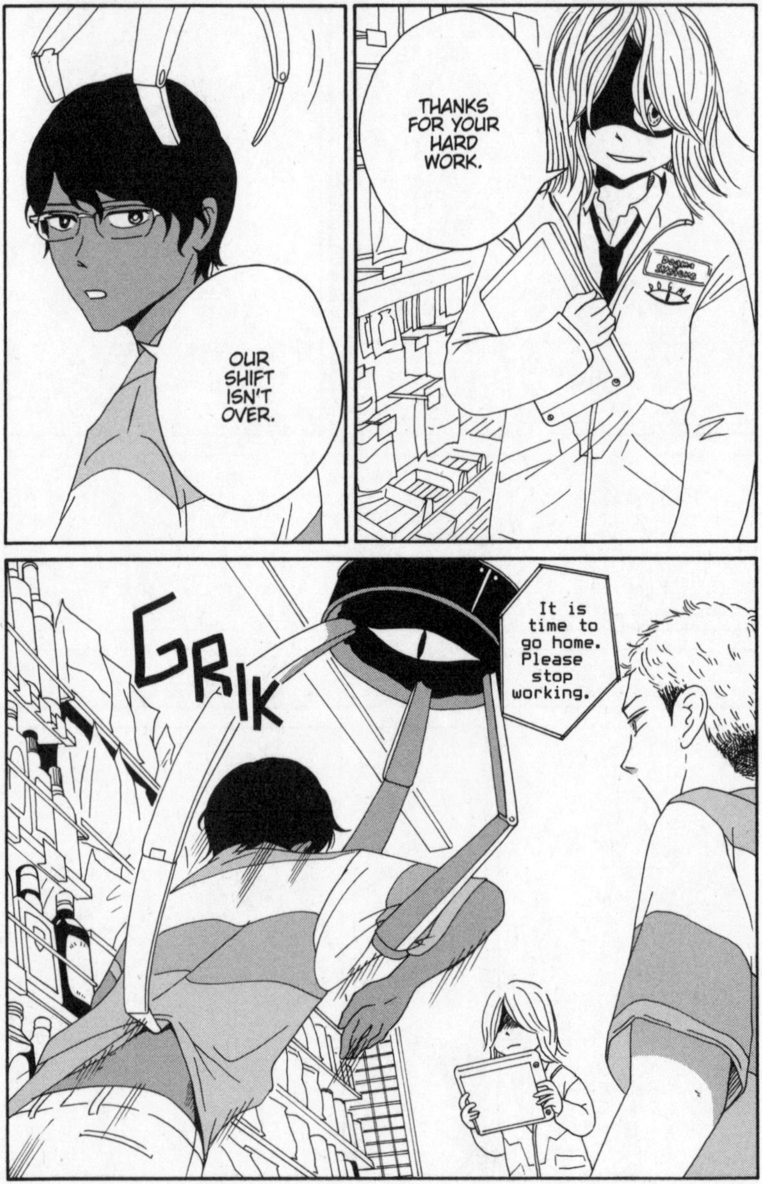
THANKS FOR YOUR HARD WORK.
OUR SHIFT ISN'T OVER.
It is time to go home. Please stop working.
GRIK

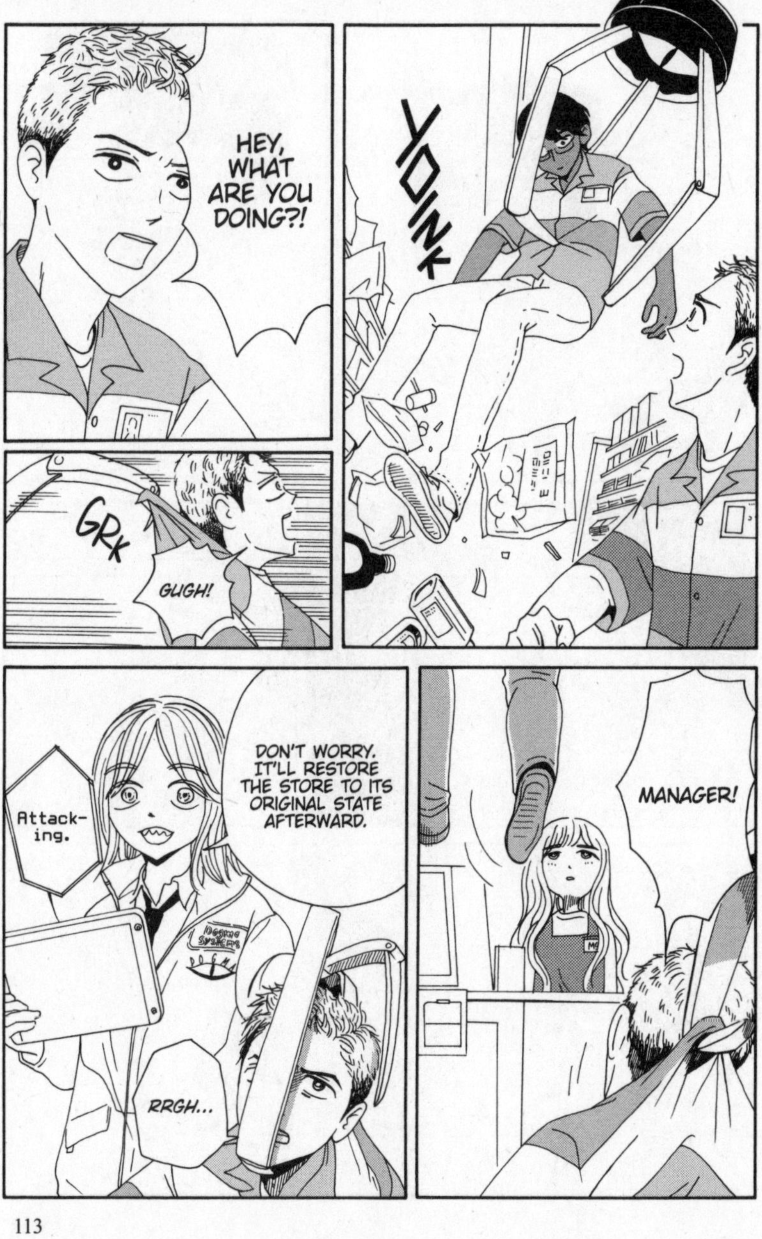
YOINK
HEY, WHAT ARE YOU DOING?!
GRk
GUGH!
MANAGER!
DON'T WORRY. IT'LL RESTORE THE STORE TO ITS ORIGINAL STATE AFTERWARD.
Attack-ing.
RRGH...

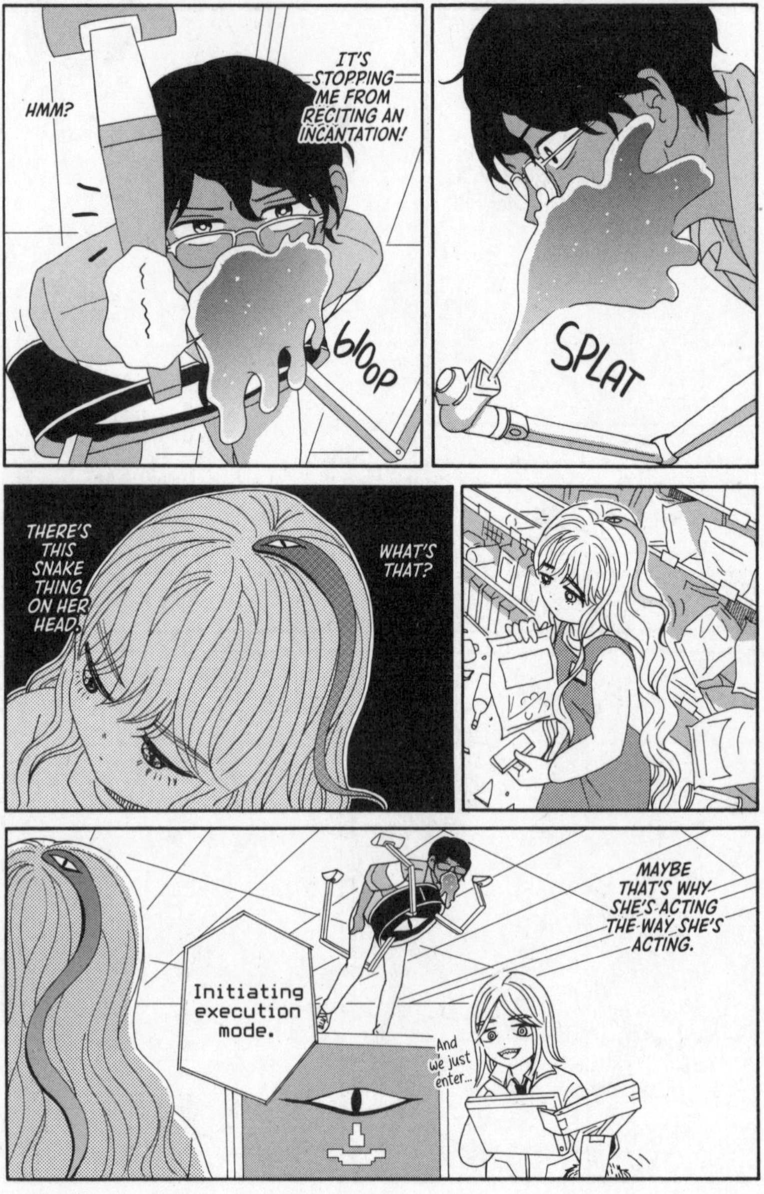
SPLAT
IT'S STOPPING ME FROM RECITING AN INCANTATION!
HMM?
bloop
WHAT'S THAT?
THERE'S THIS SNAKE THING ON HER HEAD.
MAYBE THAT'S WHY SHE'S ACTING THE WAY SHE'S ACTING.
Initiating execution mode.
And we just enter...

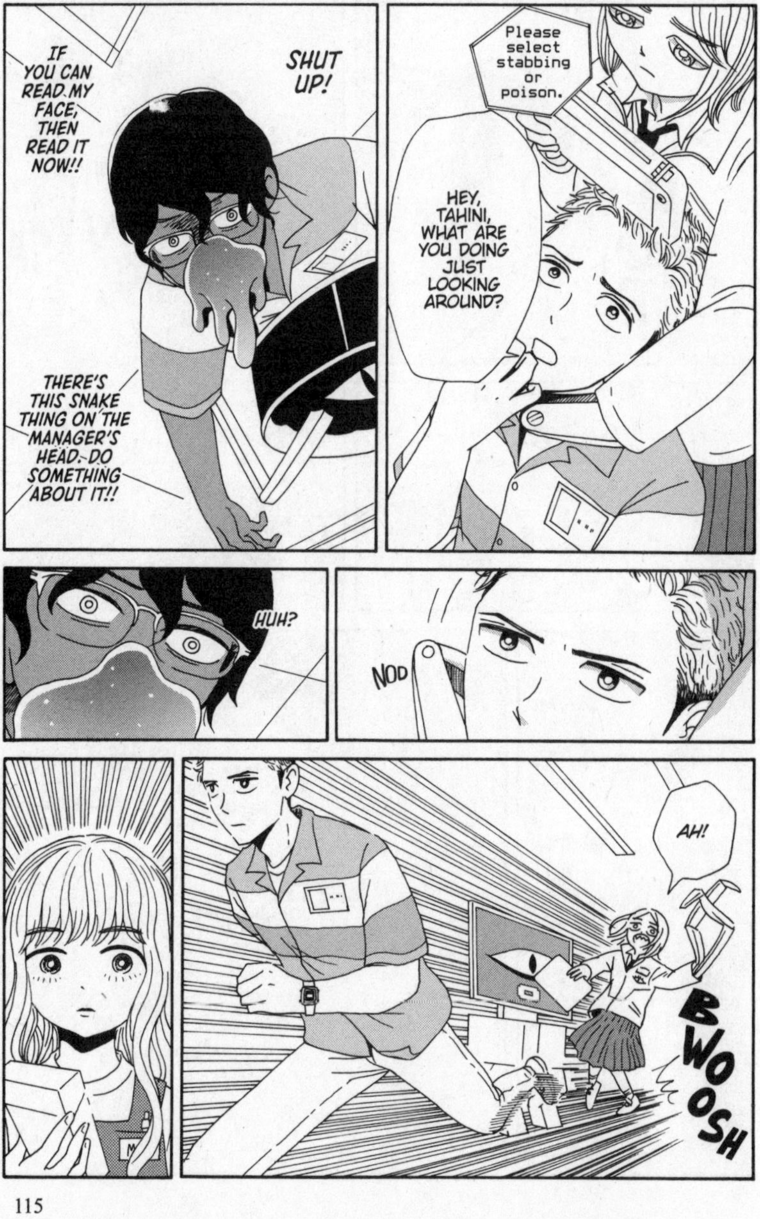
Please select stabbing or poison.
HEY, TAHINI, WHAT ARE YOU DOING JUST LOOKING AROUND?
SHUT UP!
IF YOU CAN READ MY FACE, THEN READ IT NOW!!
THERE'S THIS SNAKE THING ON THE MANAGER'S HEAD. DO SOMETHING ABOUT IT!!
NOD
HUH?
AH!
BWOOSH

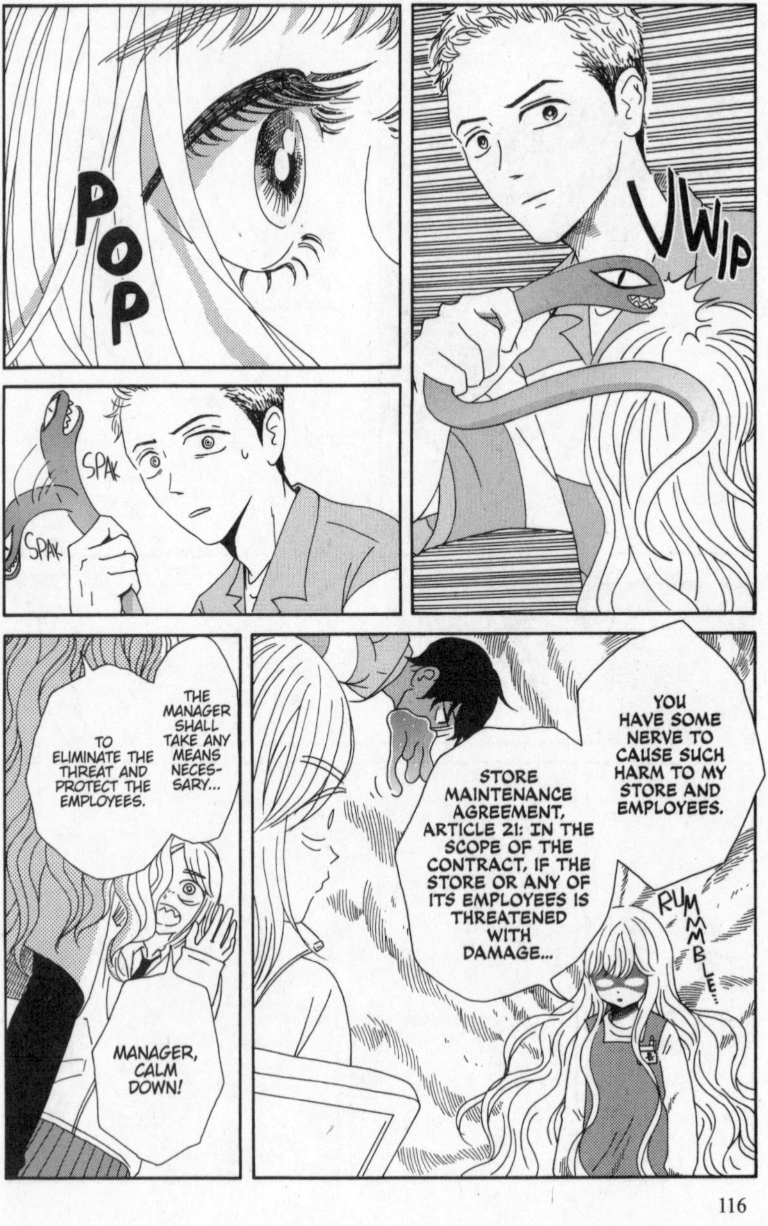
VWIP
POP
SPAK
SPAK
YOU HAVE SOME NERVE TO CAUSE SUCH HARM TO MY STORE AND EMPLOYEES.
STORE MAINTENANCE AGREEMENT, ARTICLE 21: IN THE SCOPE OF THE CONTRACT, IF THE STORE OR ANY OF ITS EMPLOYEES IS THREATENED WITH DAMAGE...
RUMMMBLE...
THE MANAGER SHALL TAKE ANY MEANS NECES-SARY...
TO ELIMINATE THE THREAT AND PROTECT THE EMPLOYEES.
MANAGER, CALM DOWN!

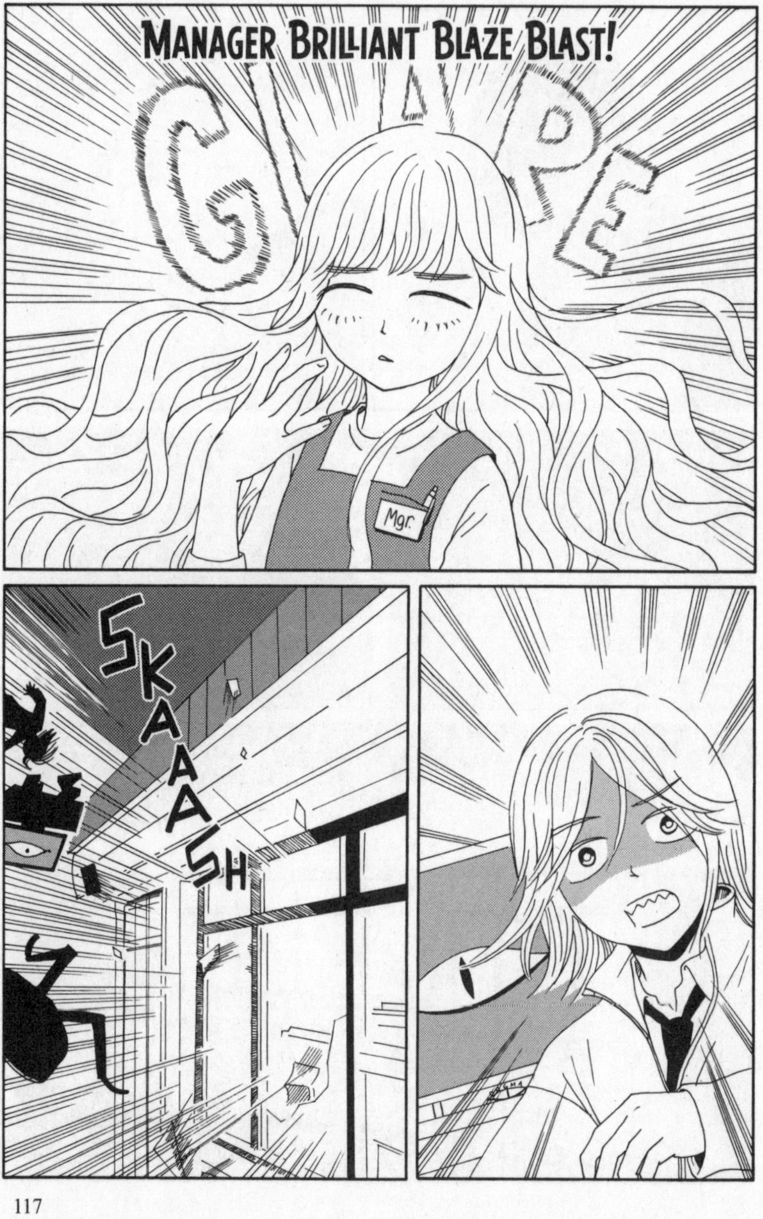
MANAGER BRILLIANT BLAZE BLAST!
Mgr.
SKAAASH

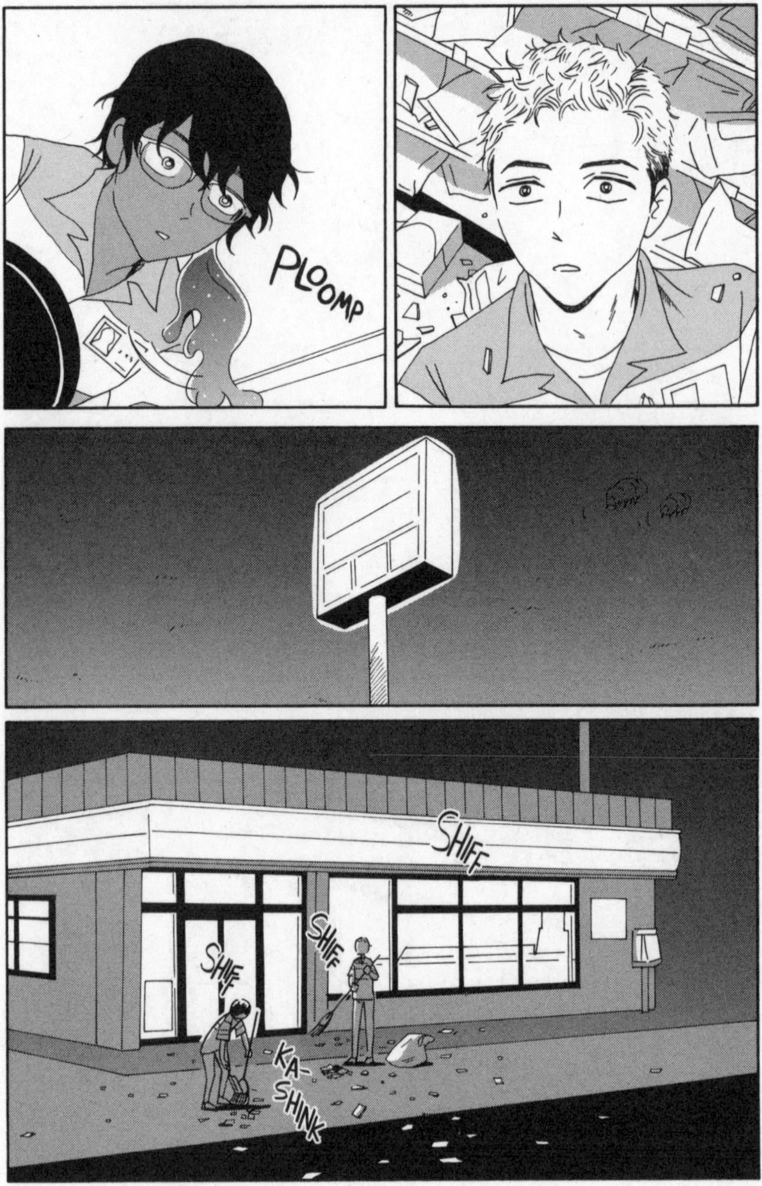
PLOOMP
SHIFF
SHIFF
SHIFF
KA-SHINK

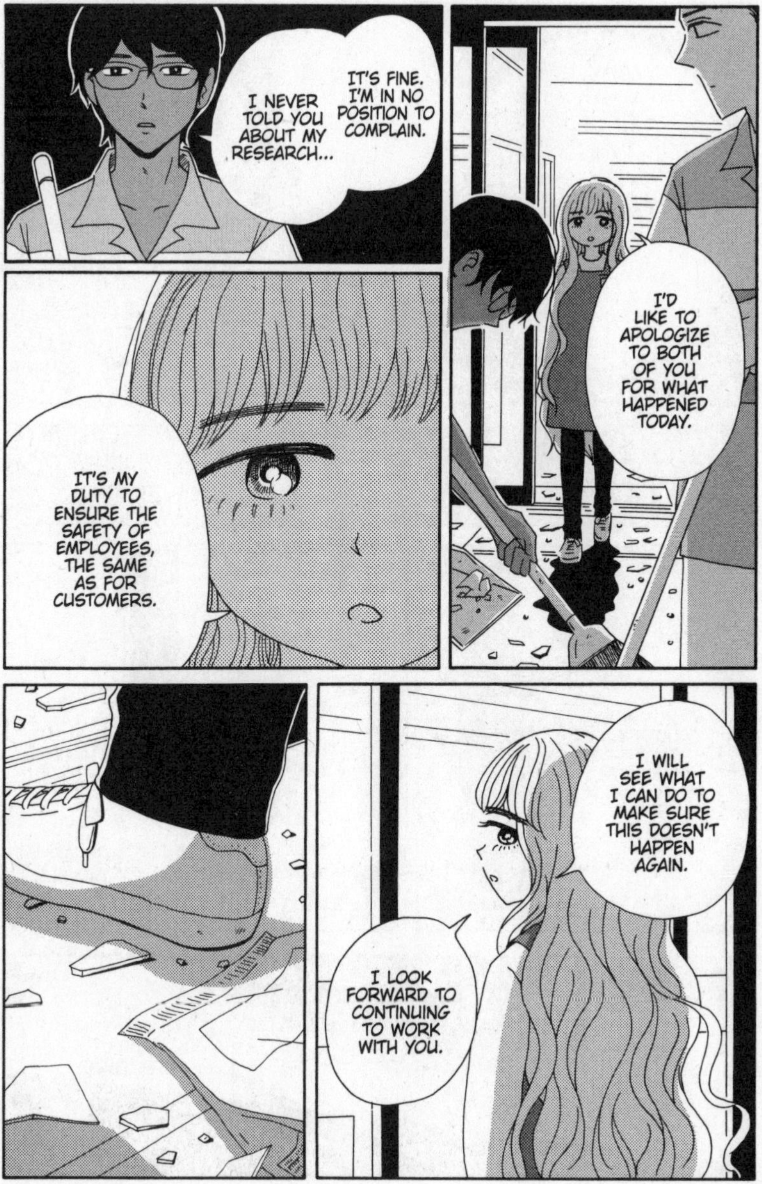
I'D LIKE TO APOLOGIZE TO BOTH OF YOU FOR WHAT HAPPENED TODAY.
IT'S FINE. I'M IN NO POSITION TO COMPLAIN.
I NEVER TOLD YOU ABOUT MY RESEARCH...
IT'S MY DUTY TO ENSURE THE SAFETY OF EMPLOYEES, THE SAME AS FOR CUSTOMERS.
I WILL SEE WHAT I CAN DO TO MAKE SURE THIS DOESN'T HAPPEN AGAIN.
I LOOK FORWARD TO CONTINUING TO WORK WITH YOU.

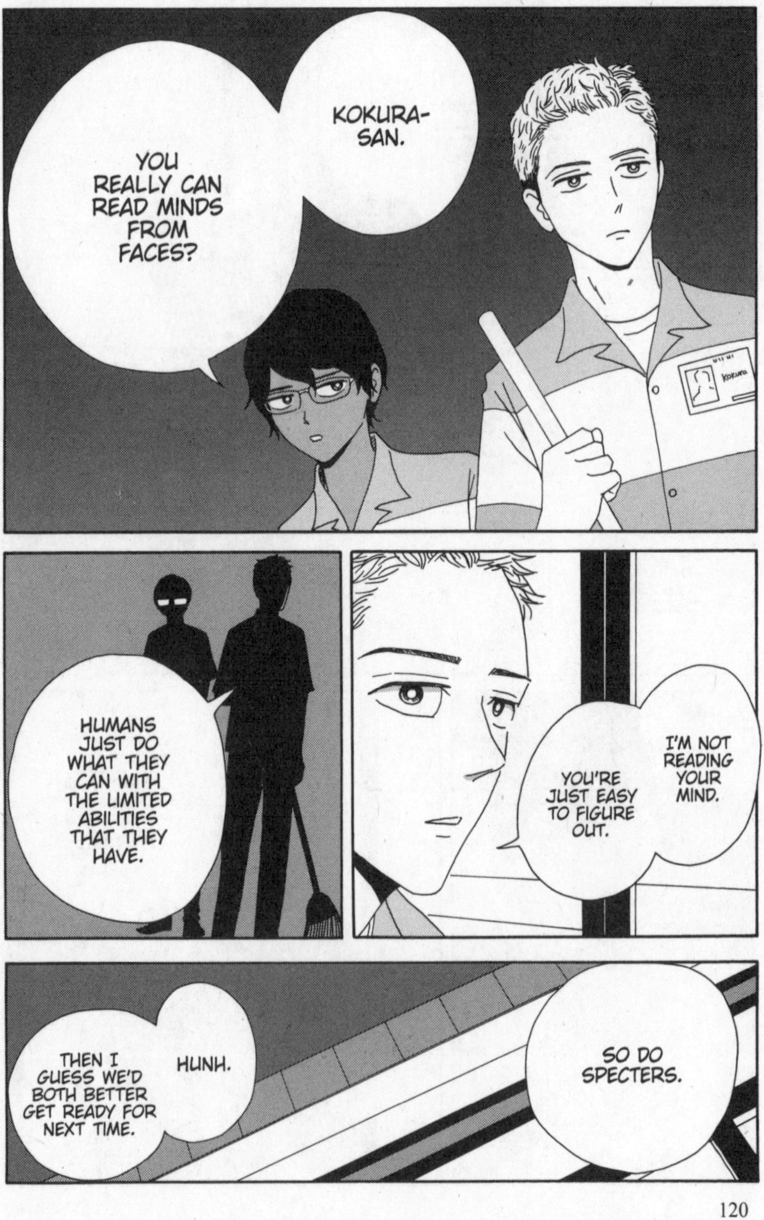
KOKURA-SAN.
YOU REALLY CAN READ MINDS FROM FACES?
I'M NOT READING YOUR MIND.
YOU'RE JUST EASY TO FIGURE OUT.
HUMANS JUST DO WHAT THEY CAN WITH THE LIMITED ABILITIES THAT THEY HAVE.
SO DO SPECTERS.
HUNH.
THEN I GUESS WE'D BOTH BETTER GET READY FOR NEXT TIME.

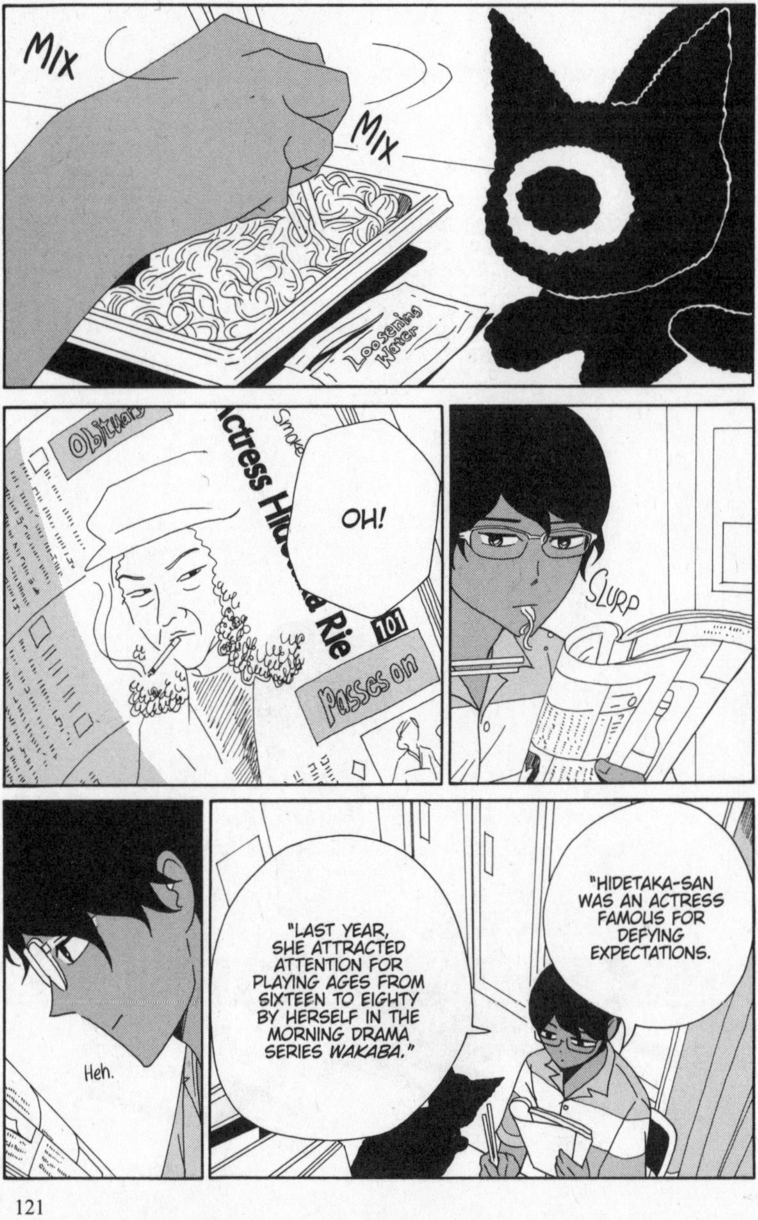
MIX
MIX
Loosening Water
SLURP
Smoke
OH!
101
passes on
"HIDETAKA-SAN WAS AN ACTRESS FAMOUS FOR DEFYING EXPECTATIONS.
"LAST YEAR, SHE ATTRACTED ATTENTION FOR PLAYING AGES FROM SIXTEEN TO EIGHTY BY HERSELF IN THE MORNING DRAMA SERIES *WAKABA*."
Heh.

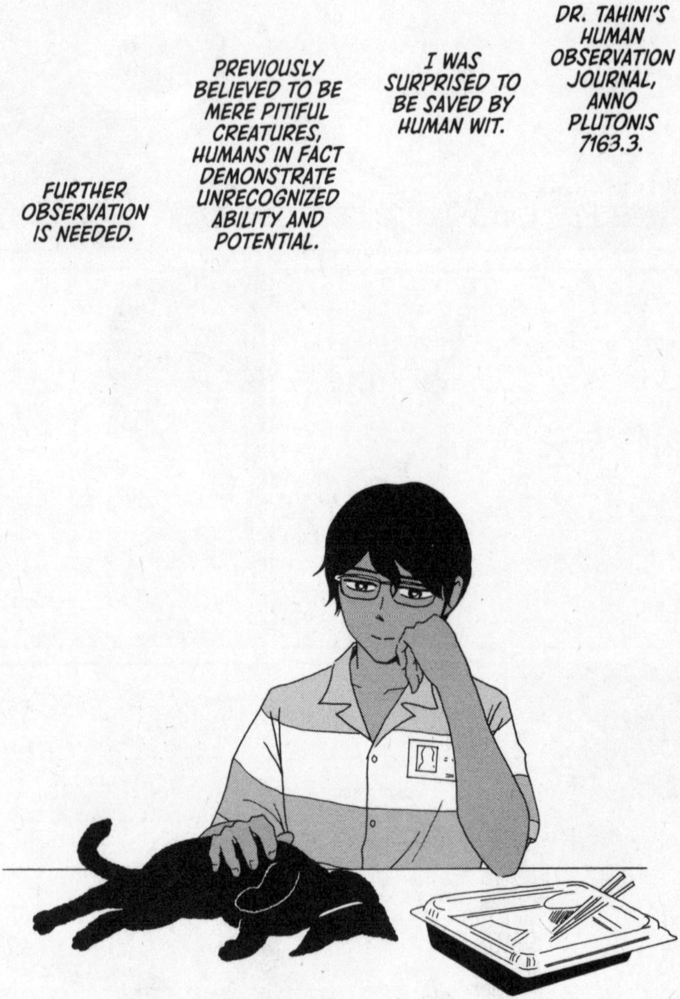
DR. TAHINI'S HUMAN OBSERVATION JOURNAL, ANNO PLUTONIS 7163.3.
I WAS SURPRISED TO BE SAVED BY HUMAN WIT.
PREVIOUSLY BELIEVED TO BE MERE PITIFUL CREATURES, HUMANS IN FACT DEMONSTRATE UNRECOGNIZED ABILITY AND POTENTIAL.
FURTHER OBSERVATION IS NEEDED.

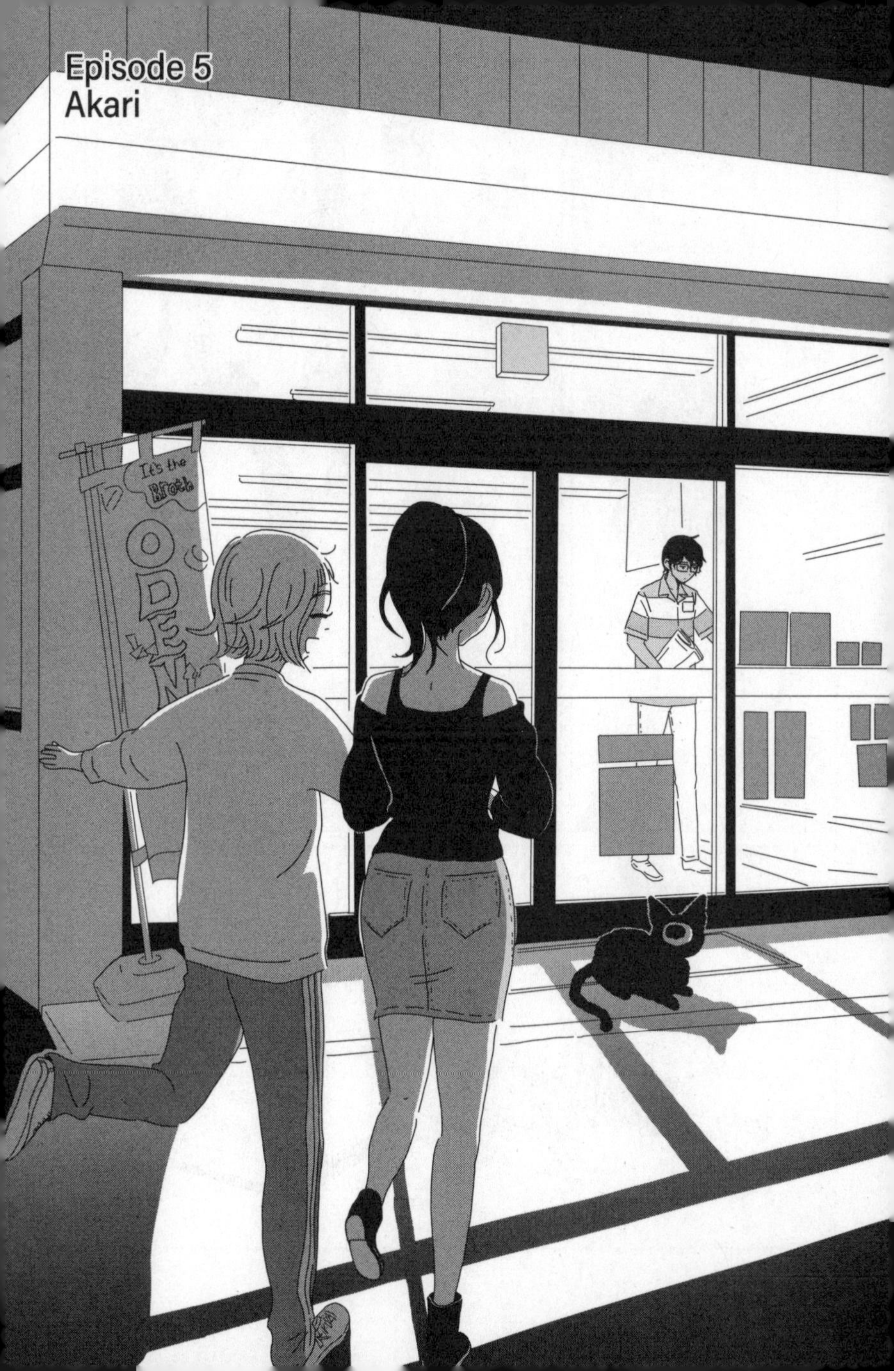
Episode 5
Akari
It's the Broth
ODEN

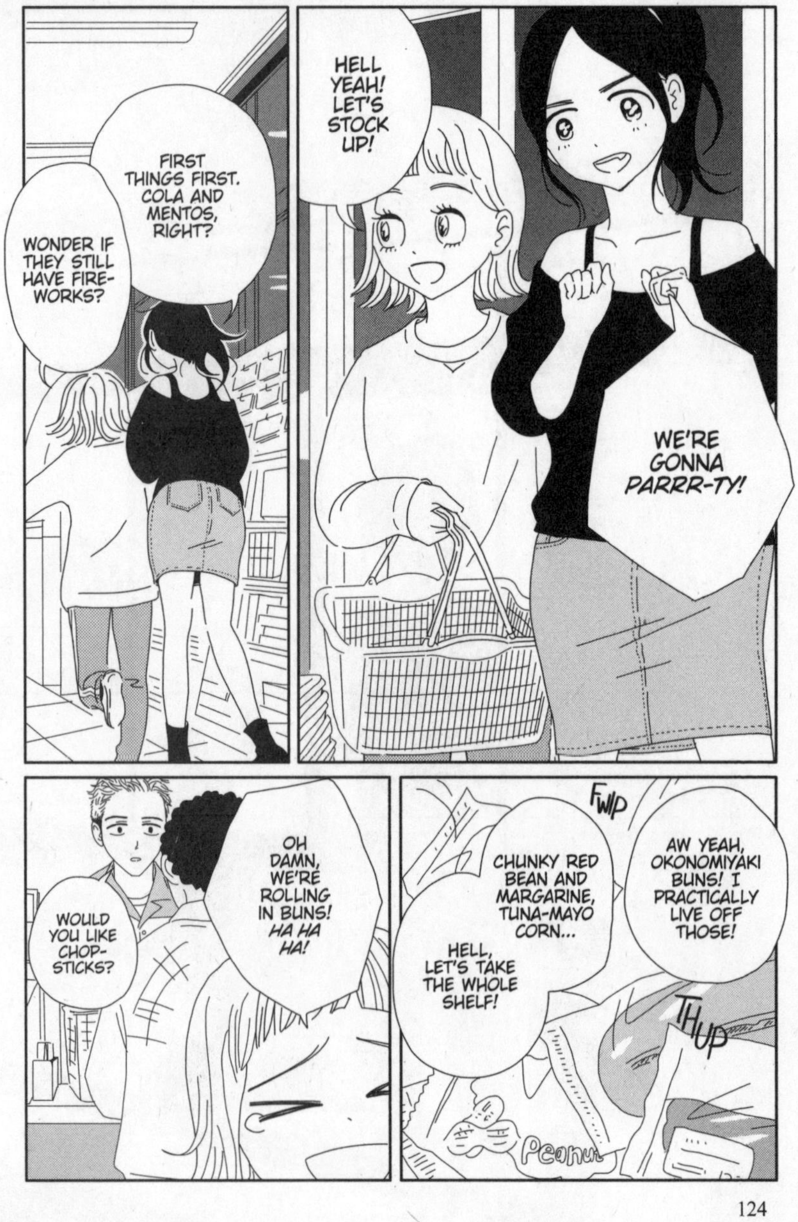
HELL YEAH! LET'S STOCK UP!
WE'RE GONNA *PARRR-TY!*
FIRST THINGS FIRST. COLA AND MENTOS, RIGHT?
WONDER IF THEY STILL HAVE FIRE-WORKS?
FWIP
AW YEAH, OKONOMIYAKI BUNS! I PRACTICALLY LIVE OFF THOSE!
CHUNKY RED BEAN AND MARGARINE, TUNA-MAYO CORN...
HELL, LET'S TAKE THE WHOLE SHELF!
THUP
OH DAMN, WE'RE ROLLING IN BUNS! *HA HA HA!*
WOULD YOU LIKE CHOP-STICKS?

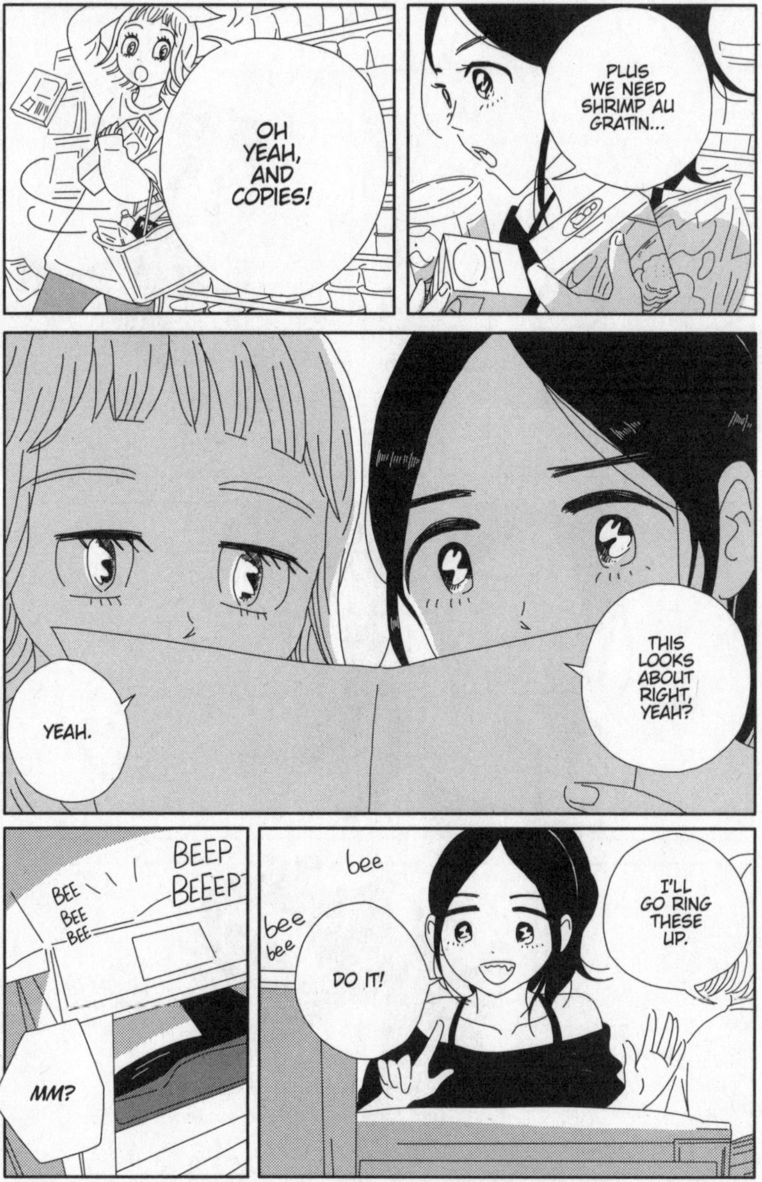
PLUS WE NEED SHRIMP AU GRATIN...
OH YEAH, AND COPIES!
THIS LOOKS ABOUT RIGHT, YEAH?
YEAH.
I'LL GO RING THESE UP.
bee
bee bee
DO IT!
BEEP BEEEP
BEE BEE BEE
MM?

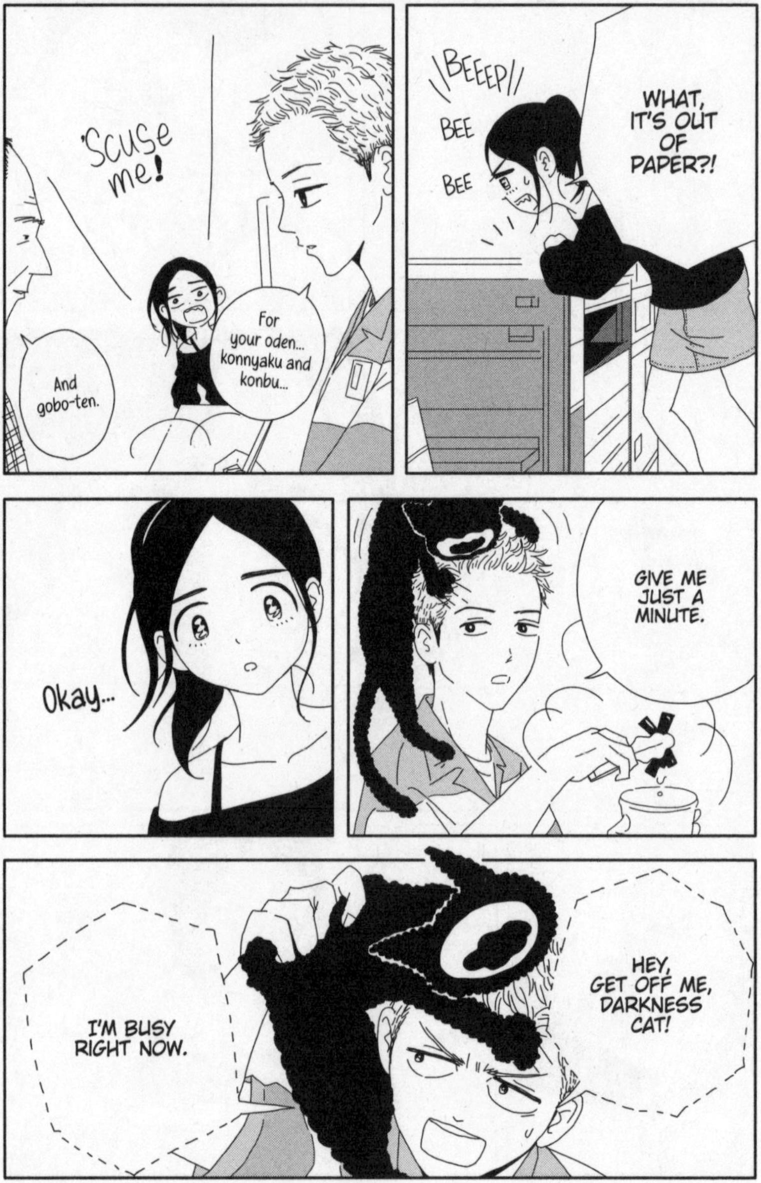
BEEEP
BEE
BEE
WHAT, IT'S OUT OF PAPER?!
'Scuse me!
For your oden... konnyaku and konbu...
And gobo-ten.
GIVE ME JUST A MINUTE.
Okay...
HEY, GET OFF ME, DARKNESS CAT!
I'M BUSY RIGHT NOW.

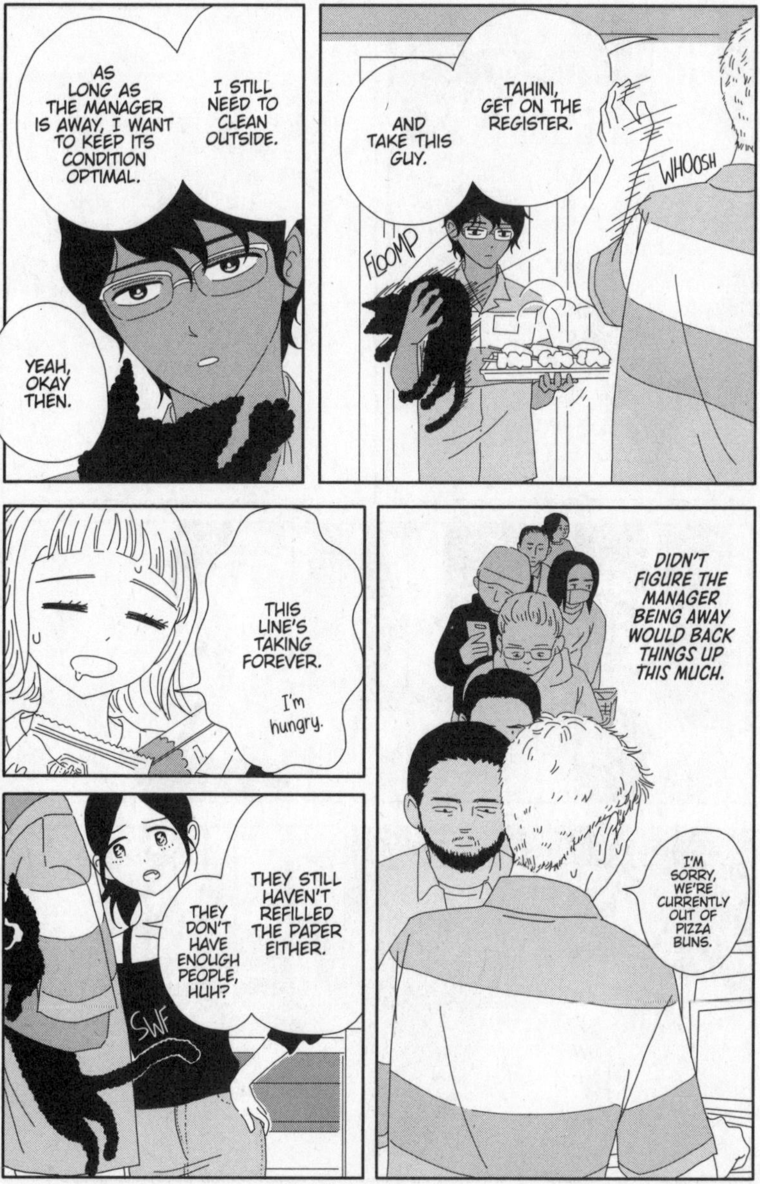
TAHINI, GET ON THE REGISTER.
AND TAKE THIS GUY.
WHOOSH
FLOOMP
I STILL NEED TO CLEAN OUTSIDE.
AS LONG AS THE MANAGER IS AWAY, I WANT TO KEEP ITS CONDITION OPTIMAL.
YEAH, OKAY THEN.
DIDN'T FIGURE THE MANAGER BEING AWAY WOULD BACK THINGS UP THIS MUCH.
I'M SORRY, WE'RE CURRENTLY OUT OF PIZZA BUNS.
THIS LINE'S TAKING FOREVER.
I'm hungry.
THEY STILL HAVEN'T REFILLED THE PAPER EITHER.
THEY DON'T HAVE ENOUGH PEOPLE, HUH?

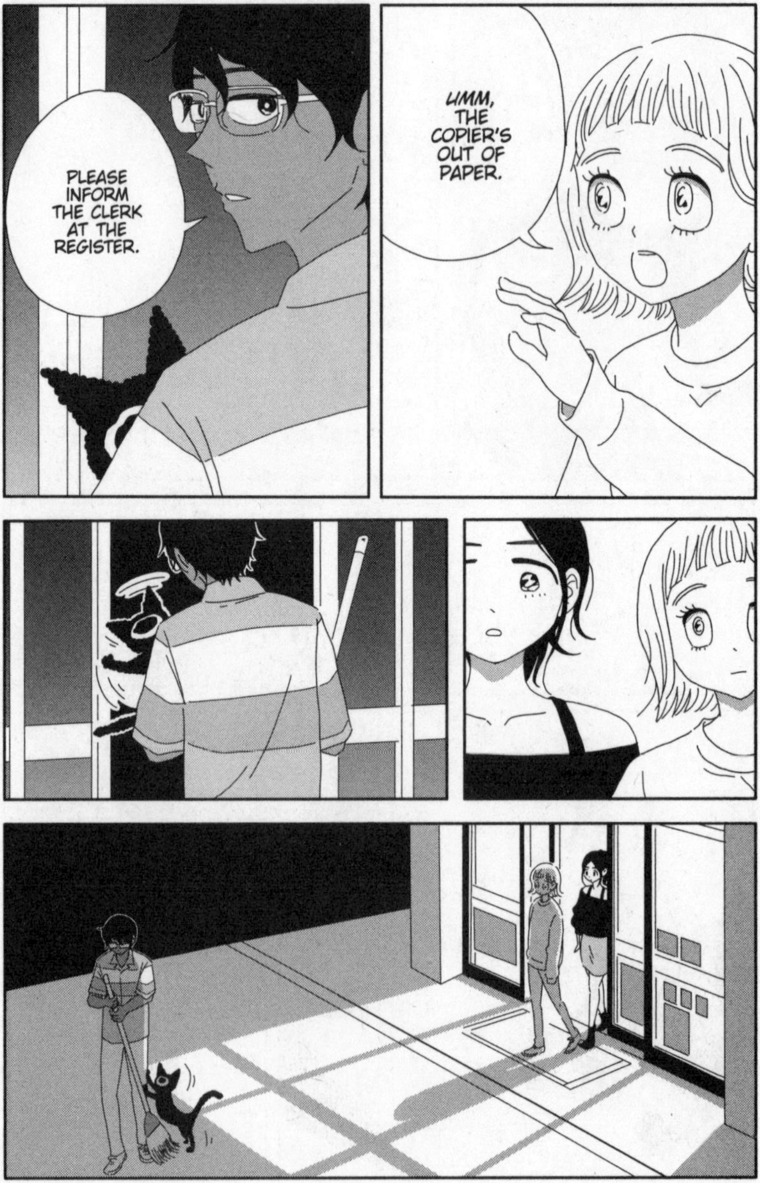
UMM, THE COPIER'S OUT OF PAPER.
PLEASE INFORM THE CLERK AT THE REGISTER.

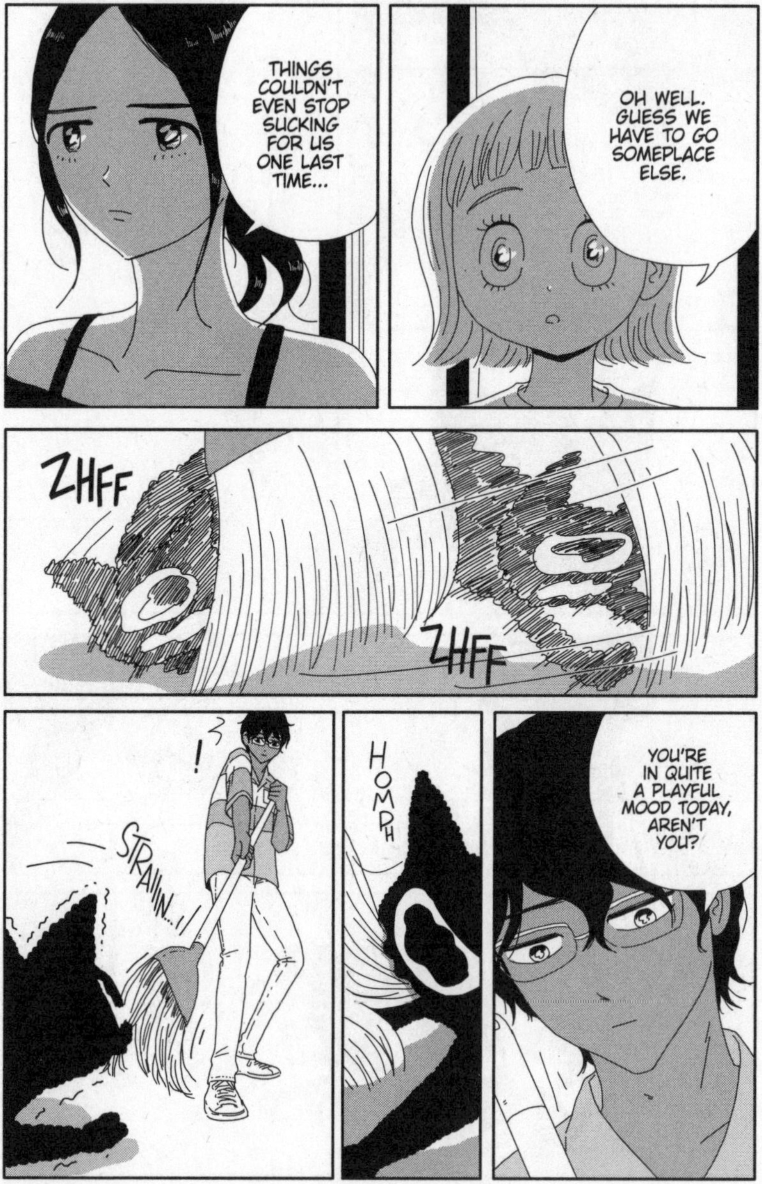
OH WELL. GUESS WE HAVE TO GO SOMEPLACE ELSE.
THINGS COULDN'T EVEN STOP SUCKING FOR US ONE LAST TIME...
ZHFF
ZHFF
YOU'RE IN QUITE A PLAYFUL MOOD TODAY, AREN'T YOU?
HOMPH
!
STRAIIN...

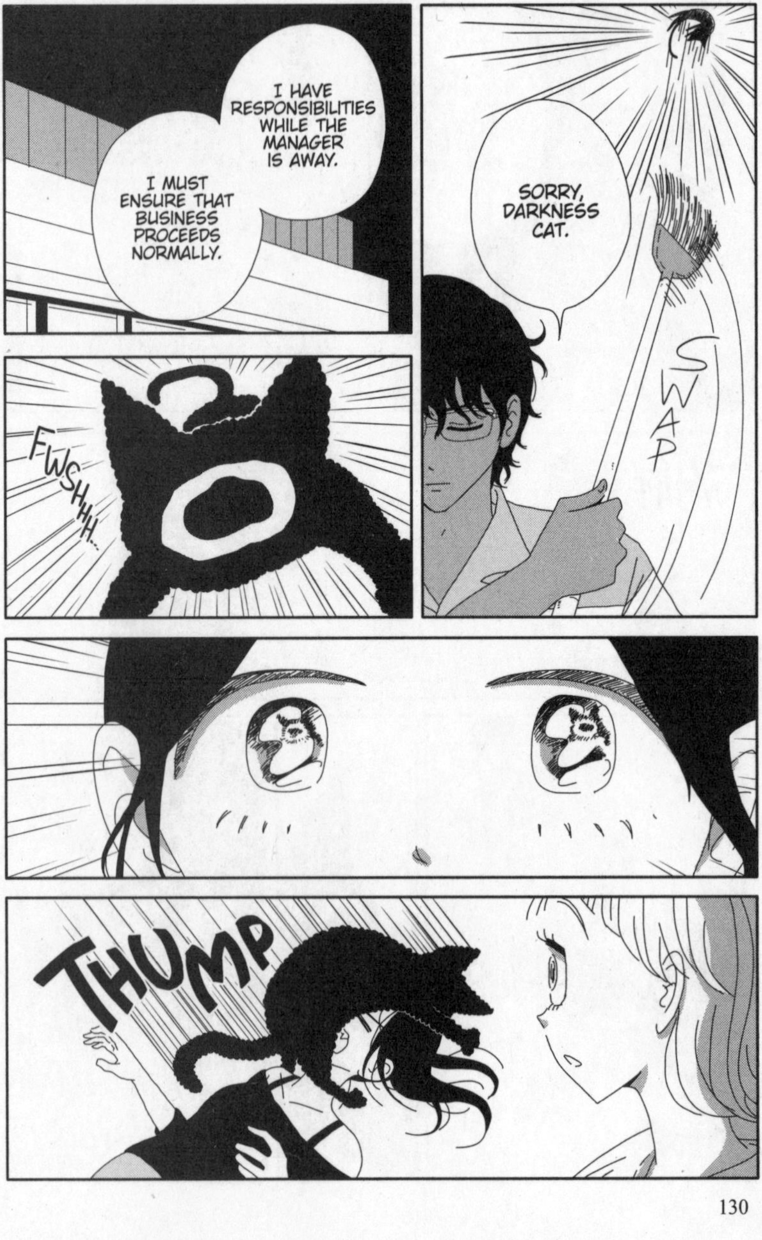
SORRY, DARKNESS CAT.
SWAP
I HAVE RESPONSIBILITIES WHILE THE MANAGER IS AWAY.
I MUST ENSURE THAT BUSINESS PROCEEDS NORMALLY.
FWSHHH...
THUMP

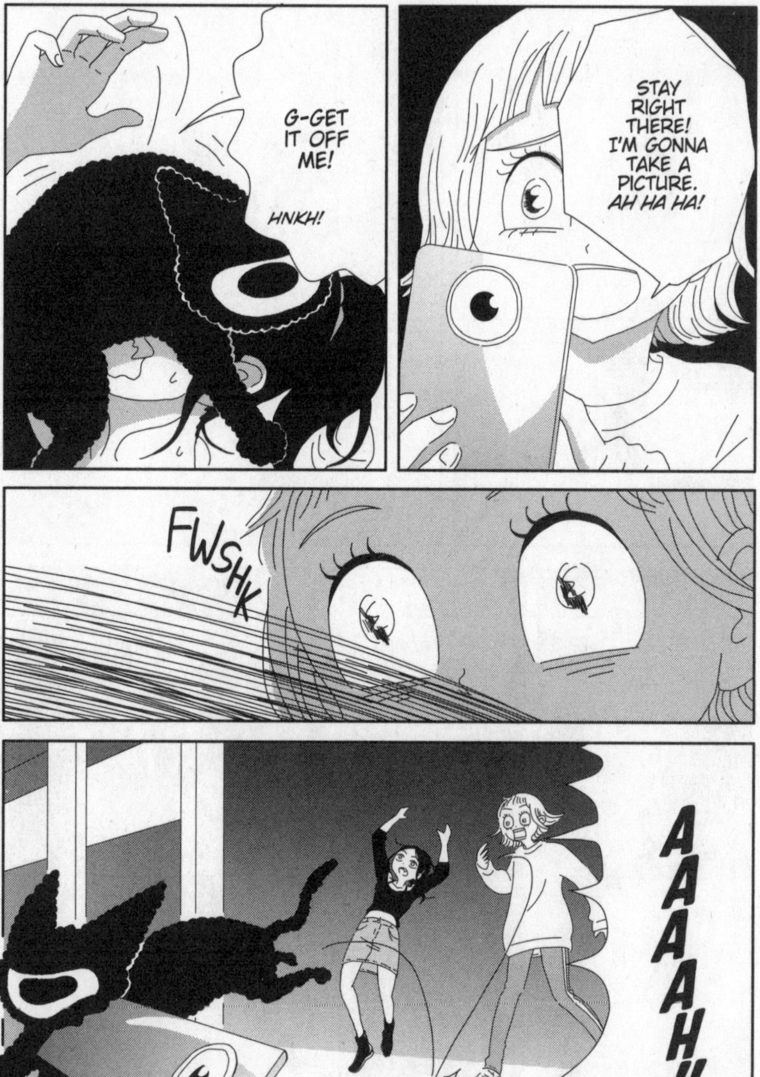
STAY RIGHT THERE! I'M GONNA TAKE A PICTURE. AH HA HA!
G-GET IT OFF ME!
HNKH!
FWSHK
AAAAAH!!

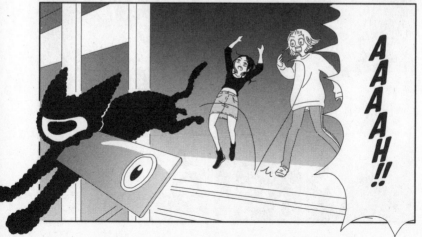

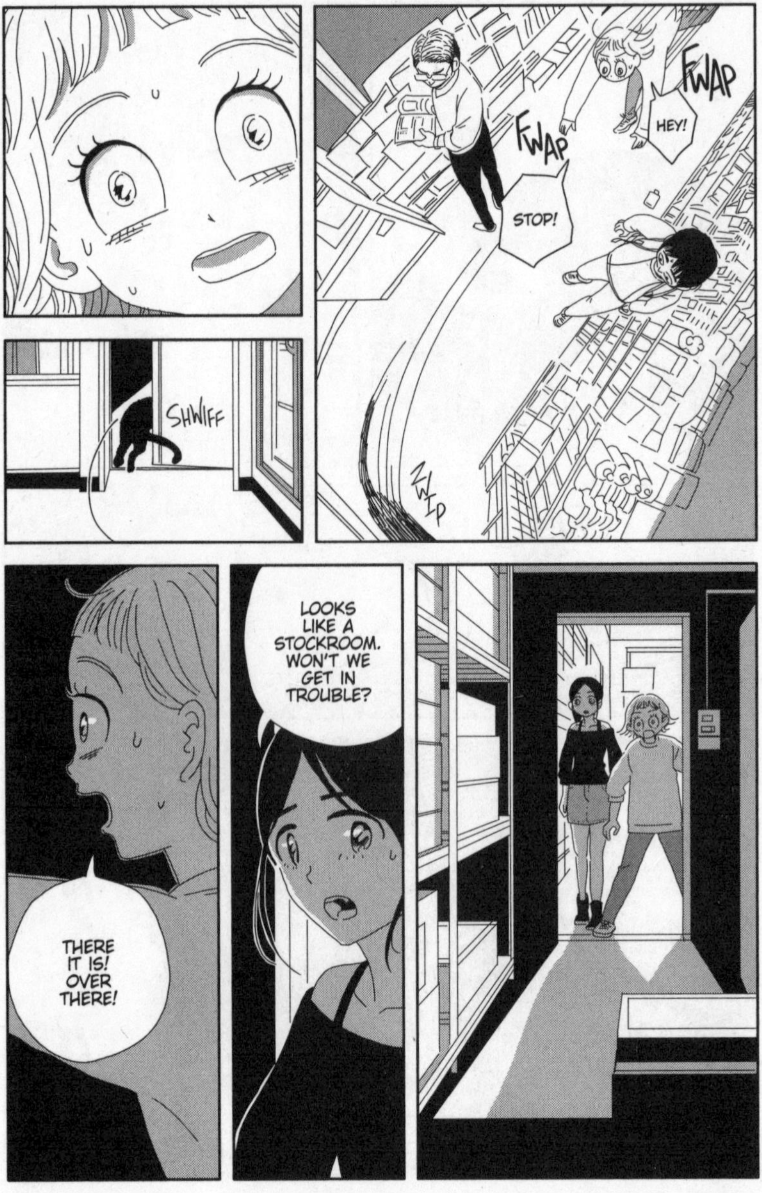
FWAP
HEY!
FWAP
STOP!
ZWIP
SHWIFF
LOOKS LIKE A STOCKROOM. WON'T WE GET IN TROUBLE?
THERE IT IS! OVER THERE!

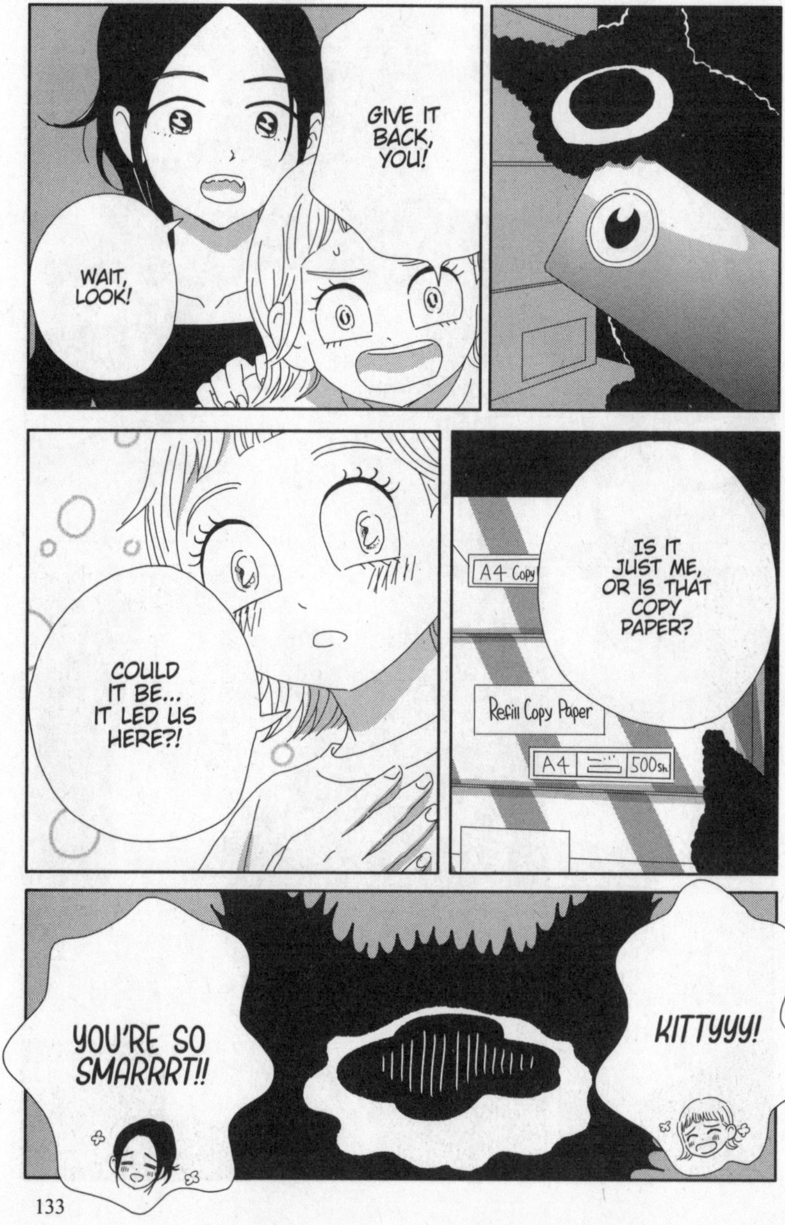
GIVE IT BACK, YOU!
WAIT, LOOK!
IS IT JUST ME, OR IS THAT COPY PAPER?
A4 Copy
Refill Copy Paper
A4 500sh.
COULD IT BE... IT LED US HERE?!
KITTYYY!
YOU'RE SO SMARRRT!!

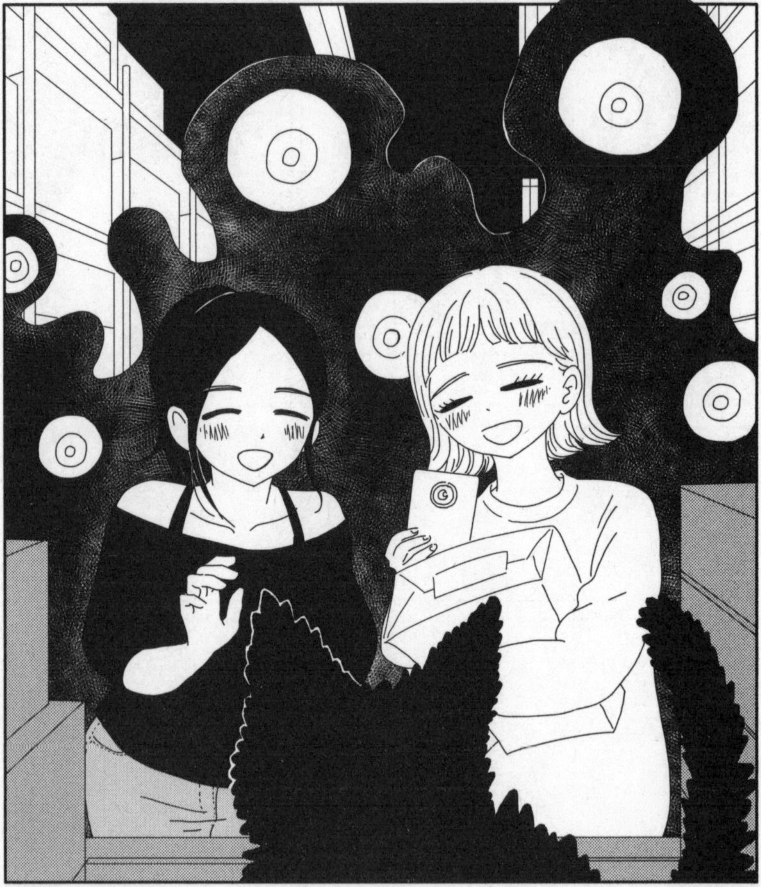

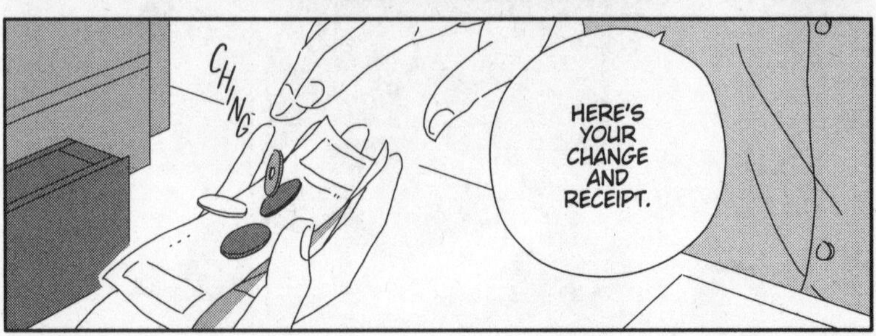
HERE'S YOUR CHANGE AND RECEIPT.
CHING

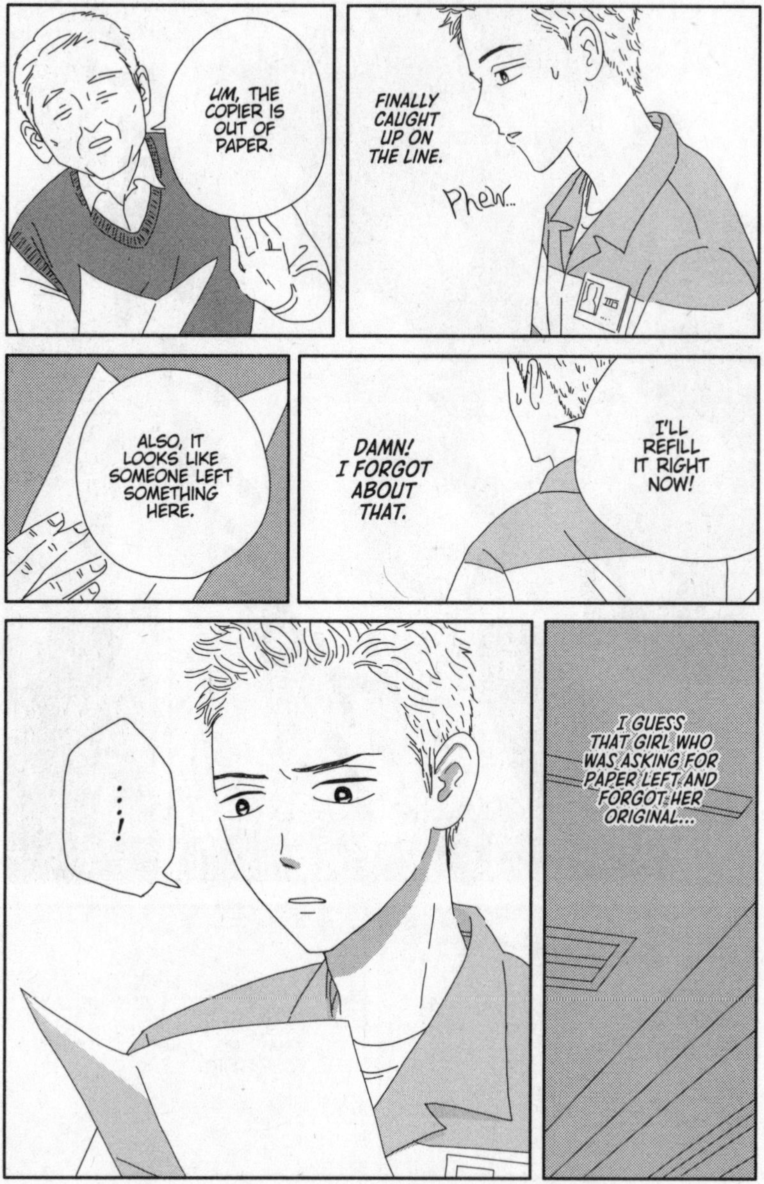
FINALLY CAUGHT UP ON THE LINE.
Phew...
UM, THE COPIER IS OUT OF PAPER.
I'LL REFILL IT RIGHT NOW!
DAMN! I FORGOT ABOUT THAT.
ALSO, IT LOOKS LIKE SOMEONE LEFT SOMETHING HERE.
I GUESS THAT GIRL WHO WAS ASKING FOR PAPER LEFT AND FORGOT HER ORIGINAL...
...!

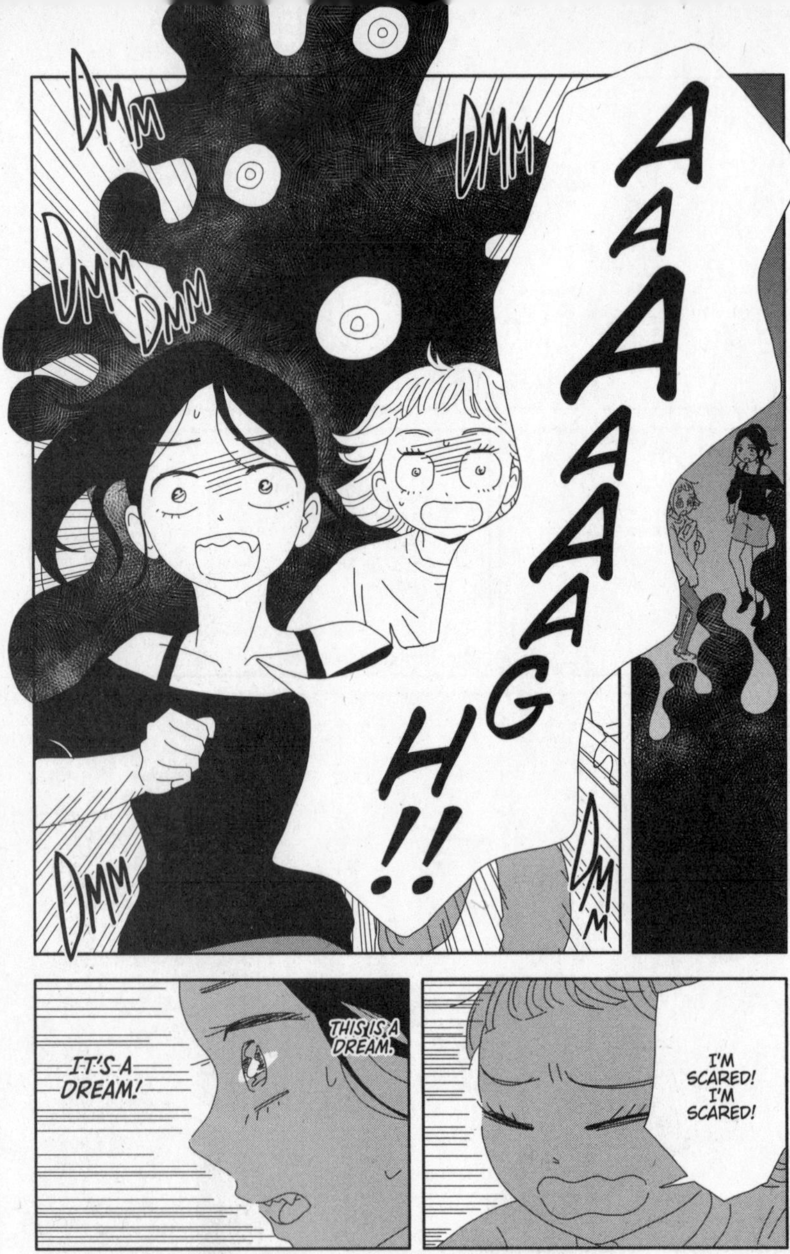
AAAAAAAAGH!!
DMM
DMM
DMMM
DMM DMM
DMM
DMMM
I'M SCARED! I'M SCARED!
THIS IS A DREAM.
IT'S A DREAM!

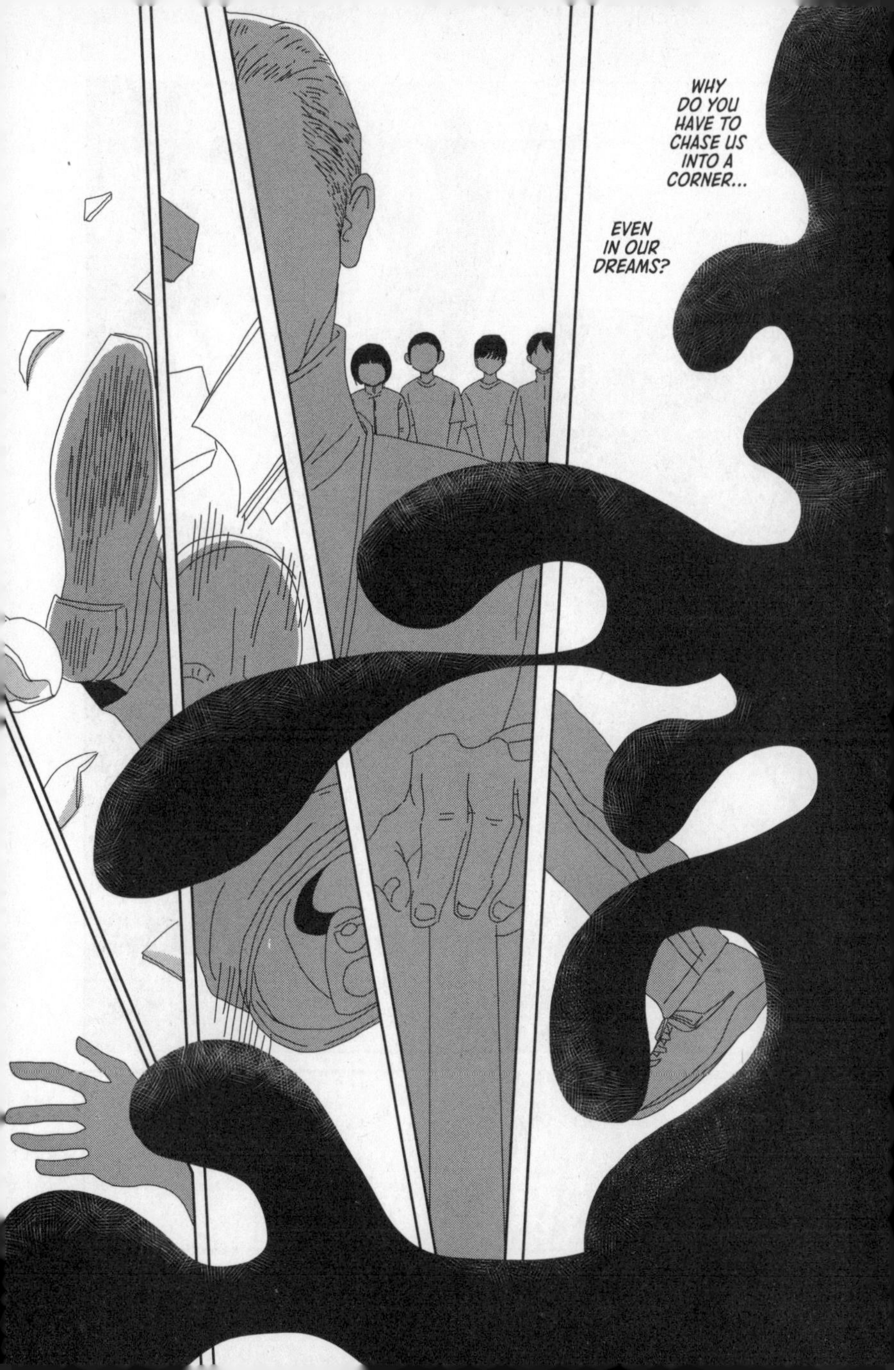
WHY DO YOU HAVE TO CHASE US INTO A CORNER...
EVEN IN OUR DREAMS?

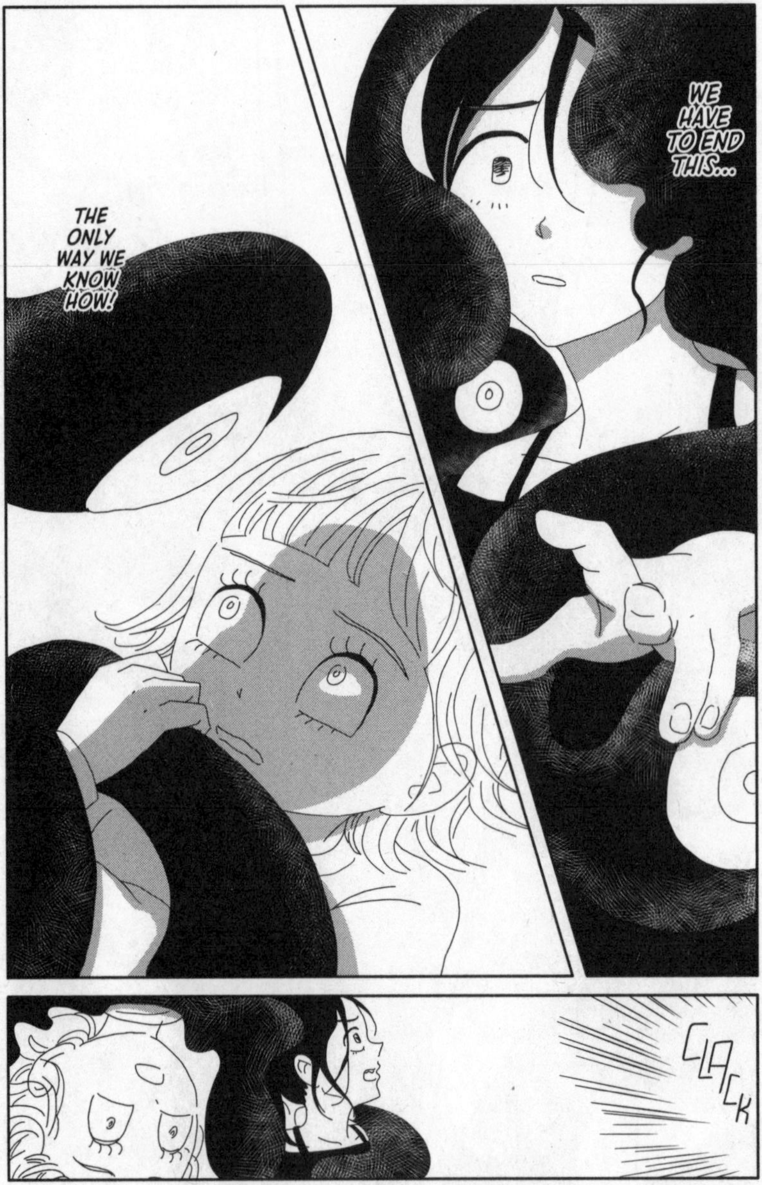
WE HAVE TO END THIS...
THE ONLY WAY WE KNOW HOW!
CLACK

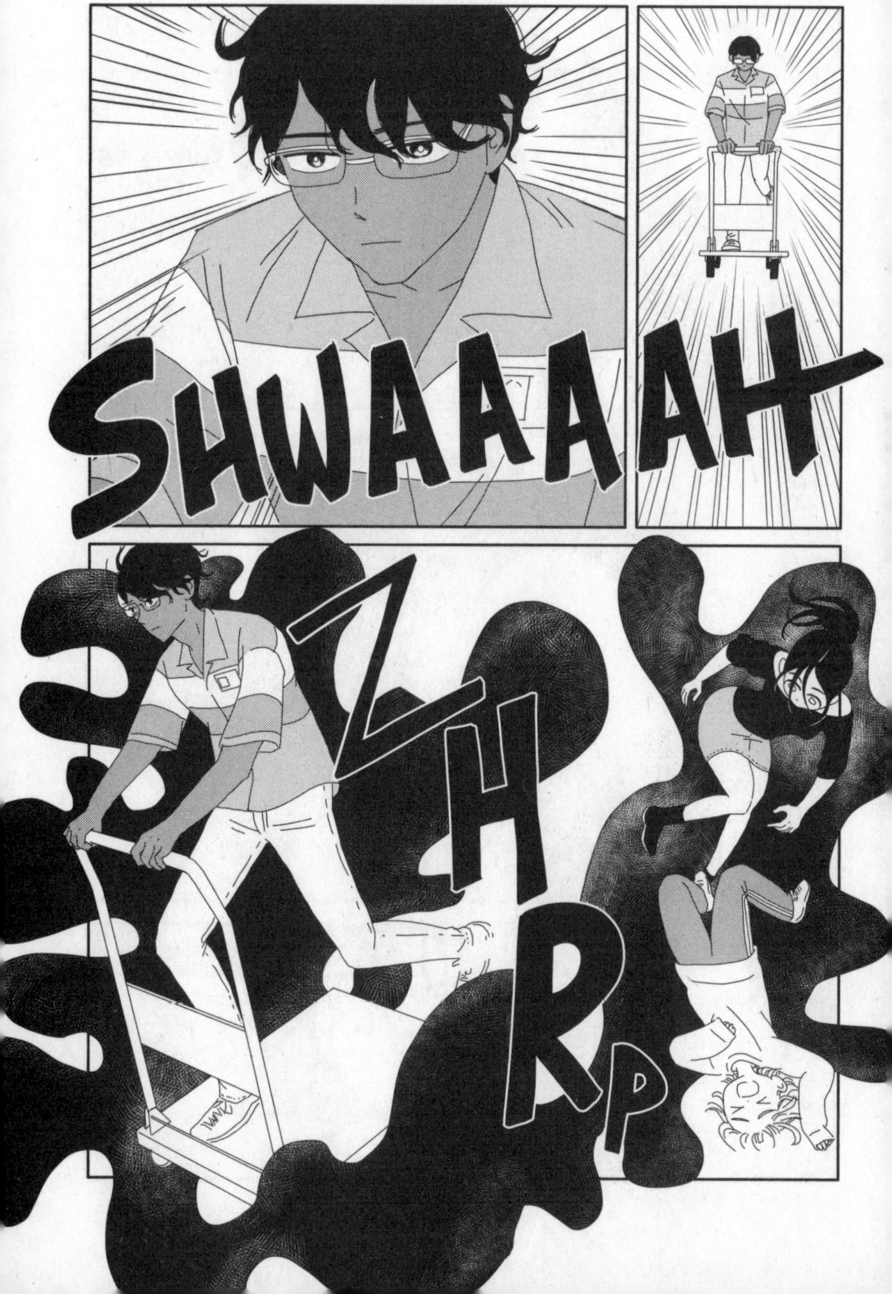
SHWAAAAH
ZHRp

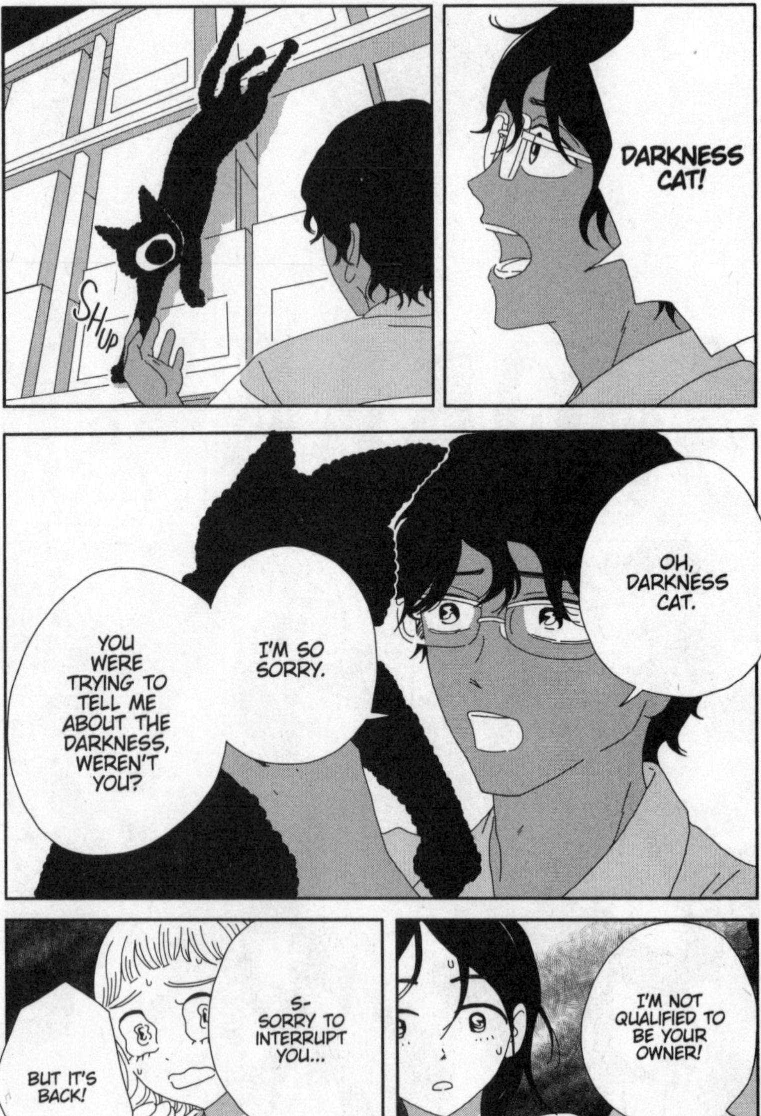
DARKNESS CAT!
SHUP
OH, DARKNESS CAT.
I'M SO SORRY.
YOU WERE TRYING TO TELL ME ABOUT THE DARKNESS, WEREN'T YOU?
I'M NOT QUALIFIED TO BE YOUR OWNER!
S- SORRY TO INTERRUPT YOU...
BUT IT'S BACK!

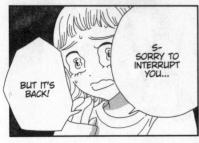

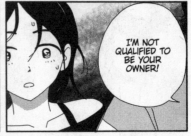

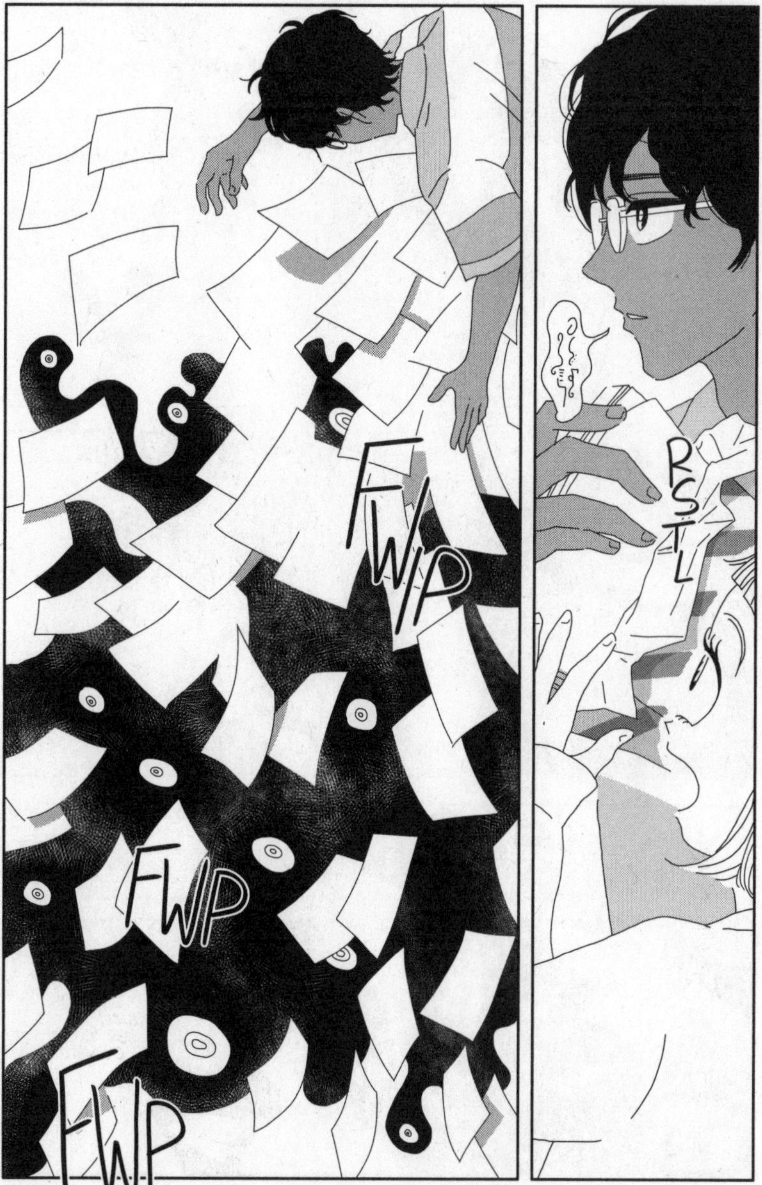
RSTL
FWIP
FWP
FWP

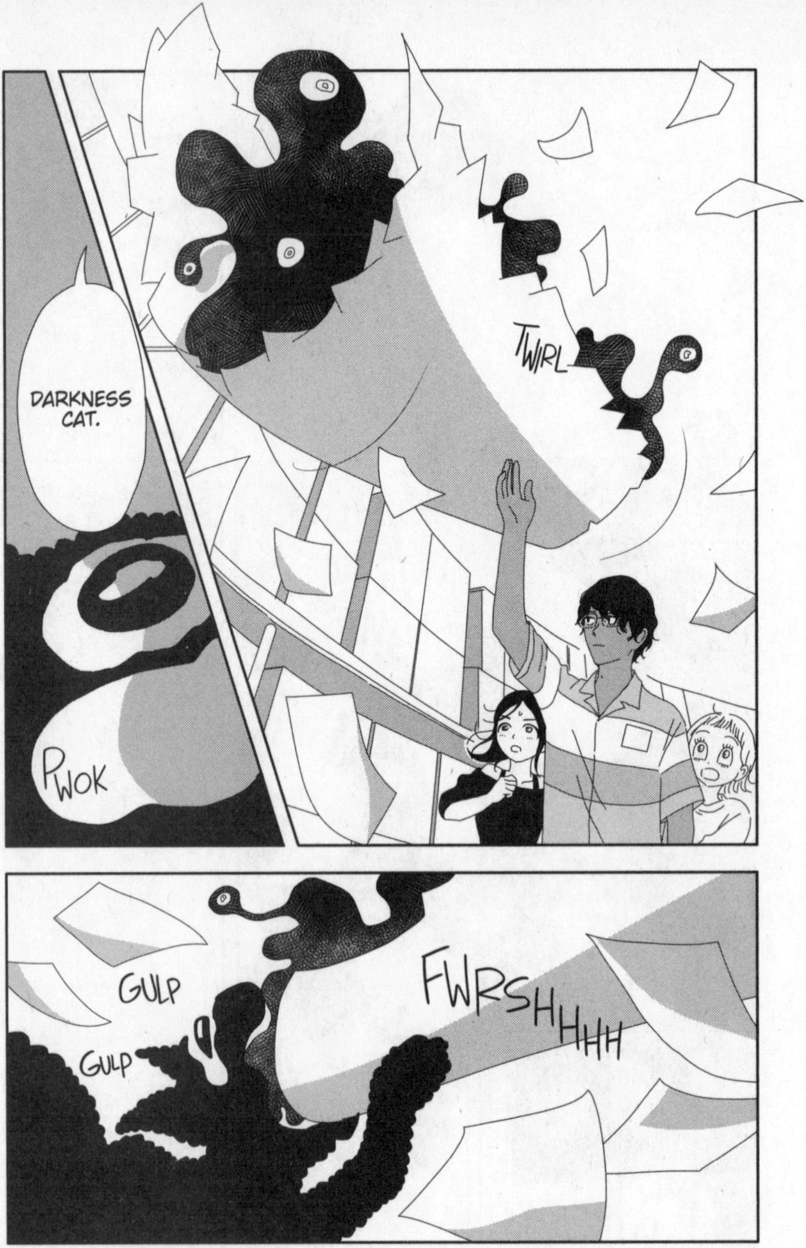
TWIRL
DARKNESS CAT.
PWOK
FWRSHHHH
GULP
GULP

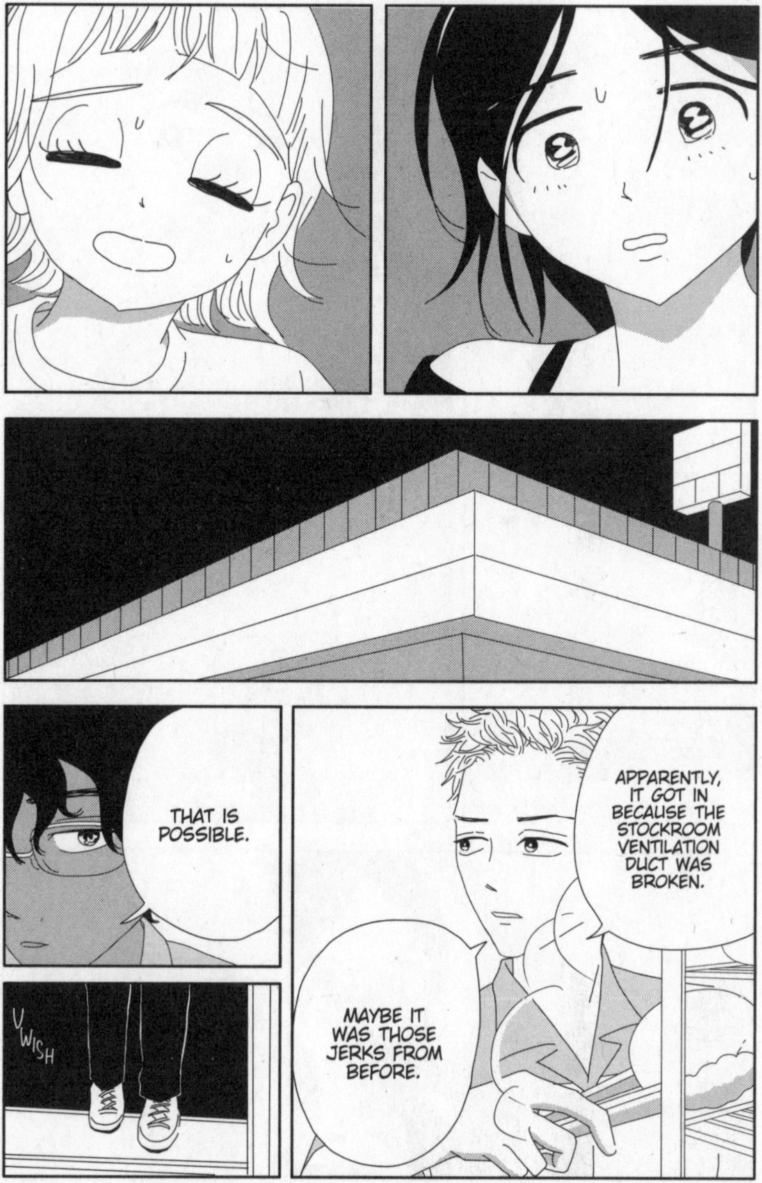
APPARENTLY, IT GOT IN BECAUSE THE STOCKROOM VENTILATION DUCT WAS BROKEN.
MAYBE IT WAS THOSE JERKS FROM BEFORE.
THAT IS POSSIBLE.
VWISH

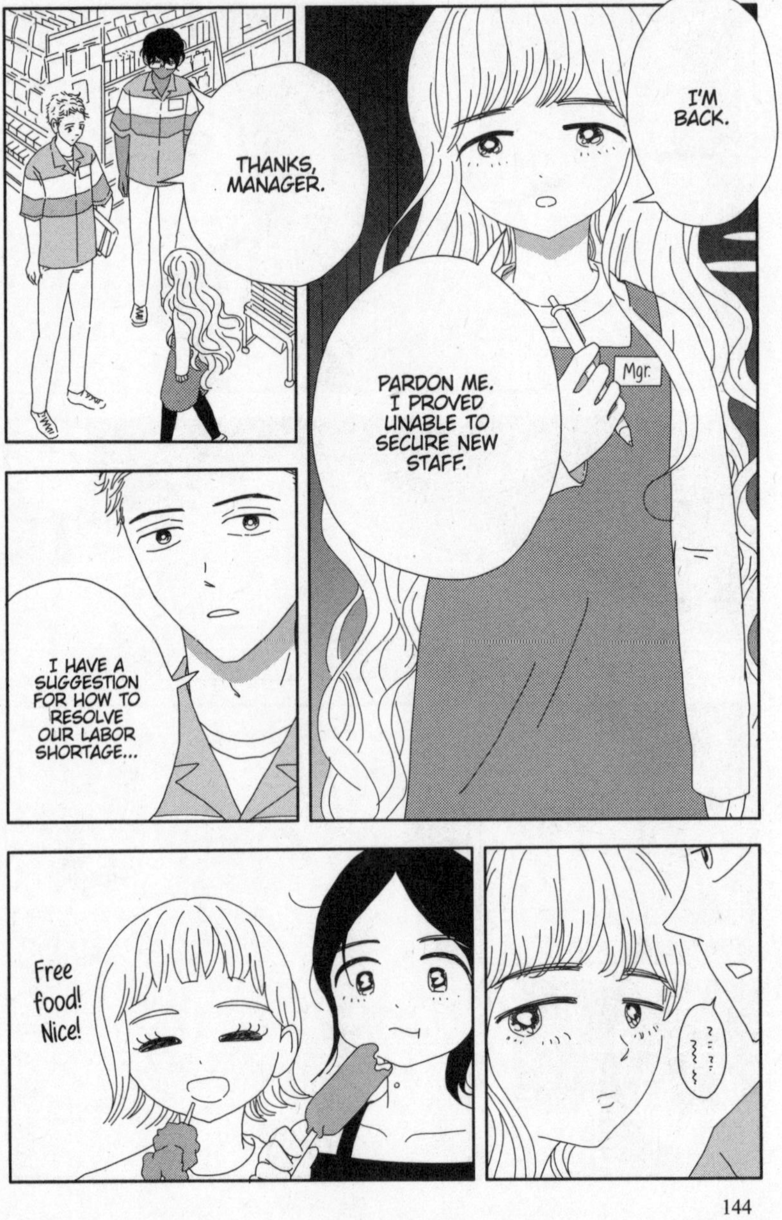
I'M BACK.
PARDON ME. I PROVED UNABLE TO SECURE NEW STAFF.
THANKS, MANAGER.
Mgr.
I HAVE A SUGGESTION FOR HOW TO RESOLVE OUR LABOR SHORTAGE...
Free food! Nice!

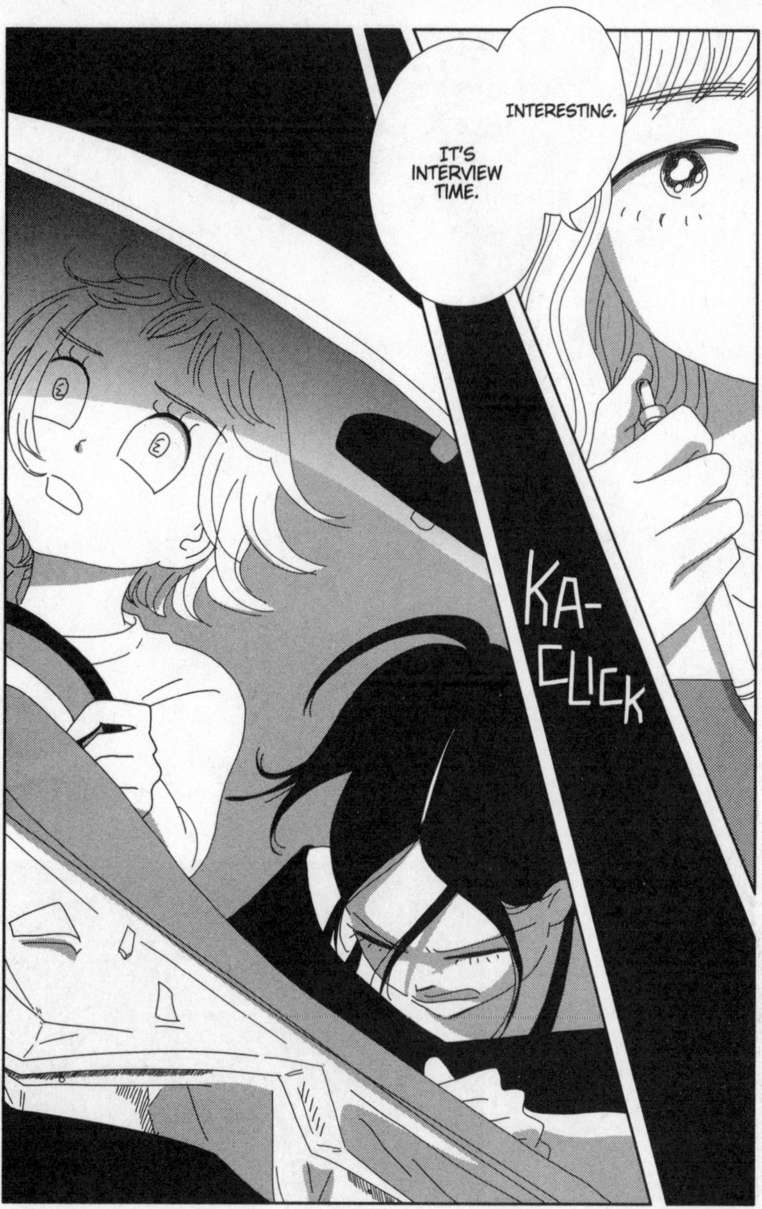
INTERESTING.
IT'S INTERVIEW TIME.
KA-CLICK

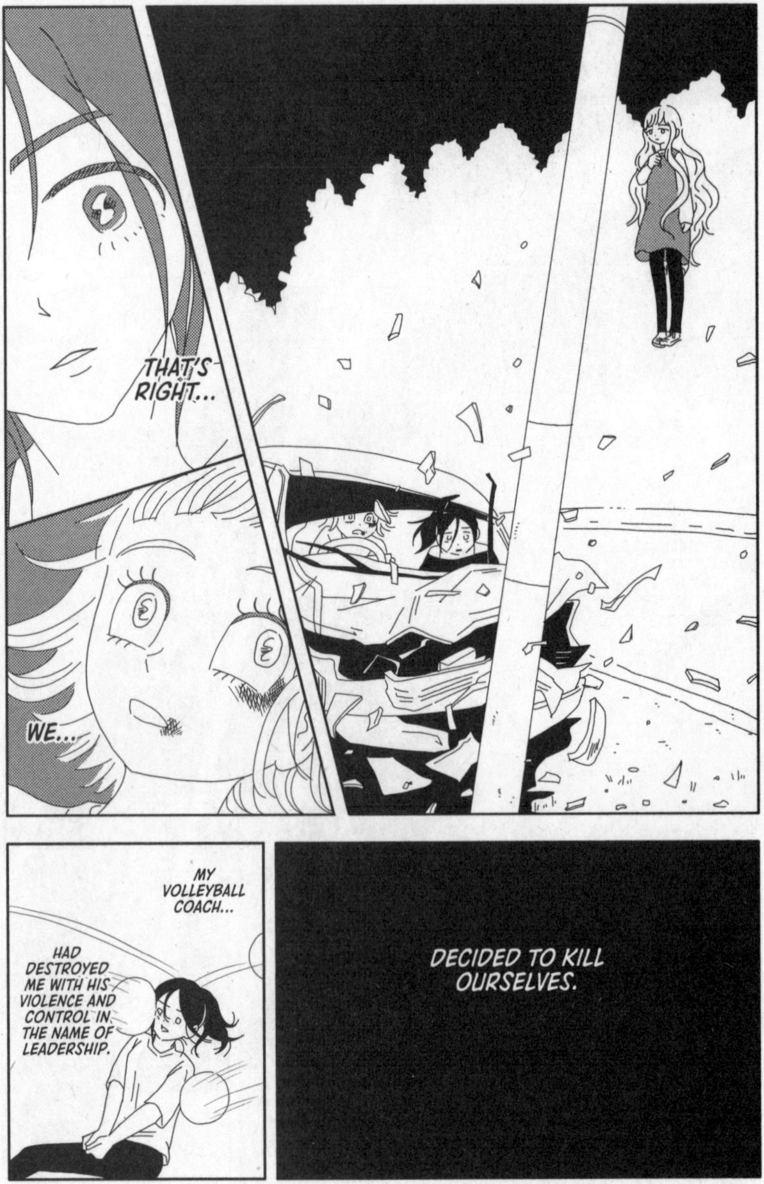
THAT'S RIGHT...
WE...
DECIDED TO KILL OURSELVES.
MY VOLLEYBALL COACH...
HAD DESTROYED ME WITH HIS VIOLENCE AND CONTROL IN THE NAME OF LEADERSHIP.

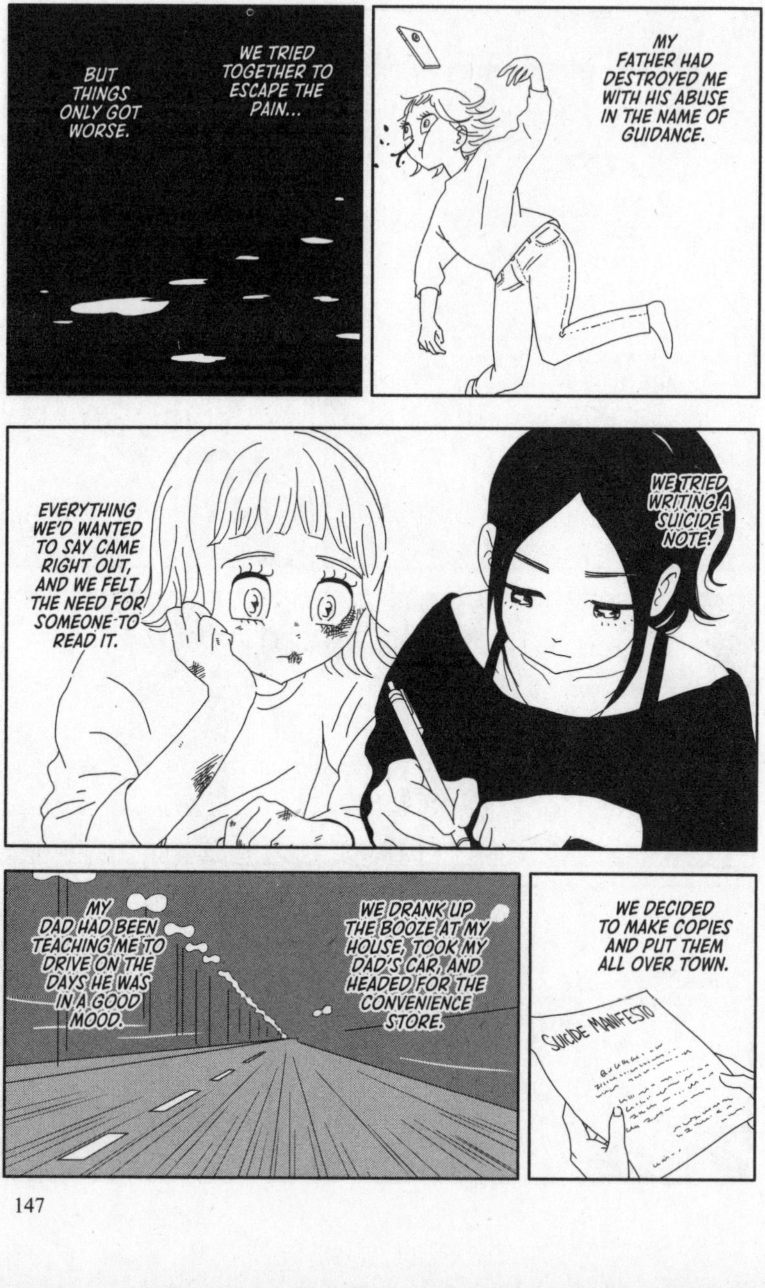
MY FATHER HAD DESTROYED ME WITH HIS ABUSE IN THE NAME OF GUIDANCE.
WE TRIED TOGETHER TO ESCAPE THE PAIN...
BUT THINGS ONLY GOT WORSE.
WE TRIED WRITING A SUICIDE NOTE.
EVERYTHING WE'D WANTED TO SAY CAME RIGHT OUT, AND WE FELT THE NEED FOR SOMEONE TO READ IT.
WE DECIDED TO MAKE COPIES AND PUT THEM ALL OVER TOWN.
SUICIDE MANIFESTO
WE DRANK UP THE BOOZE AT MY HOUSE, TOOK MY DAD'S CAR, AND HEADED FOR THE CONVENIENCE STORE.
MY DAD HAD BEEN TEACHING ME TO DRIVE ON THE DAYS HE WAS IN A GOOD MOOD.

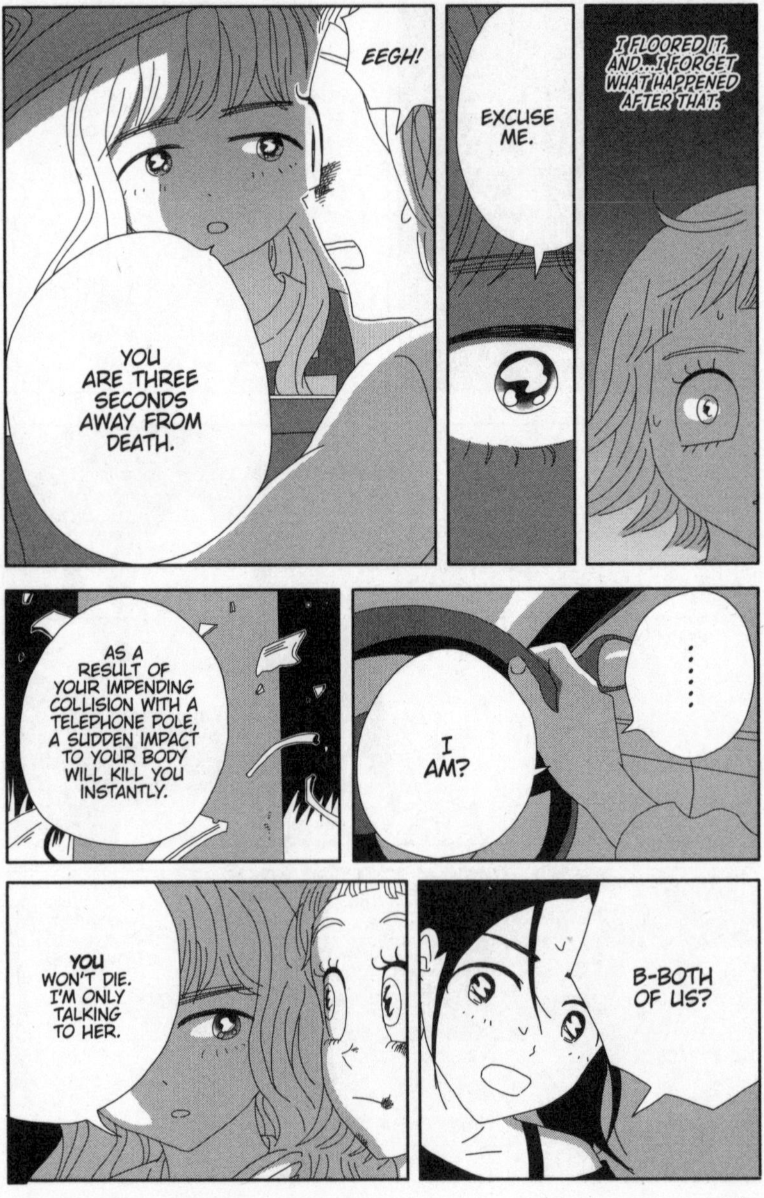
I FLOORED IT, AND...I FORGET WHAT HAPPENED AFTER THAT.
EXCUSE ME.
EEGH!
YOU ARE THREE SECONDS AWAY FROM DEATH.
......
I AM?
AS A RESULT OF YOUR IMPENDING COLLISION WITH A TELEPHONE POLE, A SUDDEN IMPACT TO YOUR BODY WILL KILL YOU INSTANTLY.
B-BOTH OF US?
YOU WON'T DIE. I'M ONLY TALKING TO HER.

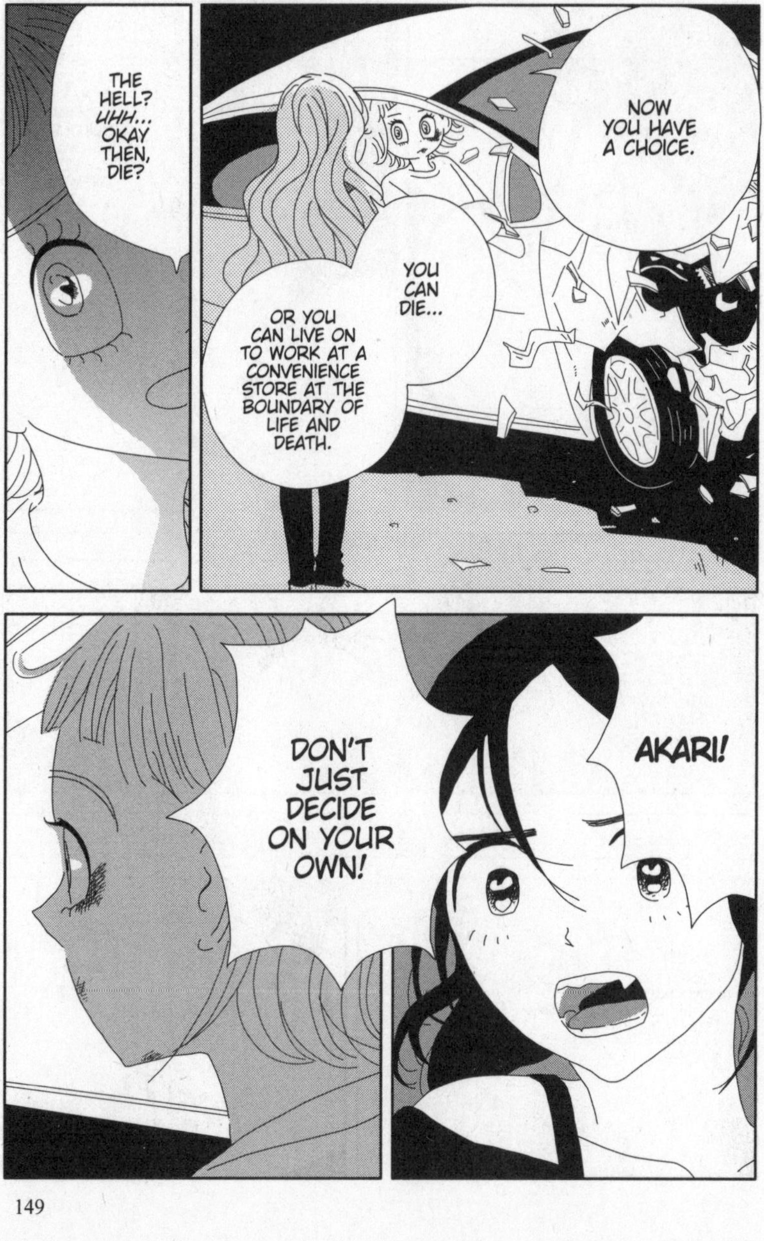
NOW YOU HAVE A CHOICE.
YOU CAN DIE...
OR YOU CAN LIVE ON TO WORK AT A CONVENIENCE STORE AT THE BOUNDARY OF LIFE AND DEATH.
THE HELL? *UHH...* OKAY THEN, DIE?
AKARI!
DON'T JUST DECIDE ON YOUR OWN!

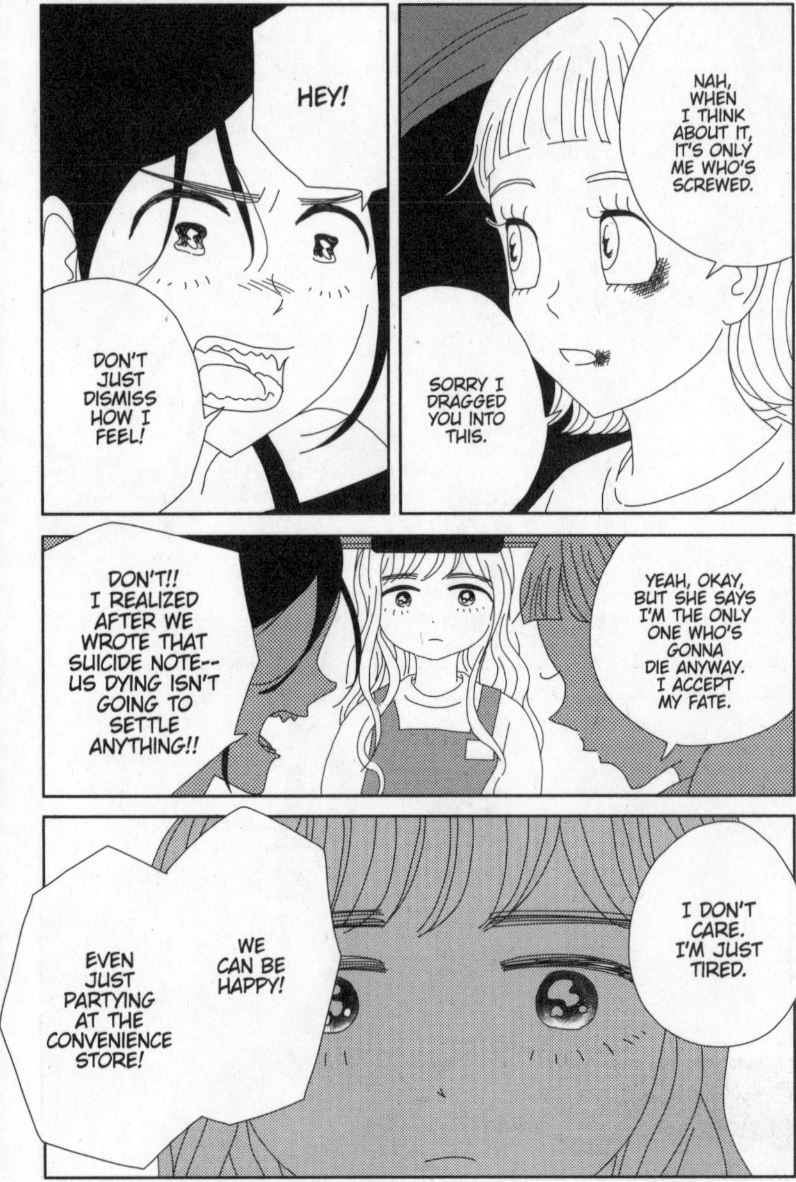
NAH, WHEN I THINK ABOUT IT, IT'S ONLY ME WHO'S SCREWED.
SORRY I DRAGGED YOU INTO THIS.
HEY!
DON'T JUST DISMISS HOW I FEEL!
YEAH, OKAY, BUT SHE SAYS I'M THE ONLY ONE WHO'S GONNA DIE ANYWAY. I ACCEPT MY FATE.
DON'T!! I REALIZED AFTER WE WROTE THAT SUICIDE NOTE-- US DYING ISN'T GOING TO SETTLE ANYTHING!!
I DON'T CARE. I'M JUST TIRED.
WE CAN BE HAPPY!
EVEN JUST PARTYING AT THE CONVENIENCE STORE!

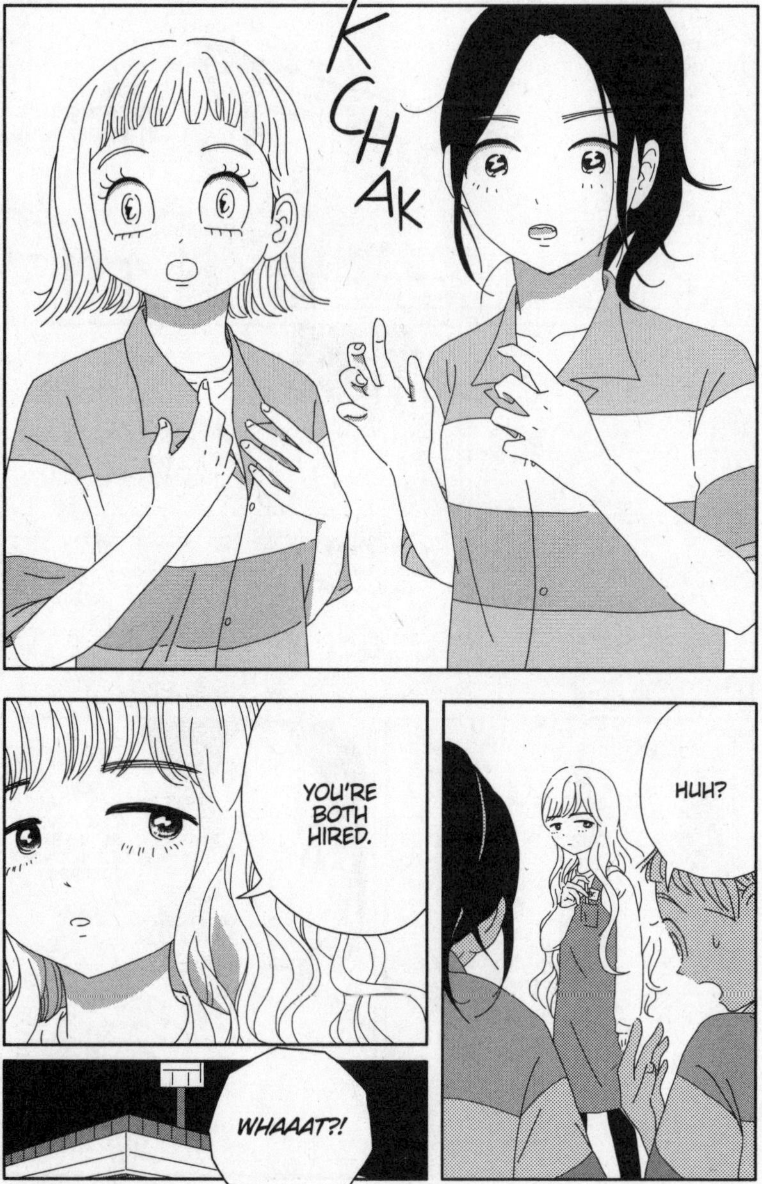
KCHAK
HUH?
YOU'RE BOTH HIRED.
WHAAAT?!

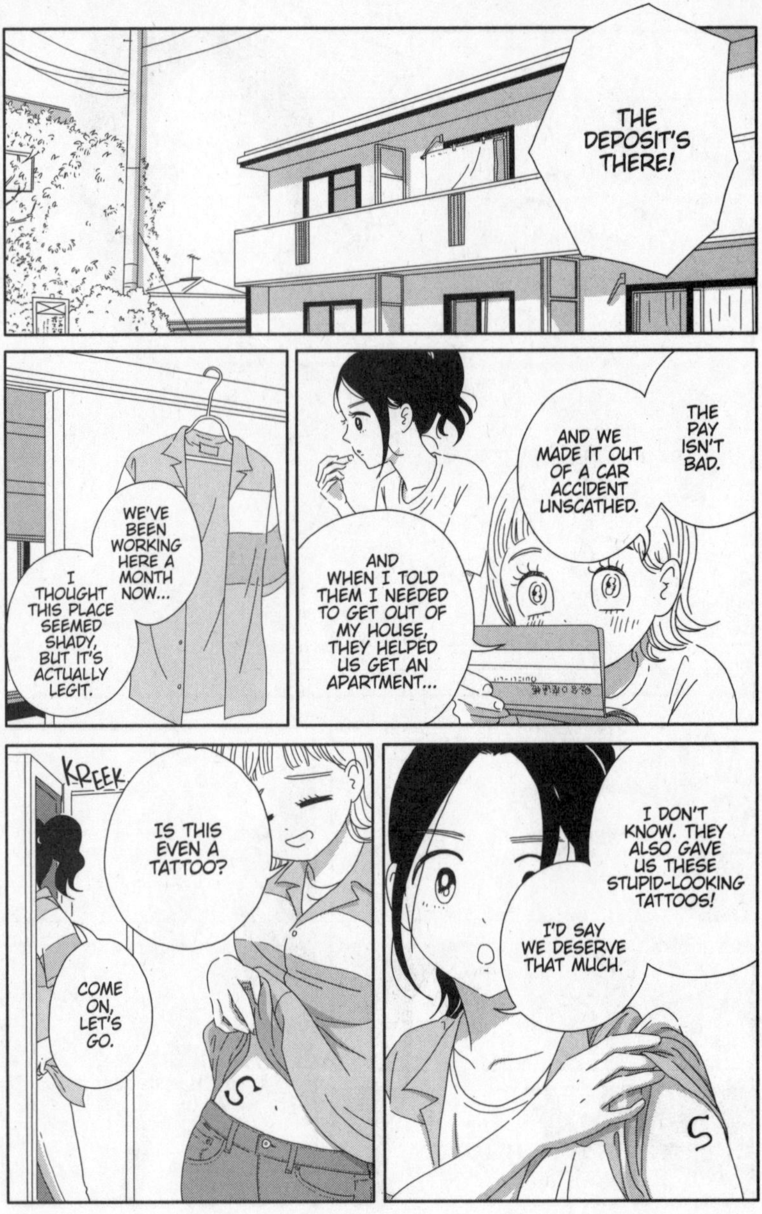
THE DEPOSIT'S THERE!
THE PAY ISN'T BAD.
AND WE MADE IT OUT OF A CAR ACCIDENT UNSCATHED.
AND WHEN I TOLD THEM I NEEDED TO GET OUT OF MY HOUSE, THEY HELPED US GET AN APARTMENT...
WE'VE BEEN WORKING HERE A MONTH NOW...
I THOUGHT THIS PLACE SEEMED SHADY, BUT IT'S ACTUALLY LEGIT.
I DON'T KNOW. THEY ALSO GAVE US THESE STUPID-LOOKING TATTOOS!
I'D SAY WE DESERVE THAT MUCH.
KREEK
IS THIS EVEN A TATTOO?
COME ON, LET'S GO.

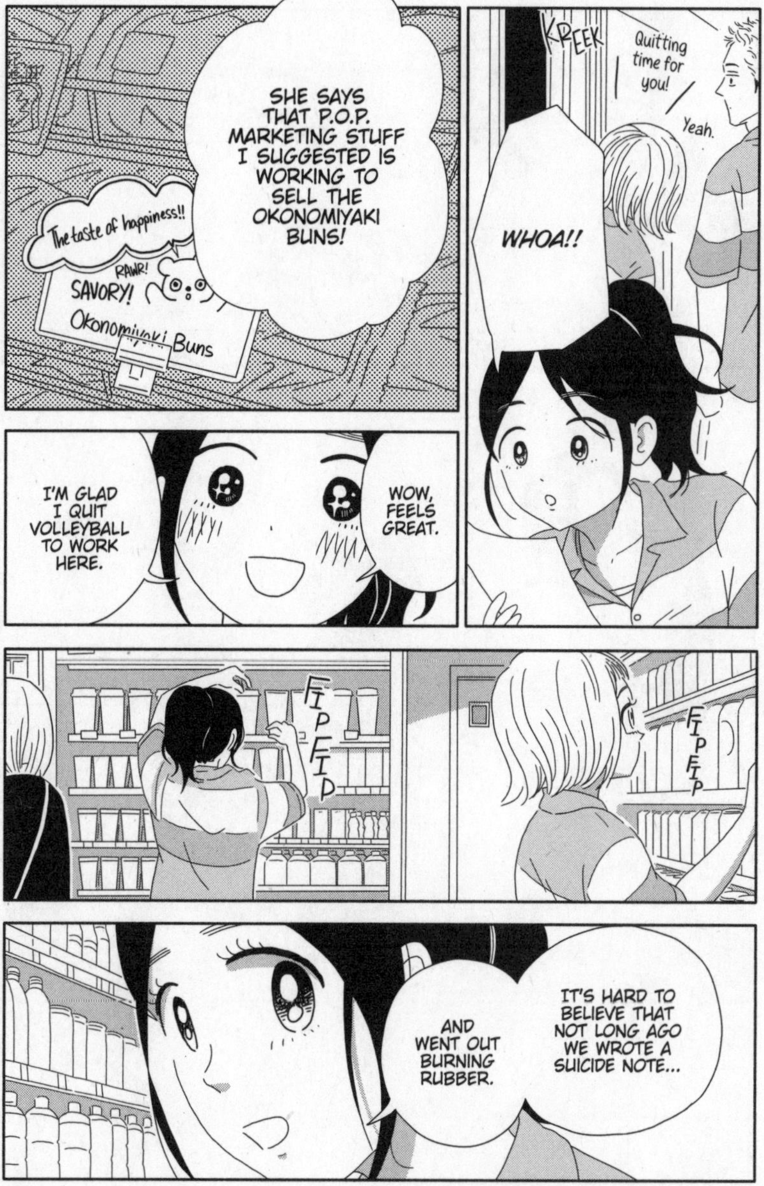
KREEK
Quitting time for you!
Yeah.
WHOA!!
SHE SAYS THAT P.O.P. MARKETING STUFF I SUGGESTED IS WORKING TO SELL THE OKONOMIYAKI BUNS!
The taste of happiness!!
RAWR!
SAVORY!
Okonomiyaki Buns
WOW, FEELS GREAT.
I'M GLAD I QUIT VOLLEYBALL TO WORK HERE.
FIP FIP
FIP FIP
IT'S HARD TO BELIEVE THAT NOT LONG AGO WE WROTE A SUICIDE NOTE...
AND WENT OUT BURNING RUBBER.

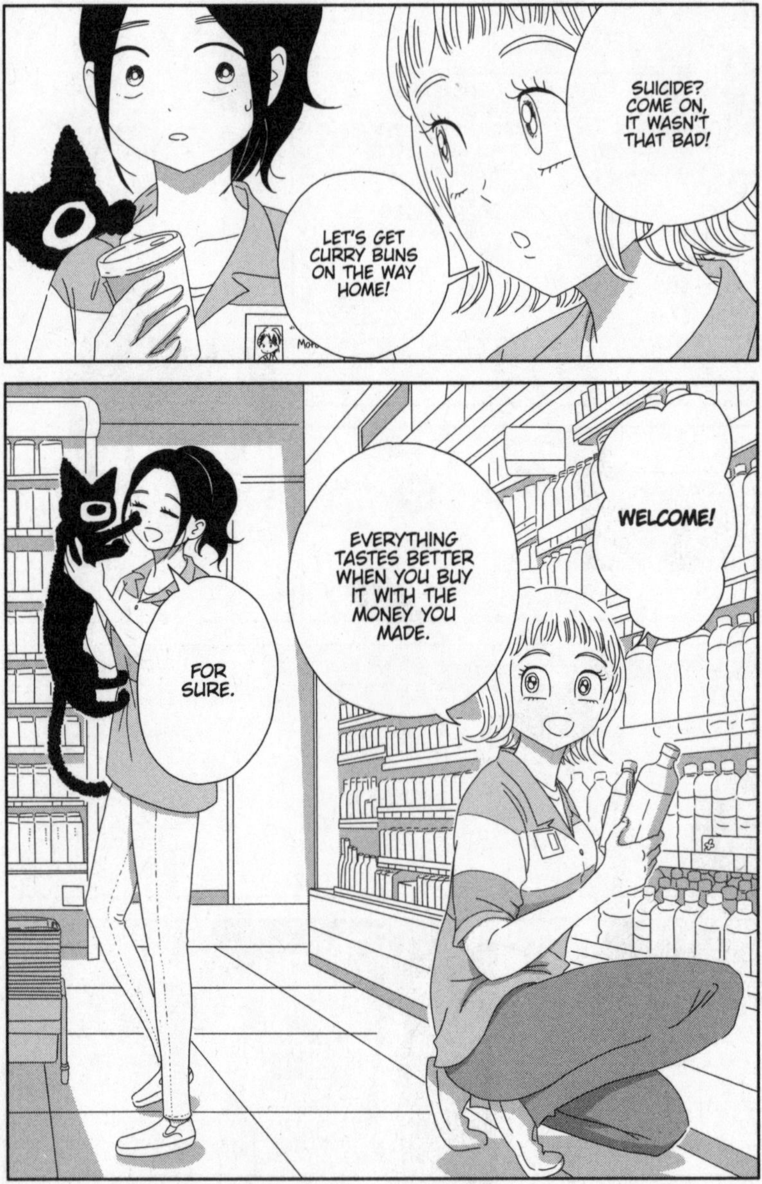
SUICIDE? COME ON, IT WASN'T THAT BAD!
LET'S GET CURRY BUNS ON THE WAY HOME!
WELCOME!
EVERYTHING TASTES BETTER WHEN YOU BUY IT WITH THE MONEY YOU MADE.
FOR SURE.

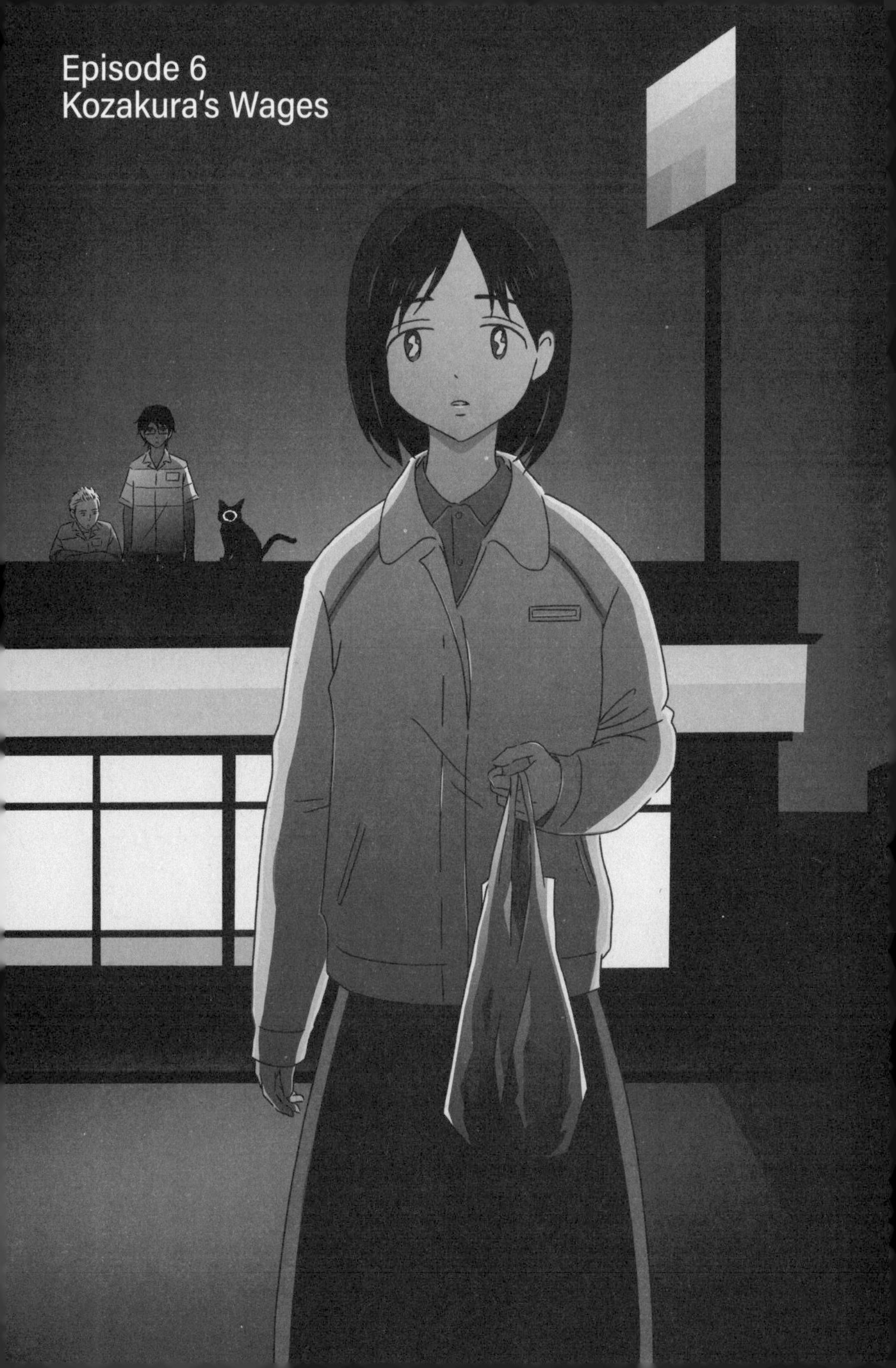
Episode 6
Kozakura's Wages

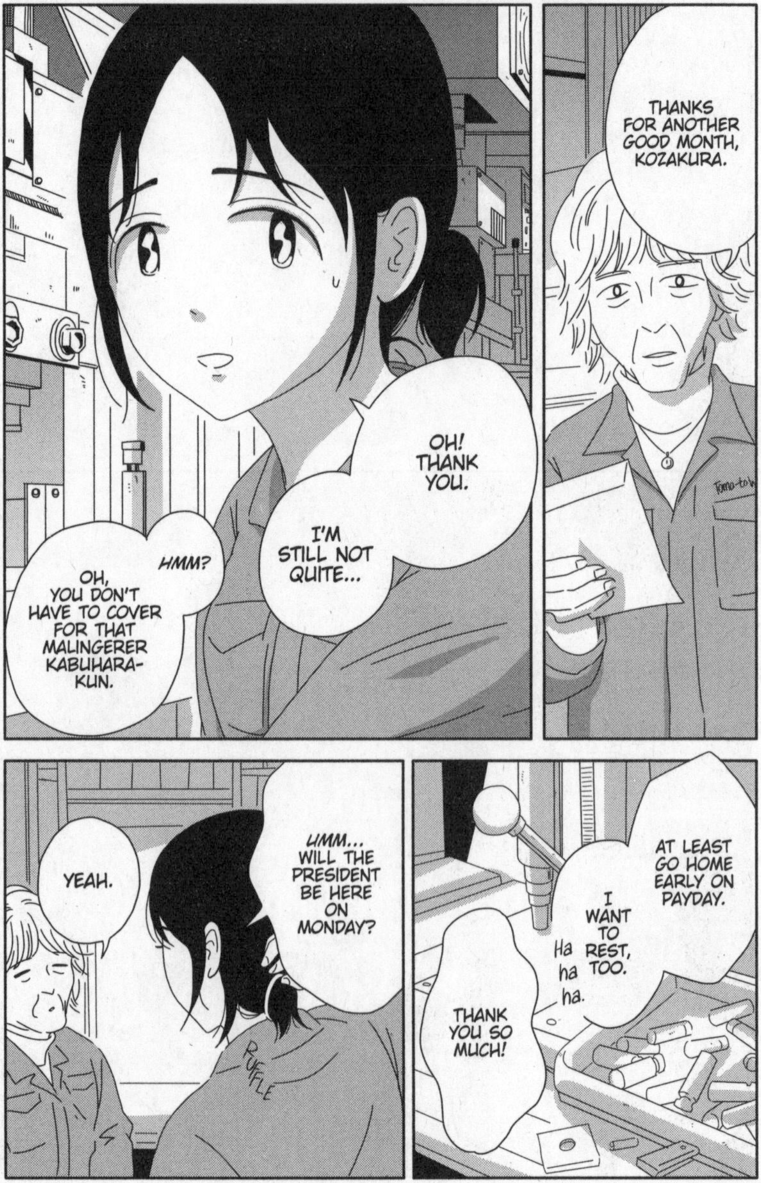
THANKS FOR ANOTHER GOOD MONTH, KOZAKURA.
OH! THANK YOU.
I'M STILL NOT QUITE...
HMM?
OH, YOU DON'T HAVE TO COVER FOR THAT MALINGERER KABUHARA-KUN.
AT LEAST GO HOME EARLY ON PAYDAY.
I WANT TO REST, TOO.
Ha ha ha.
THANK YOU SO MUCH!
UMM... WILL THE PRESIDENT BE HERE ON MONDAY?
YEAH.
RUFFLE

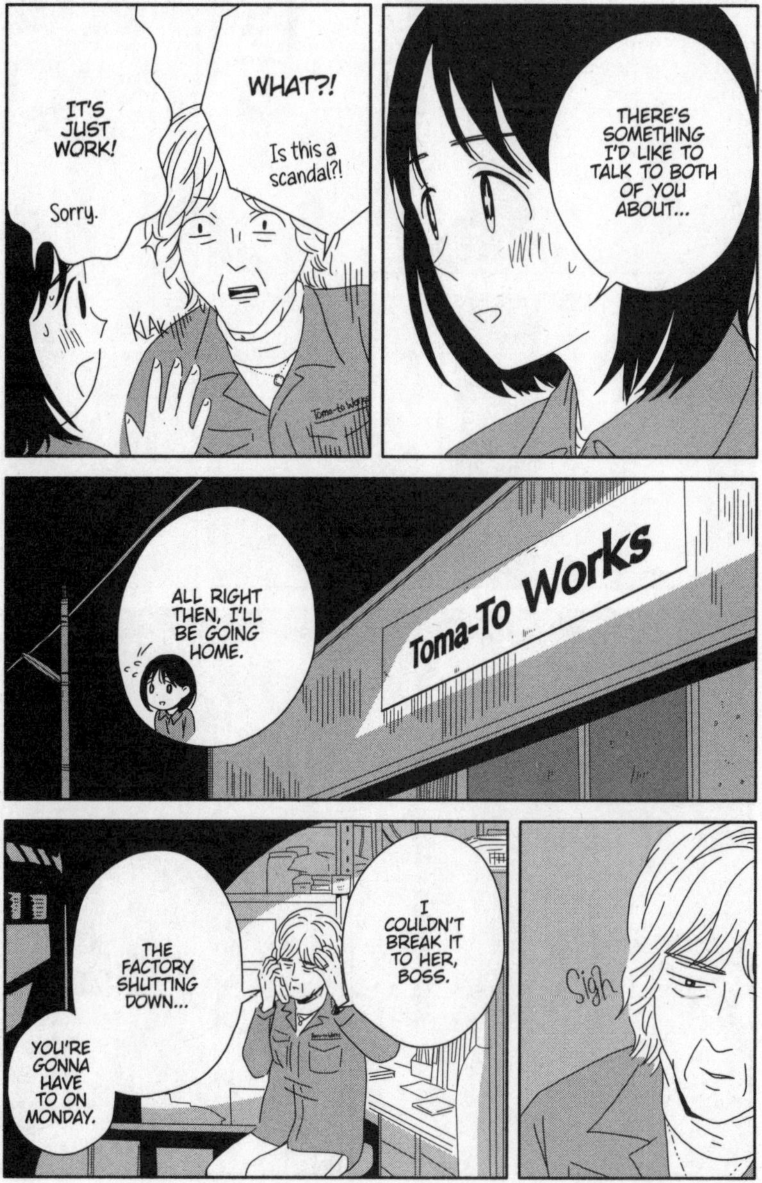

THERE'S SOMETHING I'D LIKE TO TALK TO BOTH OF YOU ABOUT...
WHAT?!
Is this a scandal?!
IT'S JUST WORK!
Sorry.
KLAK
Toma-To Works
ALL RIGHT THEN, I'LL BE GOING HOME.
Sigh
I COULDN'T BREAK IT TO HER, BOSS.
THE FACTORY SHUTTING DOWN...
YOU'RE GONNA HAVE TO ON MONDAY.

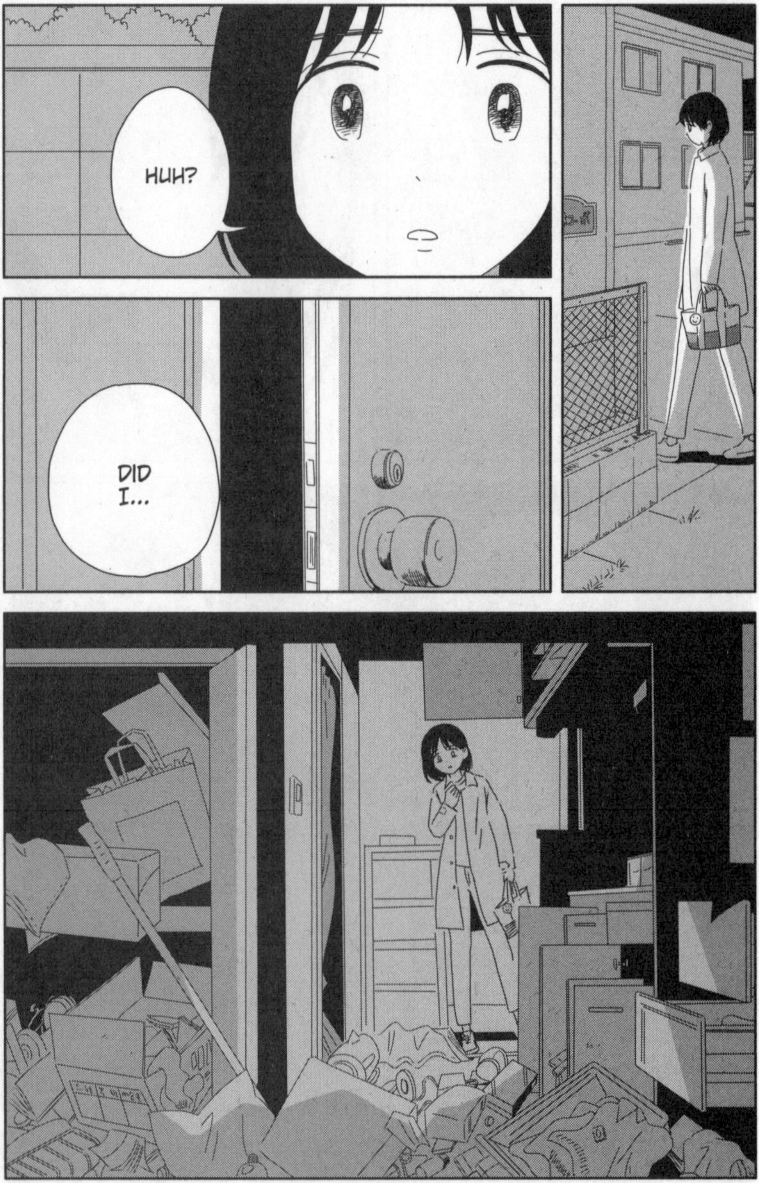
HUH?
DID I...

NO...

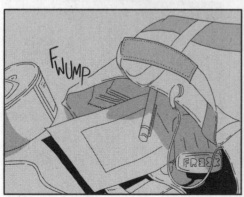

FWUMP

!!

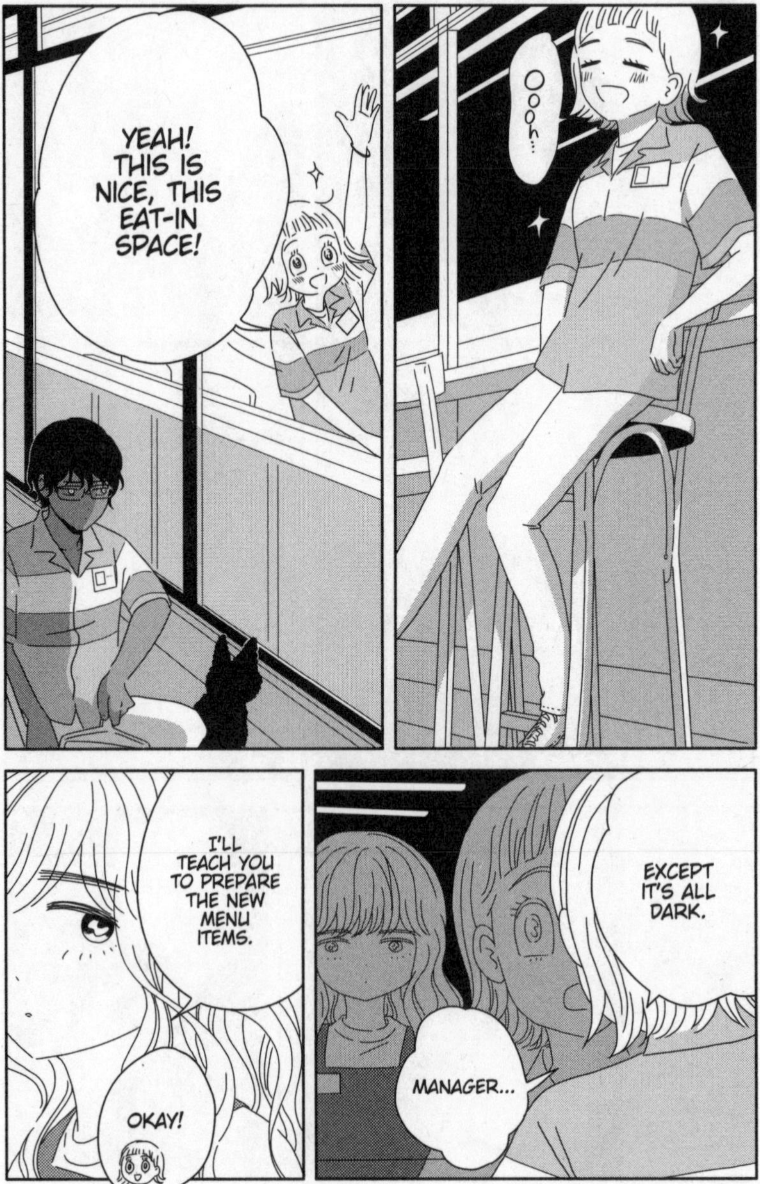
Oooh...
YEAH! THIS IS NICE, THIS EAT-IN SPACE!
EXCEPT IT'S ALL DARK.
MANAGER...
I'LL TEACH YOU TO PREPARE THE NEW MENU ITEMS.
OKAY!

IS KOKURA-SAN OFF AGAIN TODAY?

HE'S GOT THE LATE SHIFT.

OH, OH.

A CUSTOMER.

DING-DONG ♪

FRSHHH

THAT LAB SURE KEEPS HIM BUSY, HUH?

WELCOME!

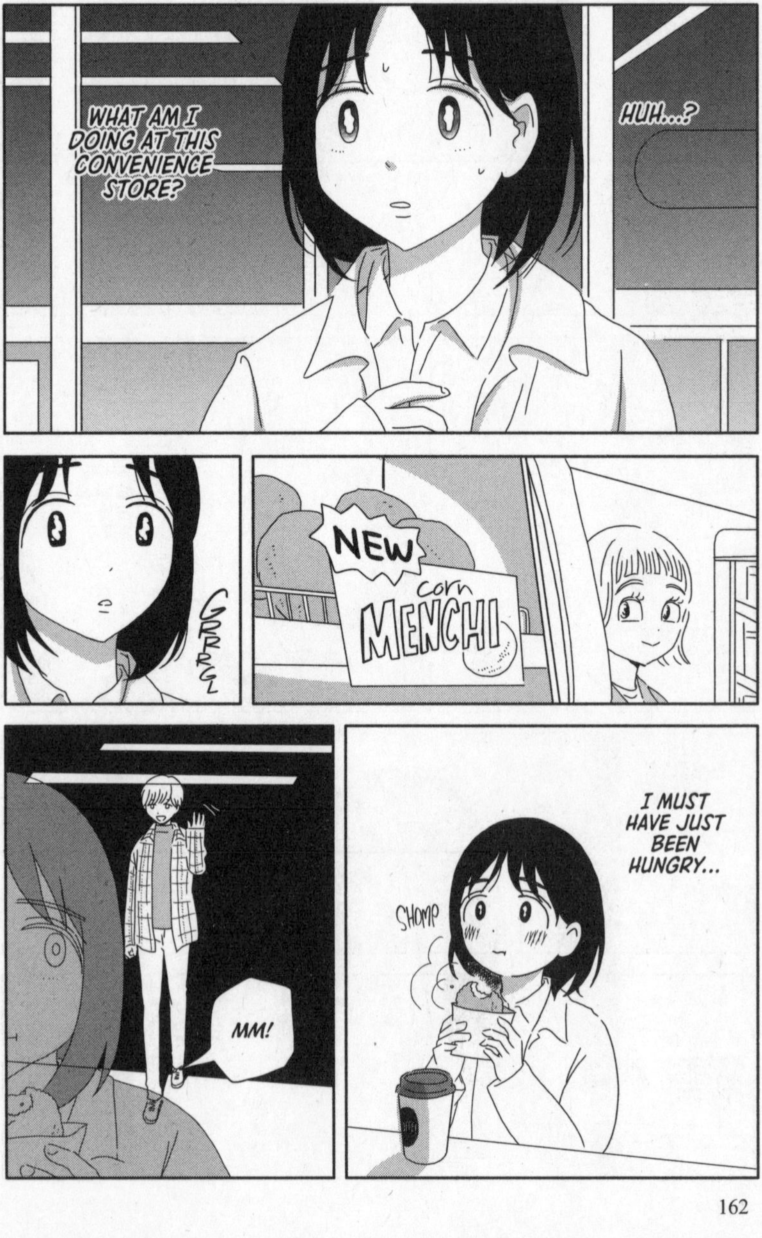
HUH...?
WHAT AM I DOING AT THIS CONVENIENCE STORE?
NEW
corn MENCHI
GRRRGL
I MUST HAVE JUST BEEN HUNGRY...
SHOMP
MM!

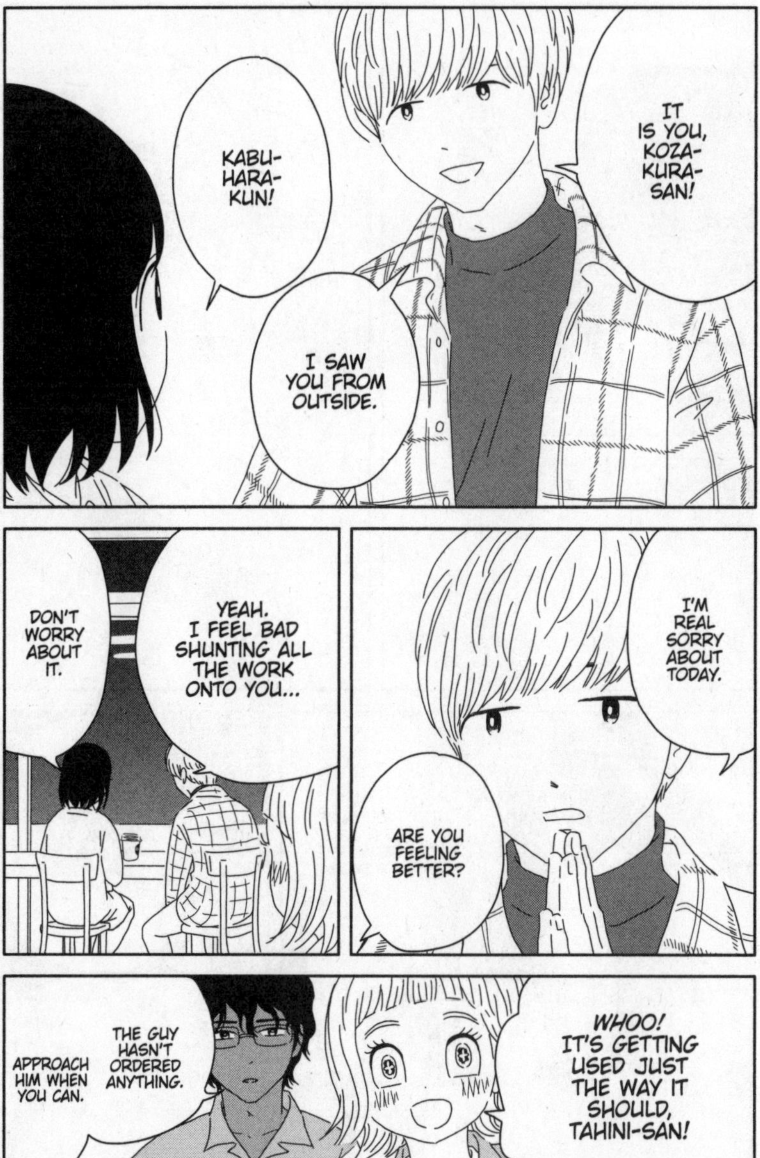
IT IS YOU, KOZA-KURA-SAN!
KABU-HARA-KUN!
I SAW YOU FROM OUTSIDE.
I'M REAL SORRY ABOUT TODAY.
ARE YOU FEELING BETTER?
YEAH. I FEEL BAD SHUNTING ALL THE WORK ONTO YOU...
DON'T WORRY ABOUT IT.
WHOO! IT'S GETTING USED JUST THE WAY IT SHOULD, TAHINI-SAN!
THE GUY HASN'T ORDERED ANYTHING.
APPROACH HIM WHEN YOU CAN.

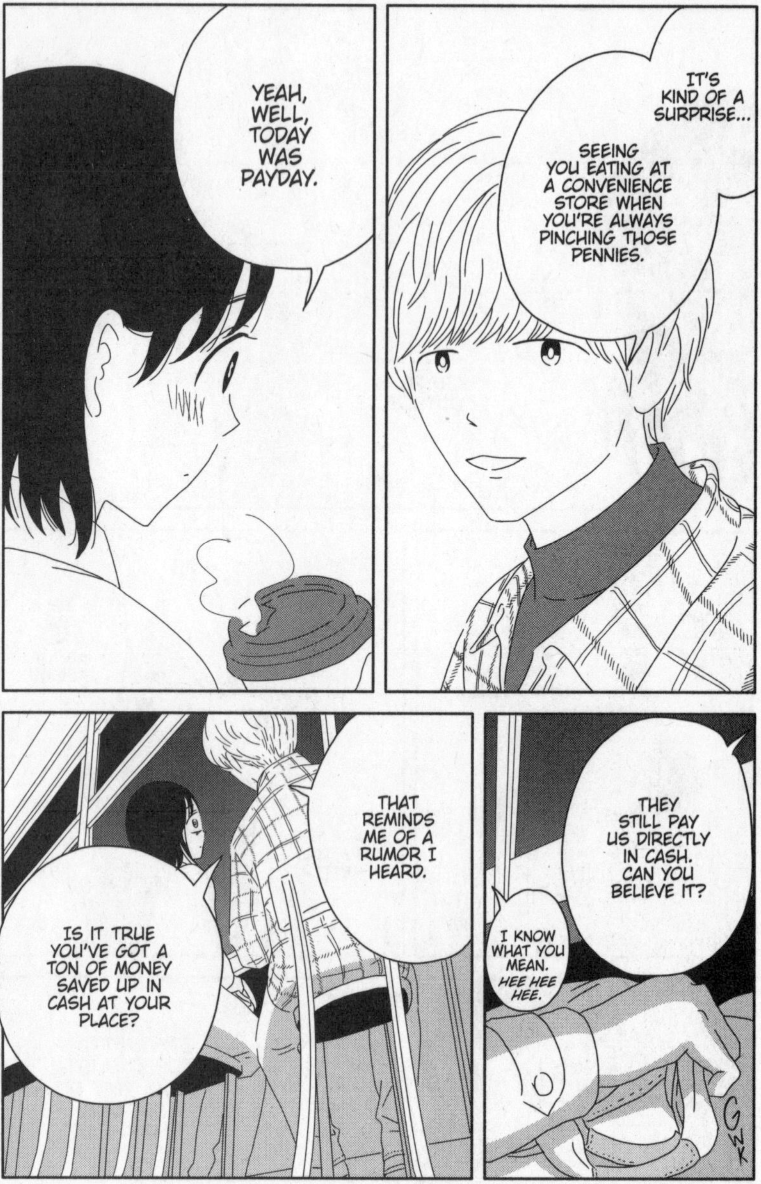
IT'S KIND OF A SURPRISE...
SEEING YOU EATING AT A CONVENIENCE STORE WHEN YOU'RE ALWAYS PINCHING THOSE PENNIES.
YEAH, WELL, TODAY WAS PAYDAY.
THEY STILL PAY US DIRECTLY IN CASH. CAN YOU BELIEVE IT?
I KNOW WHAT YOU MEAN. HEE HEE HEE.
GNK
THAT REMINDS ME OF A RUMOR I HEARD.
IS IT TRUE YOU'VE GOT A TON OF MONEY SAVED UP IN CASH AT YOUR PLACE?

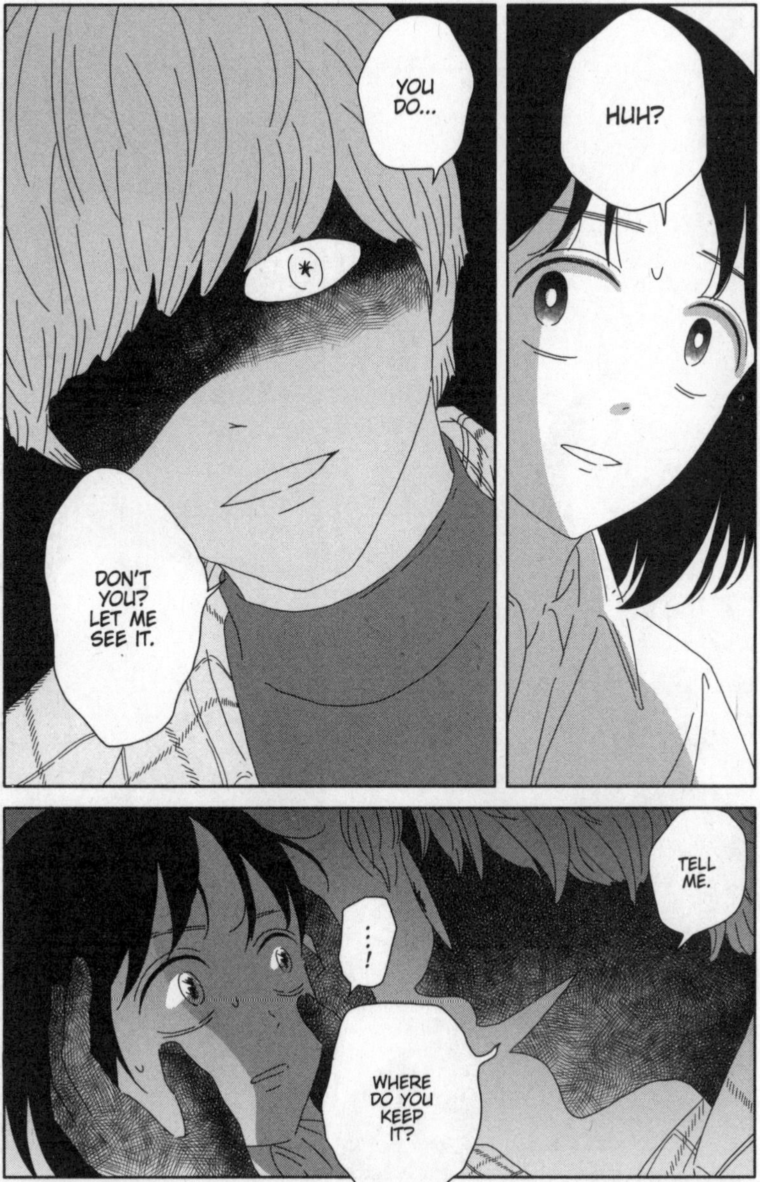
HUH?
YOU DO...
DON'T YOU? LET ME SEE IT.
TELL ME.
...!
WHERE DO YOU KEEP IT?

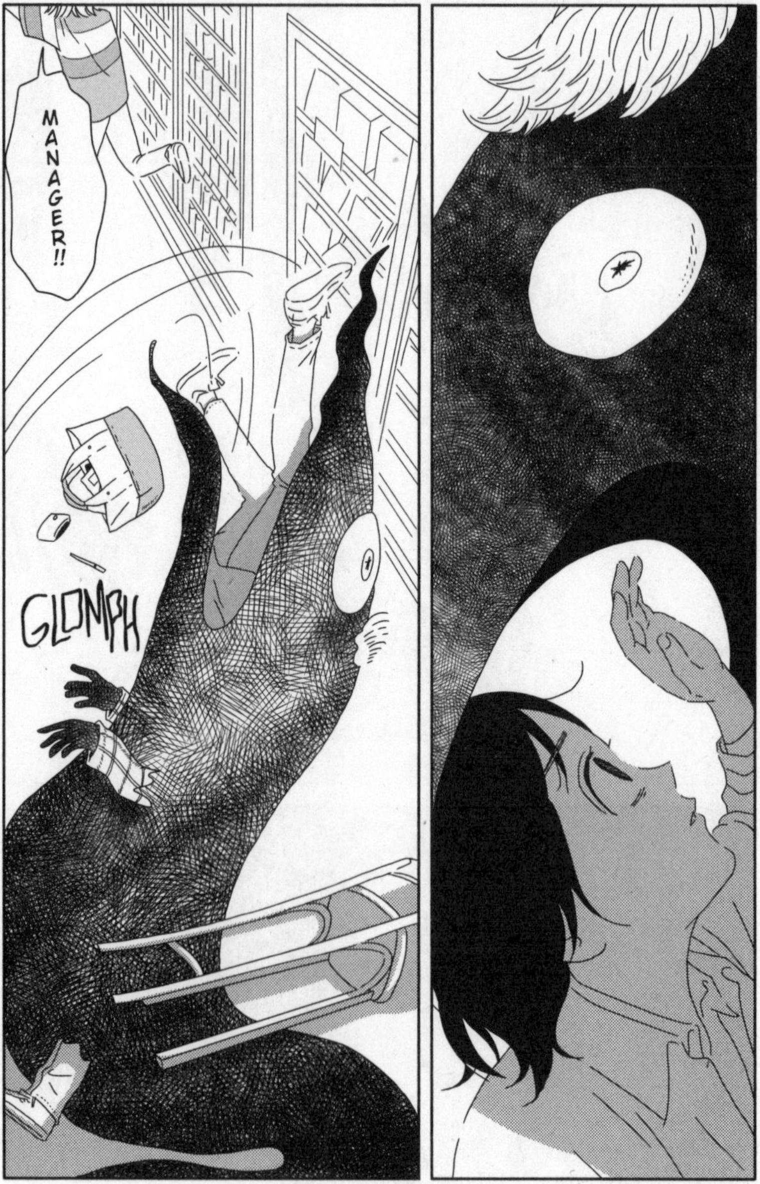
MANAGER!!
GLOMPH

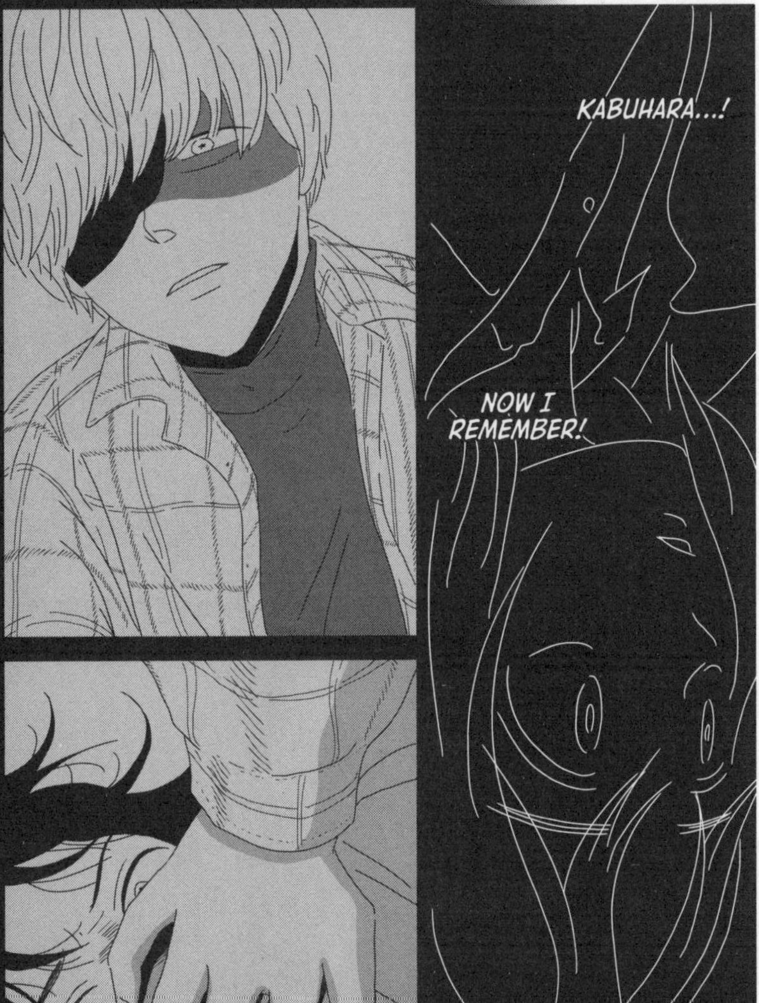
KABUHARA...!
NOW I REMEMBER!

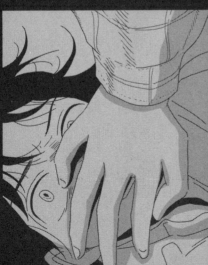

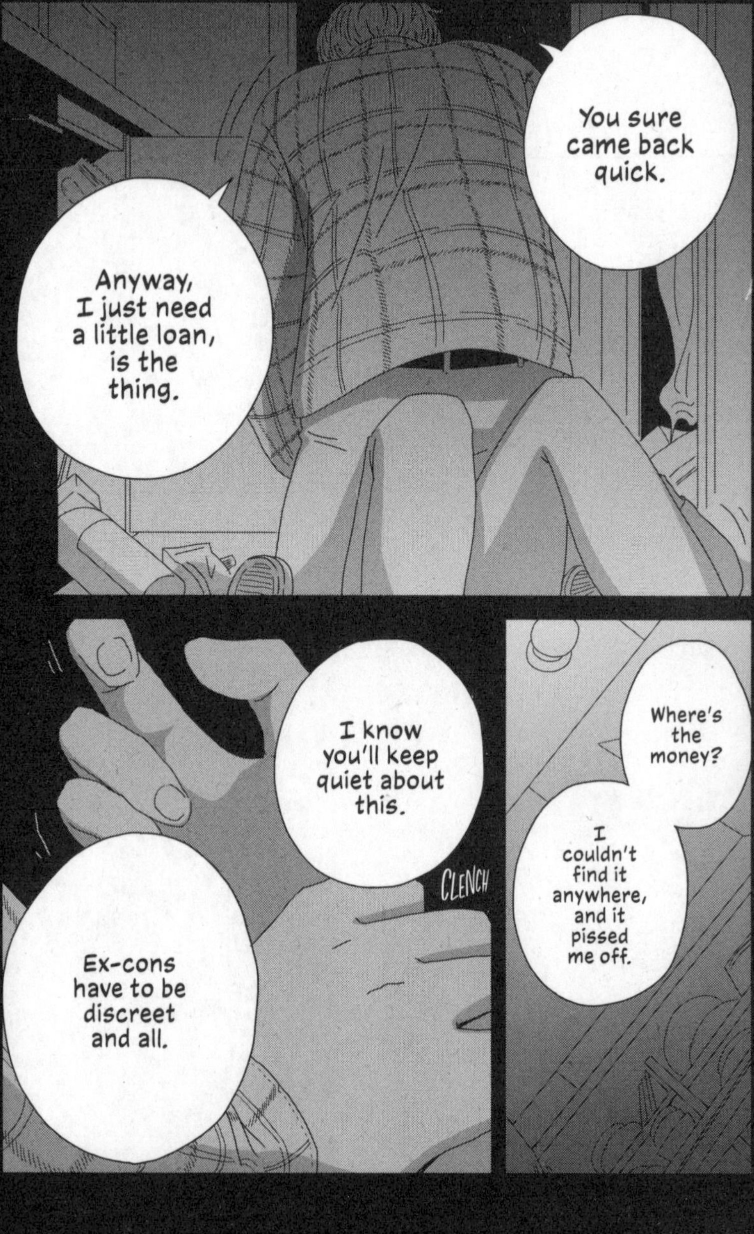
You sure came back quick.
Anyway, I just need a little loan, is the thing.
Where's the money?
I couldn't find it anywhere, and it pissed me off.
I know you'll keep quiet about this.
CLENCH
Ex-cons have to be discreet and all.

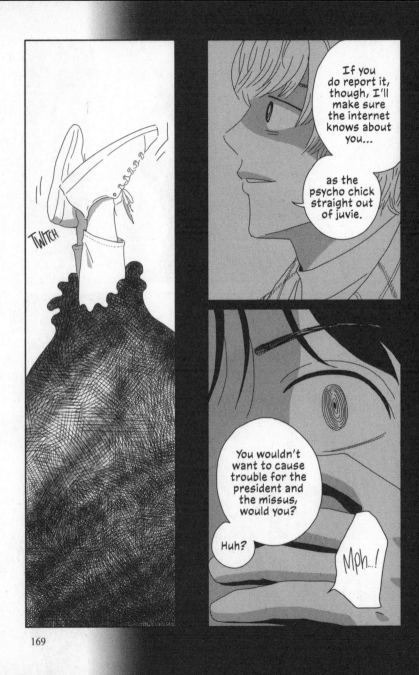

>169<

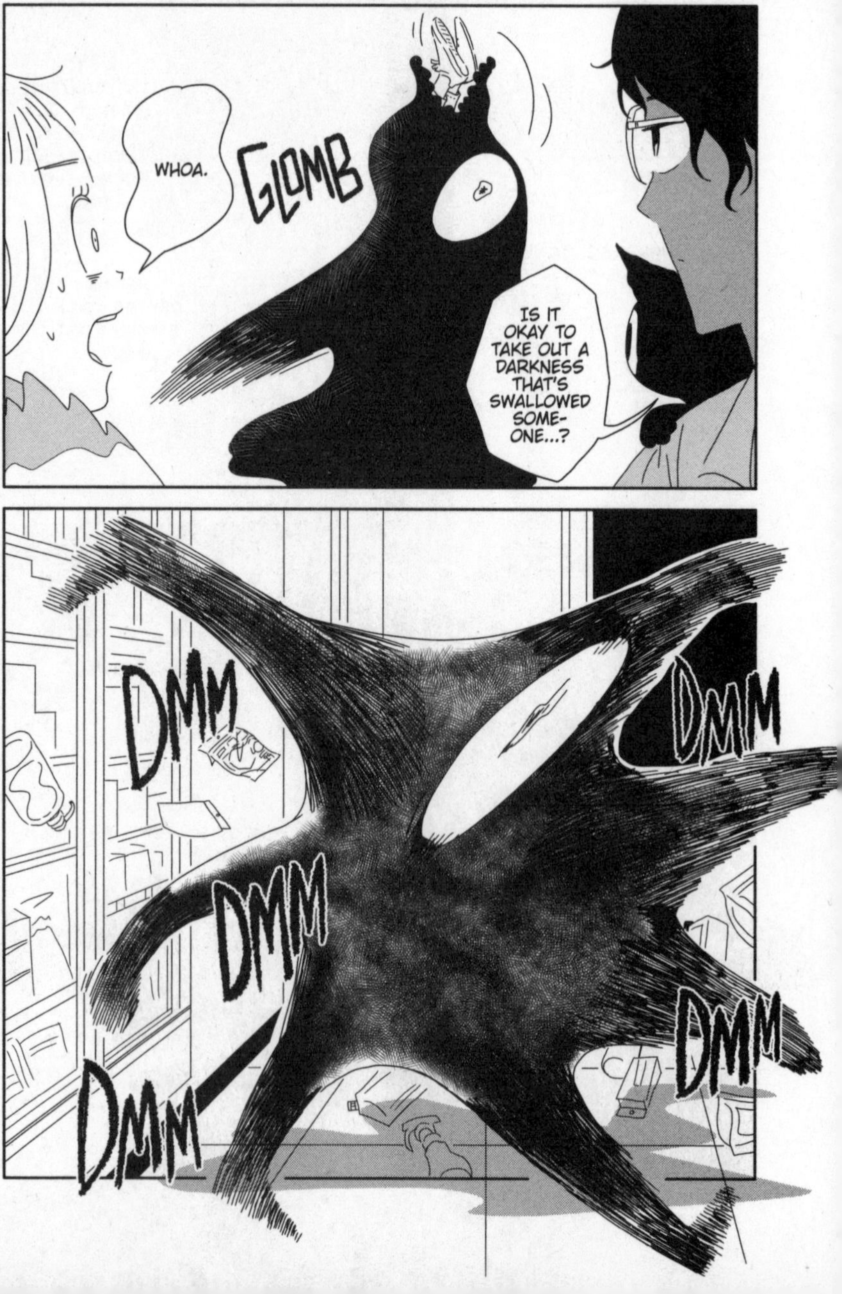
GLOMB
WHOA.
IS IT OKAY TO TAKE OUT A DARKNESS THAT'S SWALLOWED SOME-ONE...?
DMM
DMM
DMM
DMM
DMM

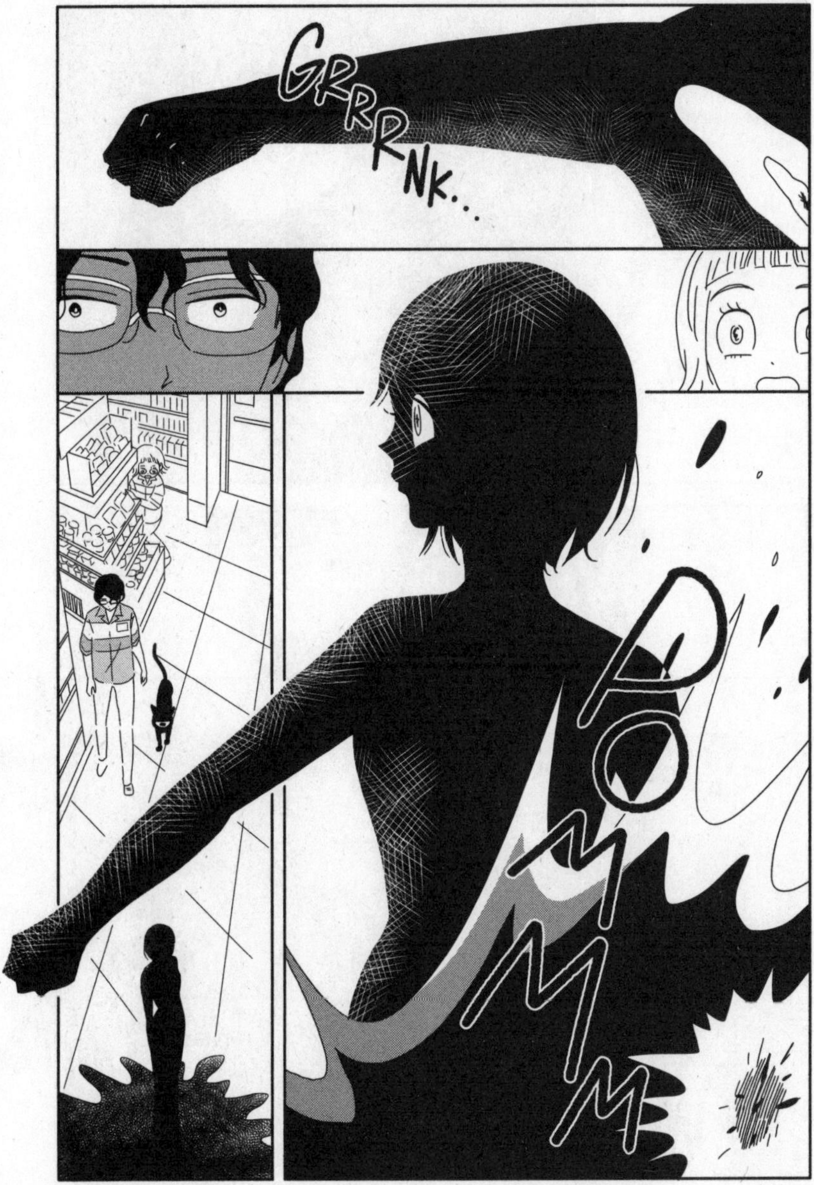
GRRRNK...
POMMM

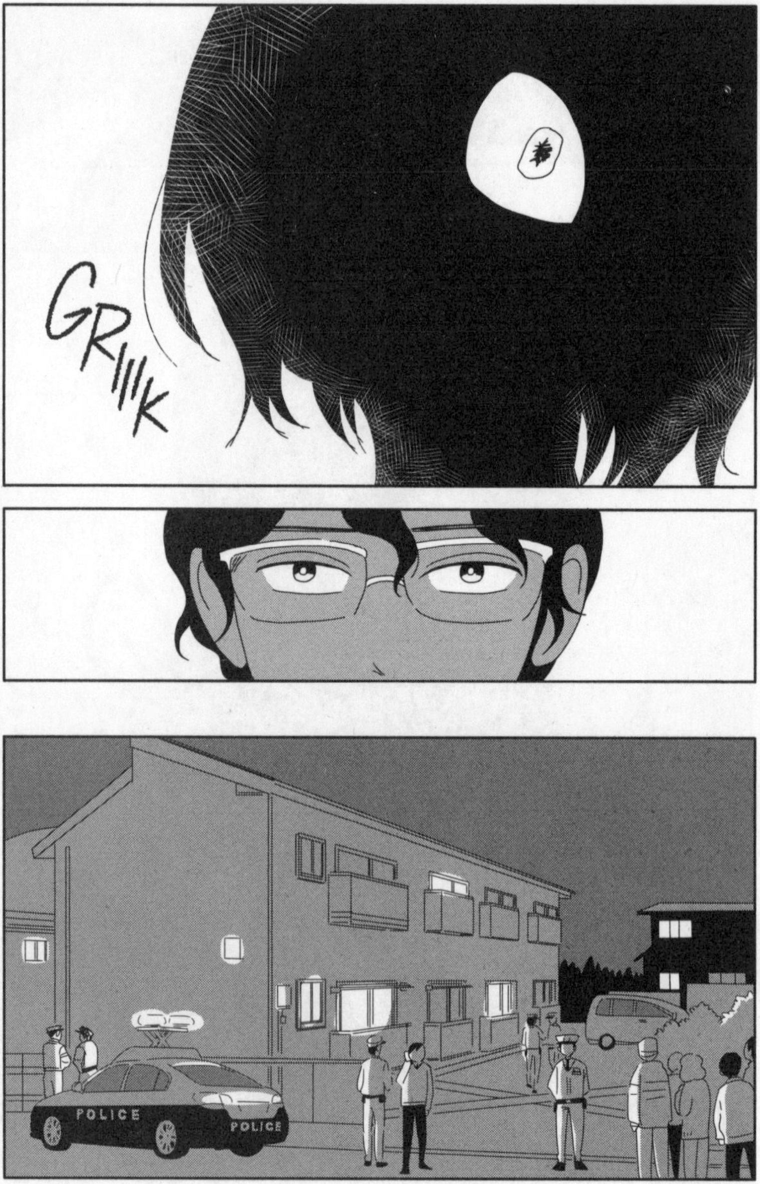
GRIIIK
POLICE
POLICE

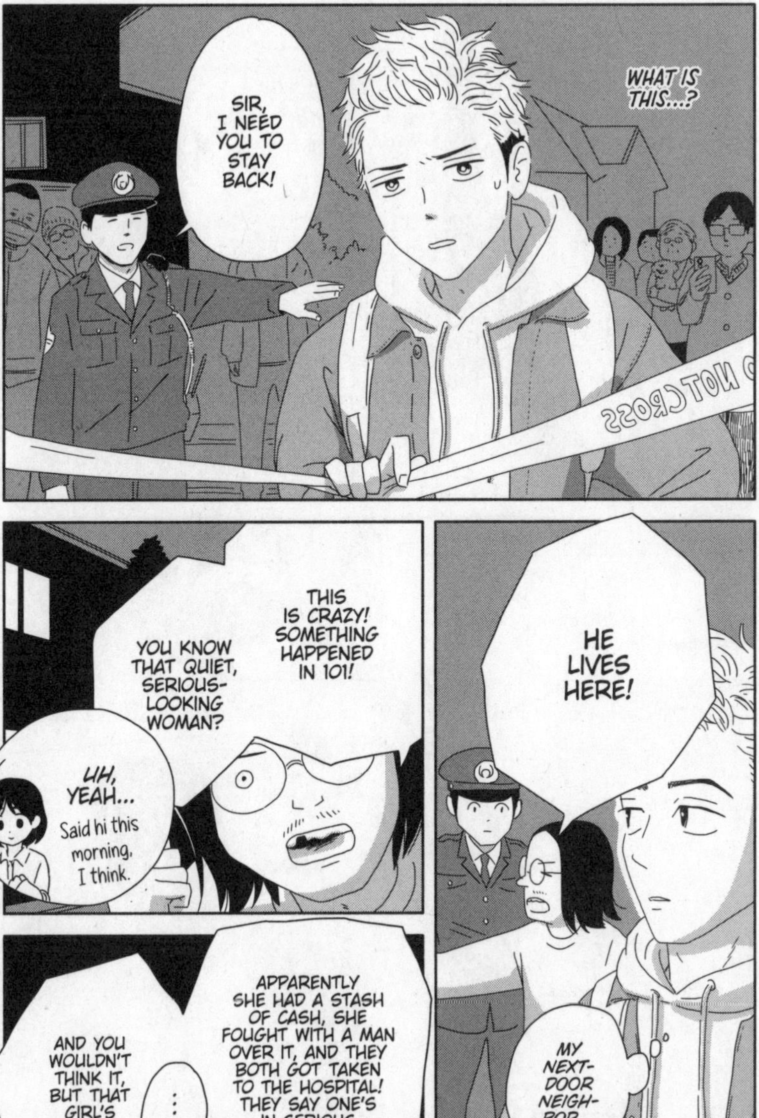
WHAT IS THIS...?
SIR, I NEED YOU TO STAY BACK!
HE LIVES HERE!
MY NEXT-DOOR NEIGHBOR...
THIS IS CRAZY! SOMETHING HAPPENED IN 101!
YOU KNOW THAT QUIET, SERIOUS-LOOKING WOMAN?
UH, YEAH... Said hi this morning, I think.
APPARENTLY SHE HAD A STASH OF CASH, SHE FOUGHT WITH A MAN OVER IT, AND THEY BOTH GOT TAKEN TO THE HOSPITAL! THEY SAY ONE'S IN SERIOUS CONDITION!!
......
AND YOU WOULDN'T THINK IT, BUT THAT GIRL'S ACTUALLY...

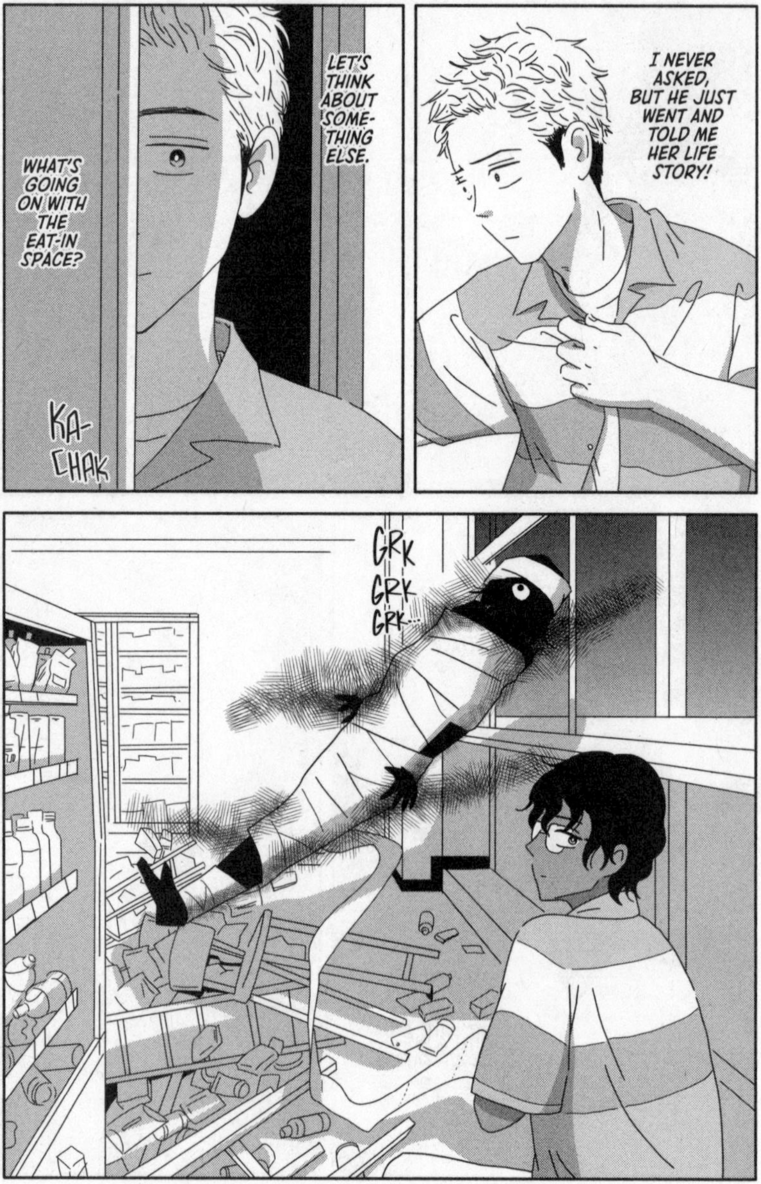
I NEVER ASKED, BUT HE JUST WENT AND TOLD ME HER LIFE STORY!
LET'S THINK ABOUT SOME-THING ELSE.
WHAT'S GOING ON WITH THE EAT-IN SPACE?
KA-CHAK
GRK GRK GRK...

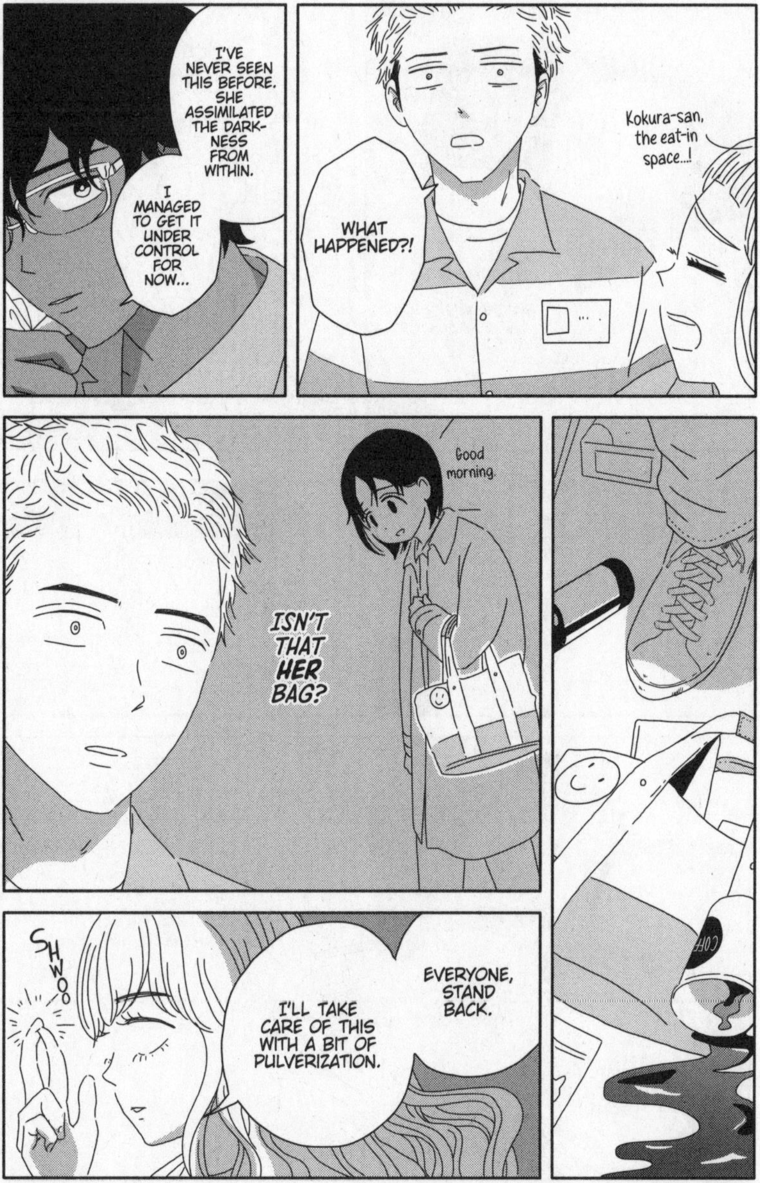
Kokura-san, the eat-in space...!
WHAT HAPPENED?!
I'VE NEVER SEEN THIS BEFORE. SHE ASSIMILATED THE DARKNESS FROM WITHIN.
I MANAGED TO GET IT UNDER CONTROL FOR NOW...
Good morning.
ISN'T THAT **HER** BAG?
EVERYONE, STAND BACK.
I'LL TAKE CARE OF THIS WITH A BIT OF PULVERIZATION.
SHWOO

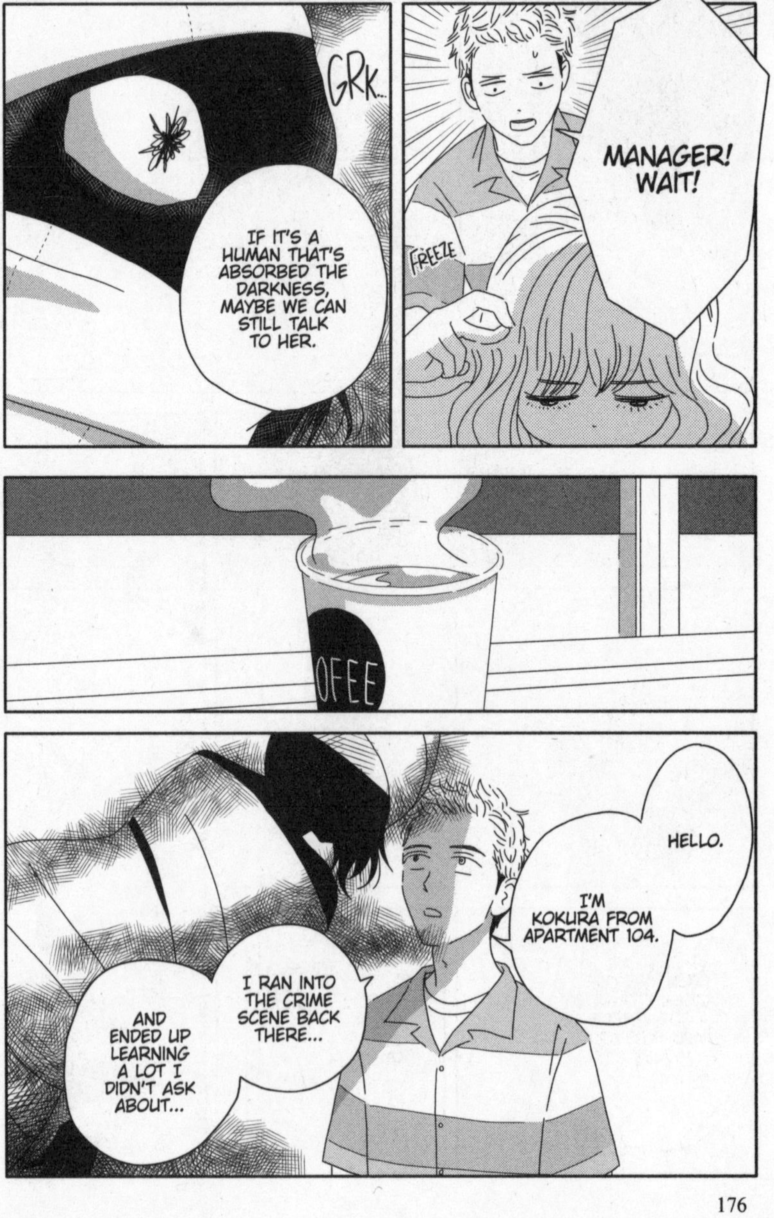
MANAGER! WAIT!
FREEZE
GRK...
IF IT'S A HUMAN THAT'S ABSORBED THE DARKNESS, MAYBE WE CAN STILL TALK TO HER.
OFEE
HELLO.
I'M KOKURA FROM APARTMENT 104.
I RAN INTO THE CRIME SCENE BACK THERE...
AND ENDED UP LEARNING A LOT I DIDN'T ASK ABOUT...

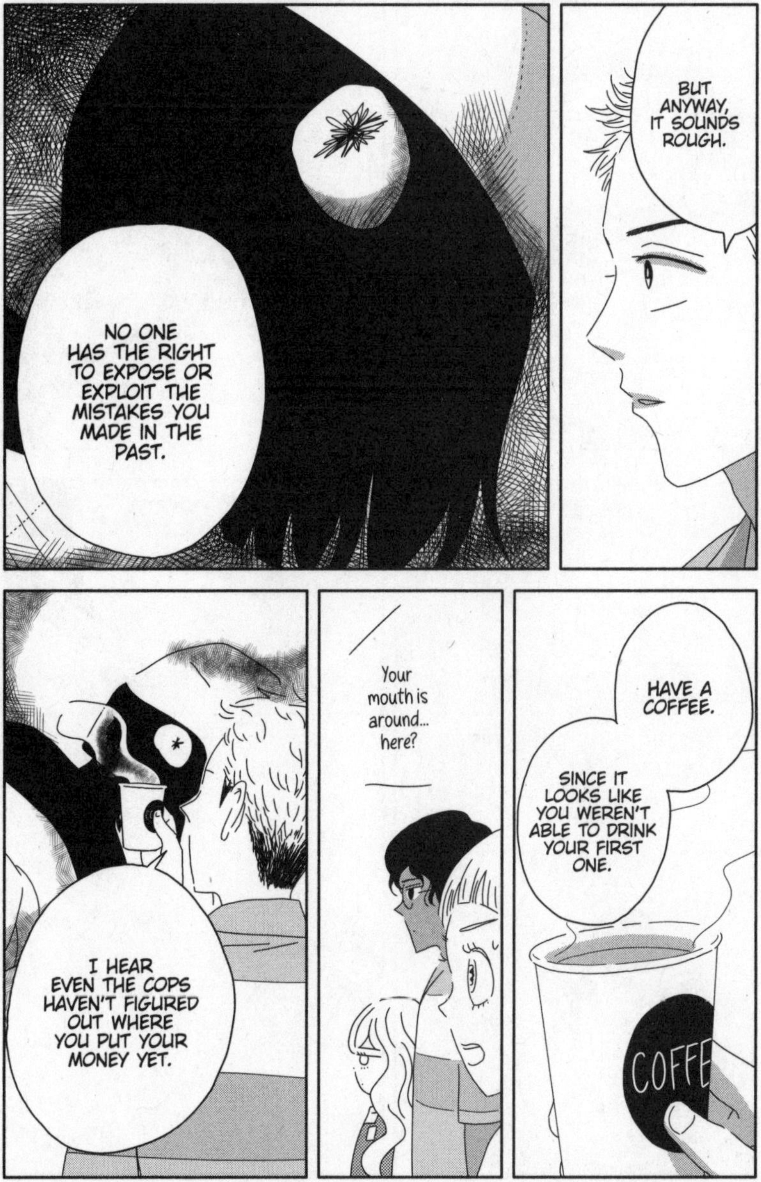
BUT ANYWAY, IT SOUNDS ROUGH.
NO ONE HAS THE RIGHT TO EXPOSE OR EXPLOIT THE MISTAKES YOU MADE IN THE PAST.
HAVE A COFFEE.
SINCE IT LOOKS LIKE YOU WEREN'T ABLE TO DRINK YOUR FIRST ONE.
COFFE
Your mouth is around... here?
I HEAR EVEN THE COPS HAVEN'T FIGURED OUT WHERE YOU PUT YOUR MONEY YET.

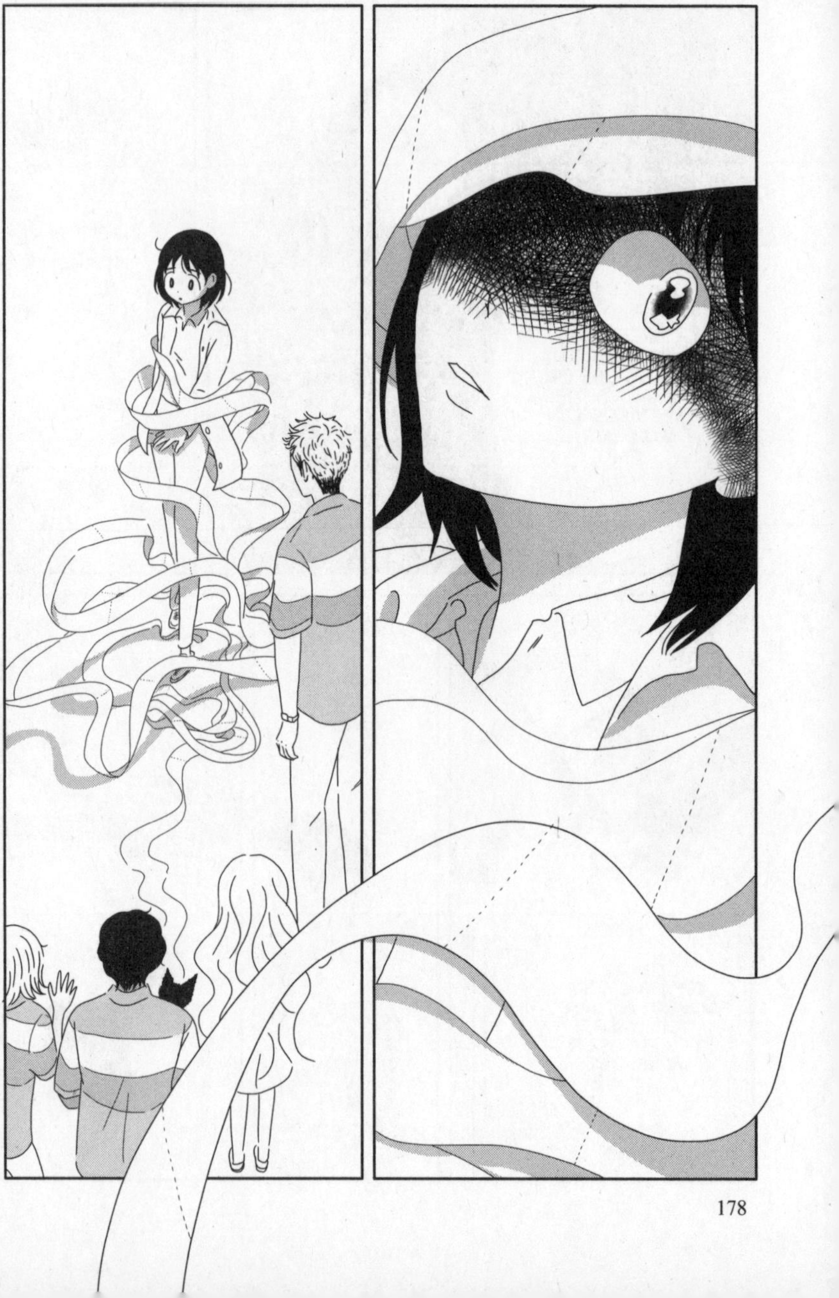

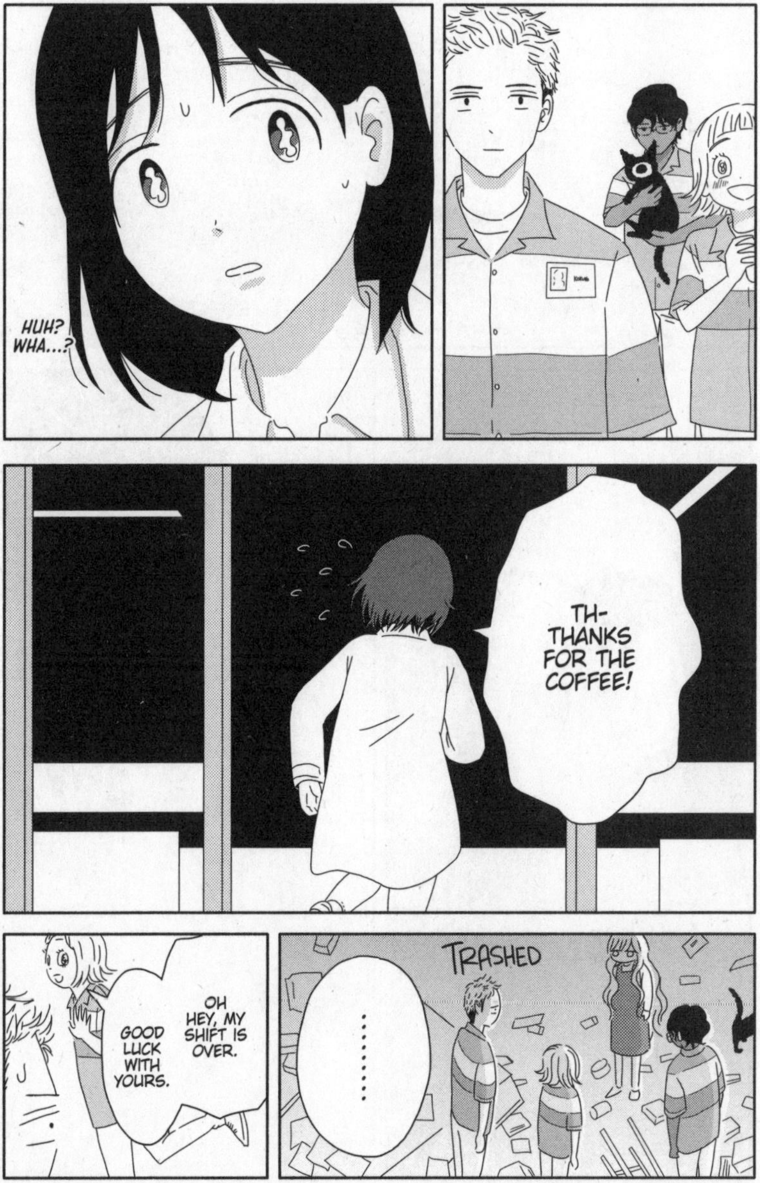
HUH? WHA...?
TH- THANKS FOR THE COFFEE!
TRASHED
......
OH HEY, MY SHIFT IS OVER.
GOOD LUCK WITH YOURS.

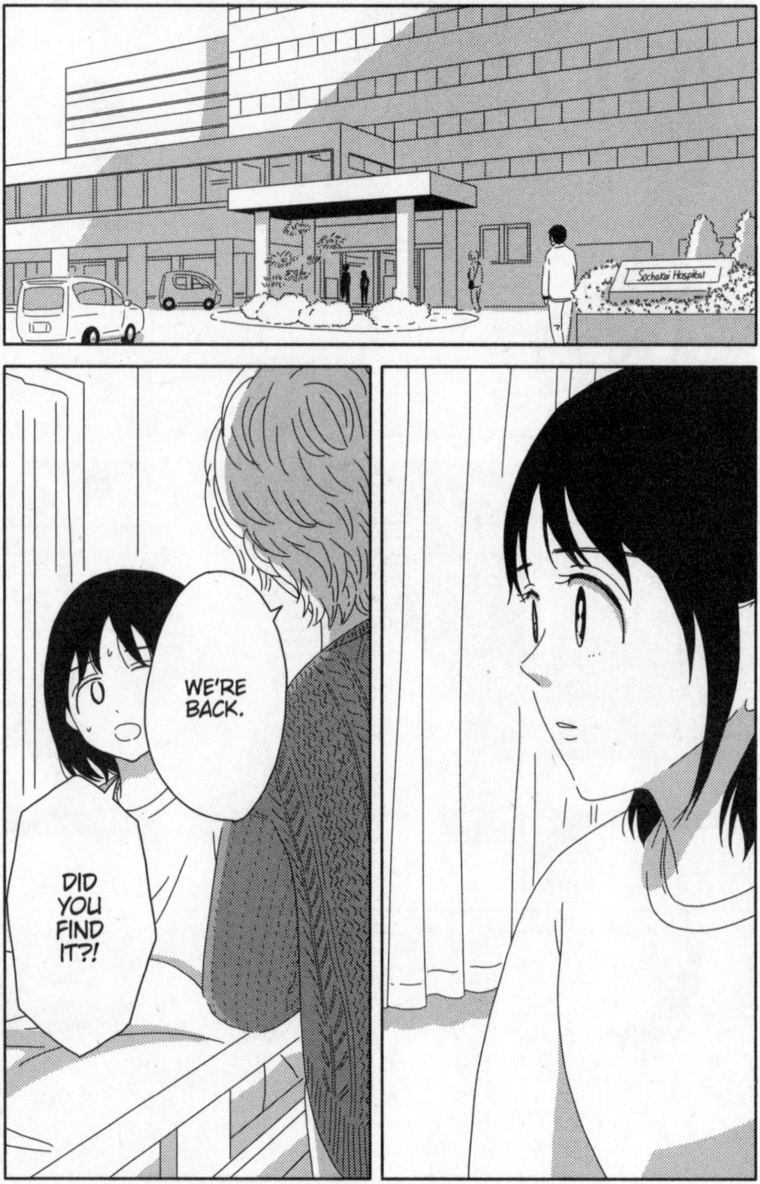
Sochakai Hospital
WE'RE BACK.
DID YOU FIND IT?!

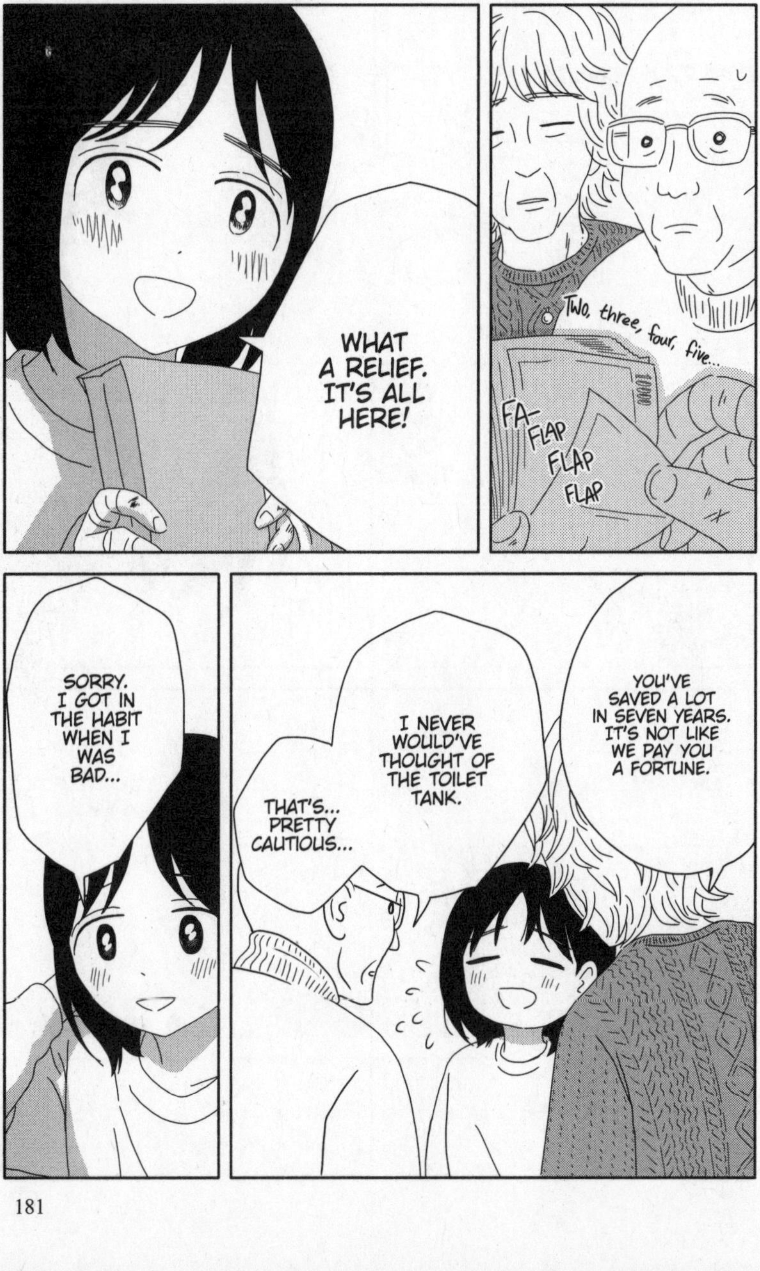
Two, three, four, five...
FA-FLAP FLAP FLAP
WHAT A RELIEF. IT'S ALL HERE!
YOU'VE SAVED A LOT IN SEVEN YEARS. IT'S NOT LIKE WE PAY YOU A FORTUNE.
I NEVER WOULD'VE THOUGHT OF THE TOILET TANK.
THAT'S... PRETTY CAUTIOUS...
SORRY. I GOT IN THE HABIT WHEN I WAS BAD...

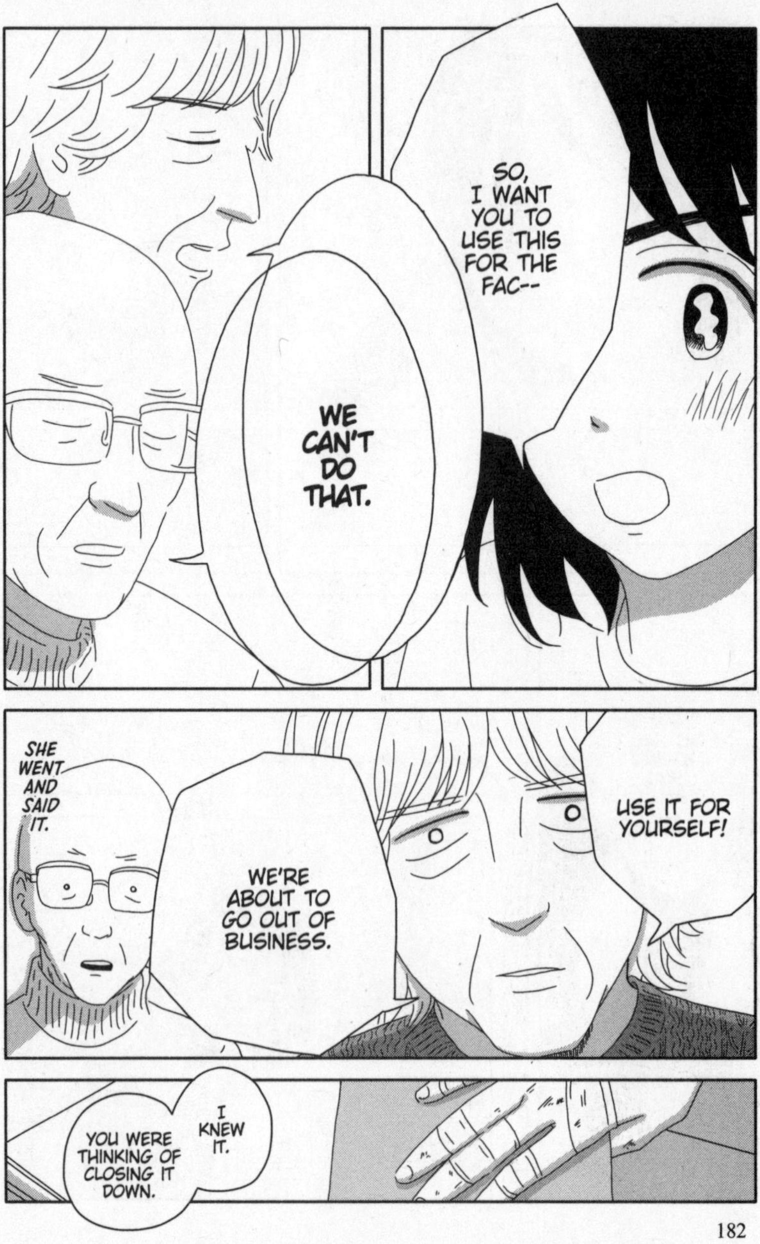
SO, I WANT YOU TO USE THIS FOR THE FAC--
WE CAN'T DO THAT.
USE IT FOR YOURSELF!
WE'RE ABOUT TO GO OUT OF BUSINESS.
SHE WENT AND SAID IT.
I KNEW IT.
YOU WERE THINKING OF CLOSING IT DOWN.

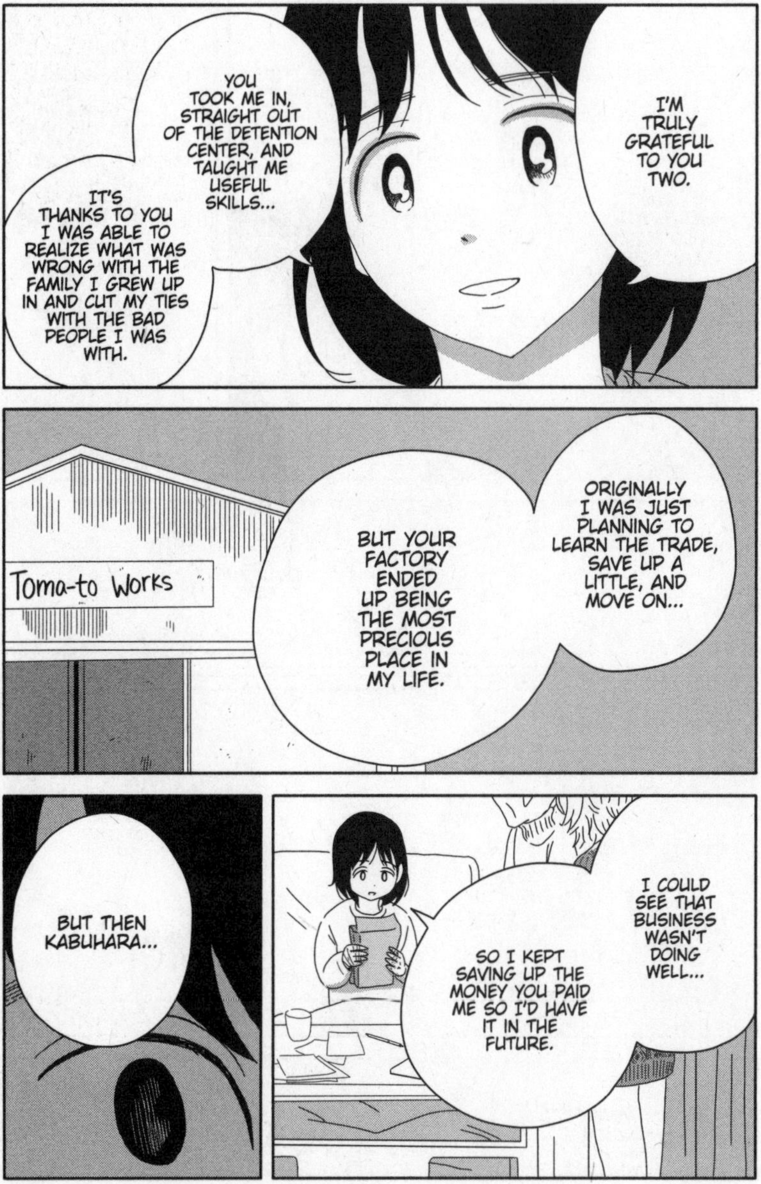
I'M TRULY GRATEFUL TO YOU TWO.
YOU TOOK ME IN, STRAIGHT OUT OF THE DETENTION CENTER, AND TAUGHT ME USEFUL SKILLS...
IT'S THANKS TO YOU I WAS ABLE TO REALIZE WHAT WAS WRONG WITH THE FAMILY I GREW UP IN AND CUT MY TIES WITH THE BAD PEOPLE I WAS WITH.
ORIGINALLY I WAS JUST PLANNING TO LEARN THE TRADE, SAVE UP A LITTLE, AND MOVE ON...
BUT YOUR FACTORY ENDED UP BEING THE MOST PRECIOUS PLACE IN MY LIFE.
Toma-to Works
I COULD SEE THAT BUSINESS WASN'T DOING WELL...
SO I KEPT SAVING UP THE MONEY YOU PAID ME SO I'D HAVE IT IN THE FUTURE.
BUT THEN KABUHARA...

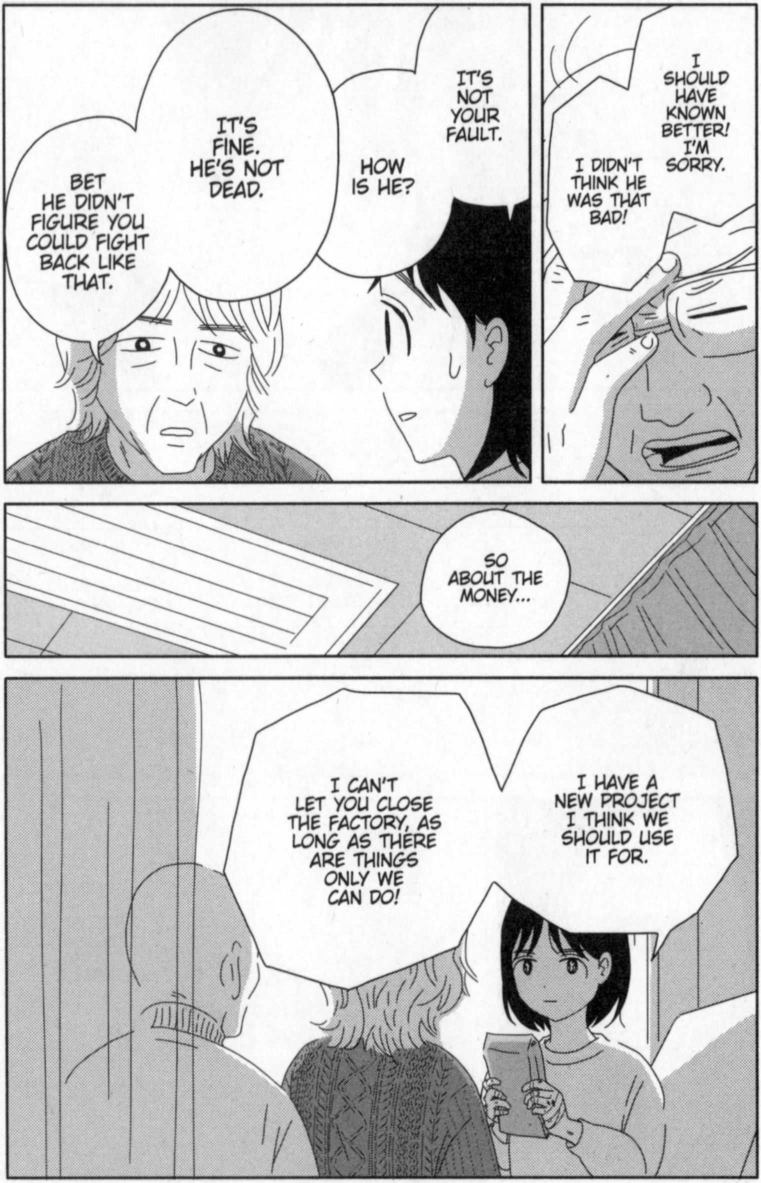
I SHOULD HAVE KNOWN BETTER! I'M SORRY.
I DIDN'T THINK HE WAS THAT BAD!
IT'S NOT YOUR FAULT.
HOW IS HE?
IT'S FINE. HE'S NOT DEAD.
BET HE DIDN'T FIGURE YOU COULD FIGHT BACK LIKE THAT.
SO ABOUT THE MONEY...
I HAVE A NEW PROJECT I THINK WE SHOULD USE IT FOR.
I CAN'T LET YOU CLOSE THE FACTORY, AS LONG AS THERE ARE THINGS ONLY WE CAN DO!

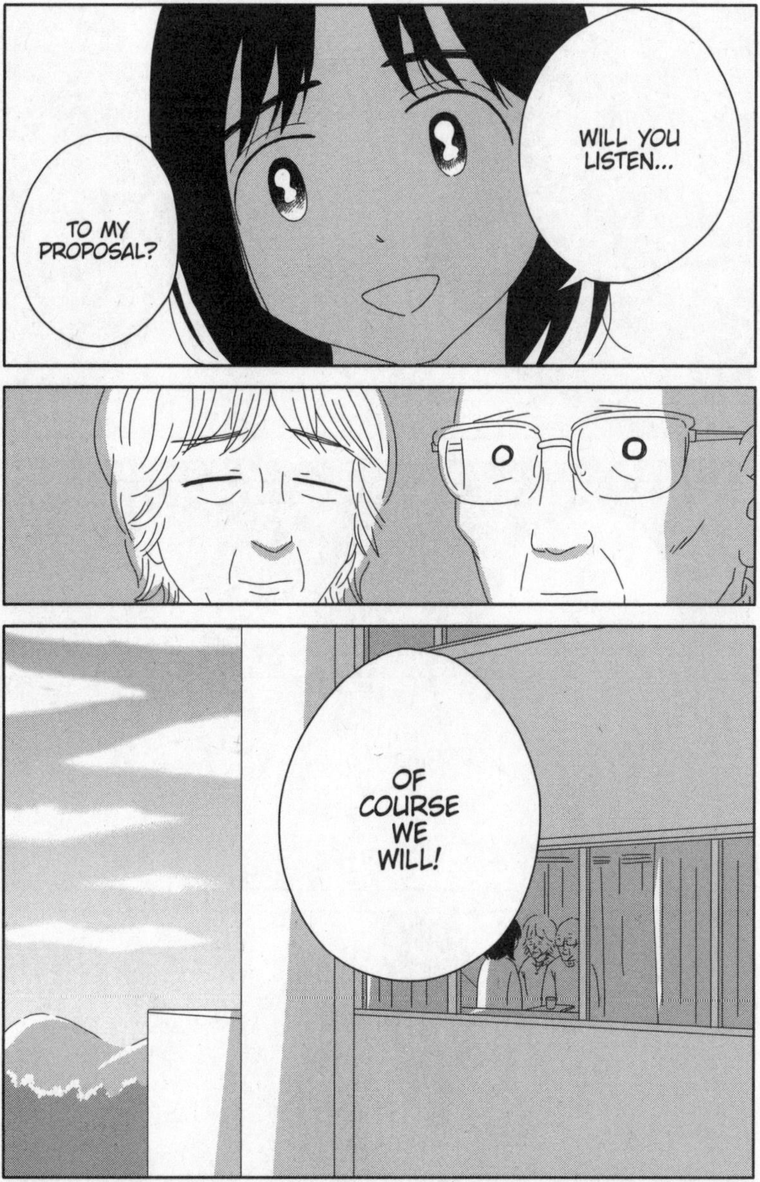
WILL YOU LISTEN...
TO MY PROPOSAL?
OF COURSE WE WILL!

SHOMP..

THANK YOU FOR YOUR HARD WORK TODAY.

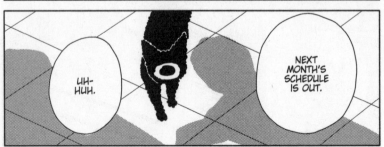

UH-HUH.

NEXT MONTH'S SCHEDULE IS OUT.

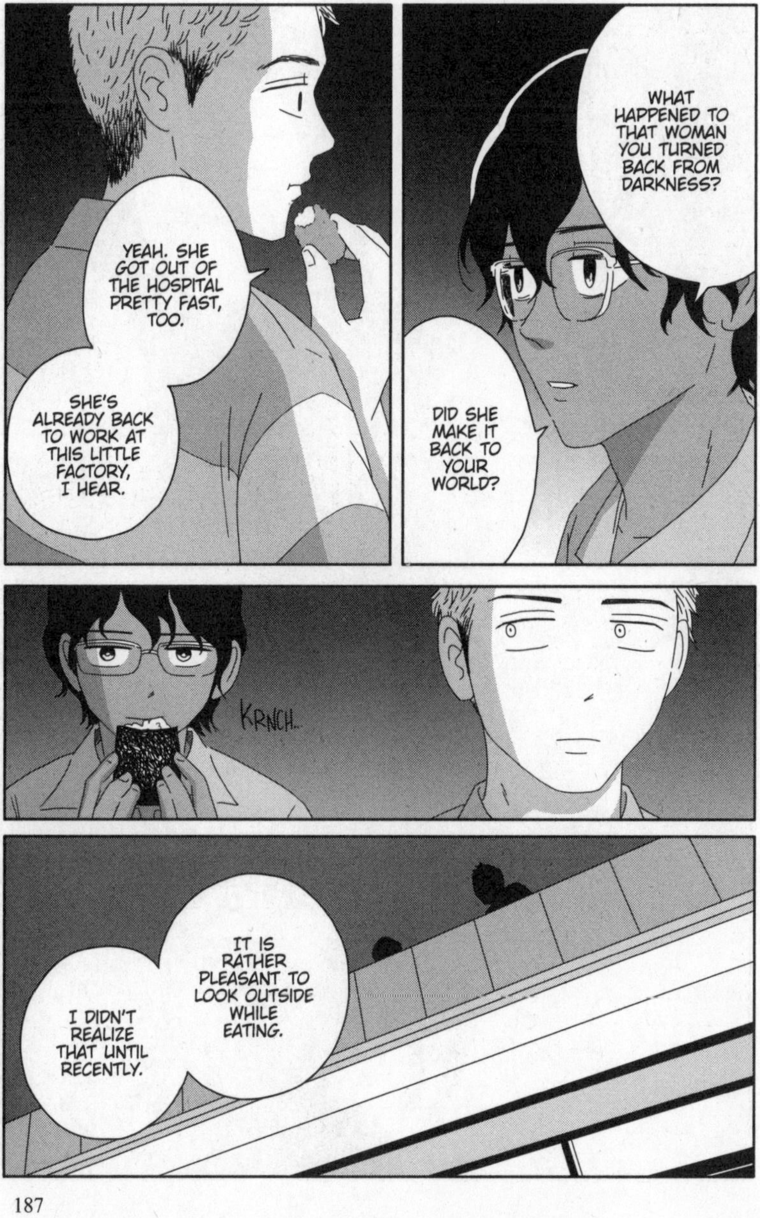
WHAT HAPPENED TO THAT WOMAN YOU TURNED BACK FROM DARKNESS?
DID SHE MAKE IT BACK TO YOUR WORLD?
YEAH. SHE GOT OUT OF THE HOSPITAL PRETTY FAST, TOO.
SHE'S ALREADY BACK TO WORK AT THIS LITTLE FACTORY, I HEAR.
KRNCH..
IT IS RATHER PLEASANT TO LOOK OUTSIDE WHILE EATING.
I DIDN'T REALIZE THAT UNTIL RECENTLY.

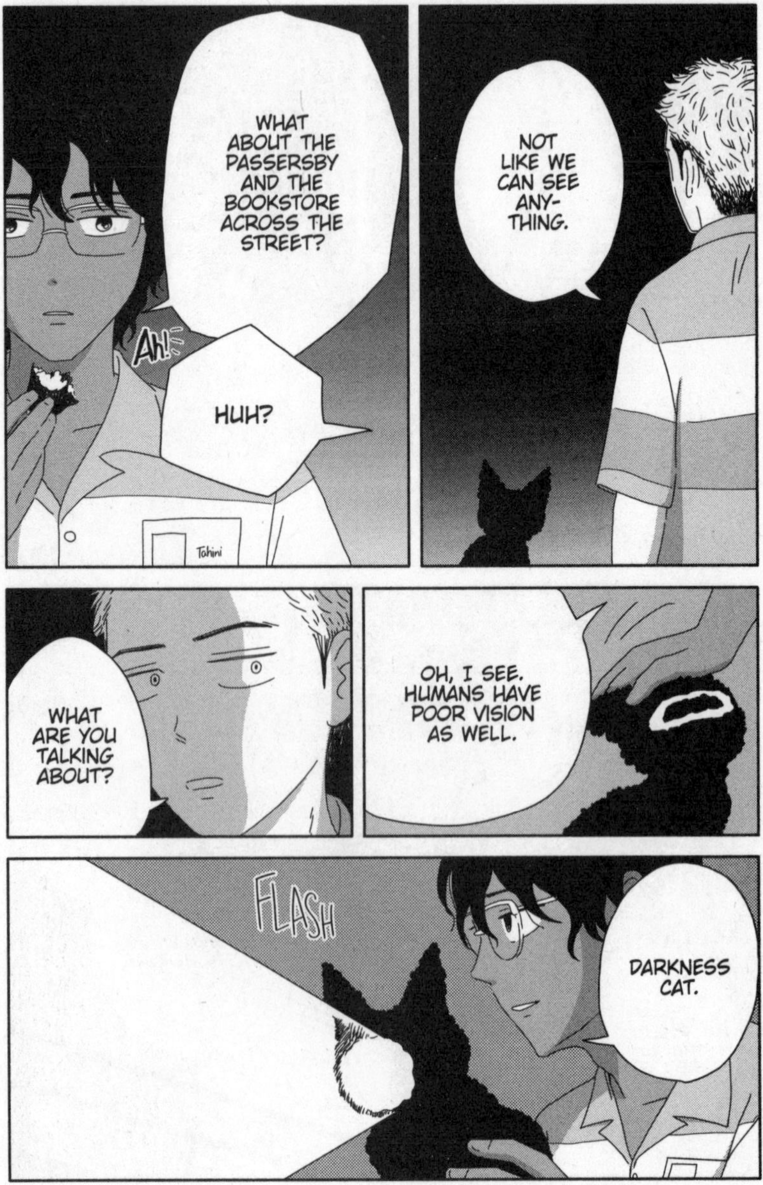
NOT LIKE WE CAN SEE ANY-THING.
WHAT ABOUT THE PASSERSBY AND THE BOOKSTORE ACROSS THE STREET?
Ah!
HUH?
Tahini
OH, I SEE. HUMANS HAVE POOR VISION AS WELL.
WHAT ARE YOU TALKING ABOUT?
FLASH
DARKNESS CAT.

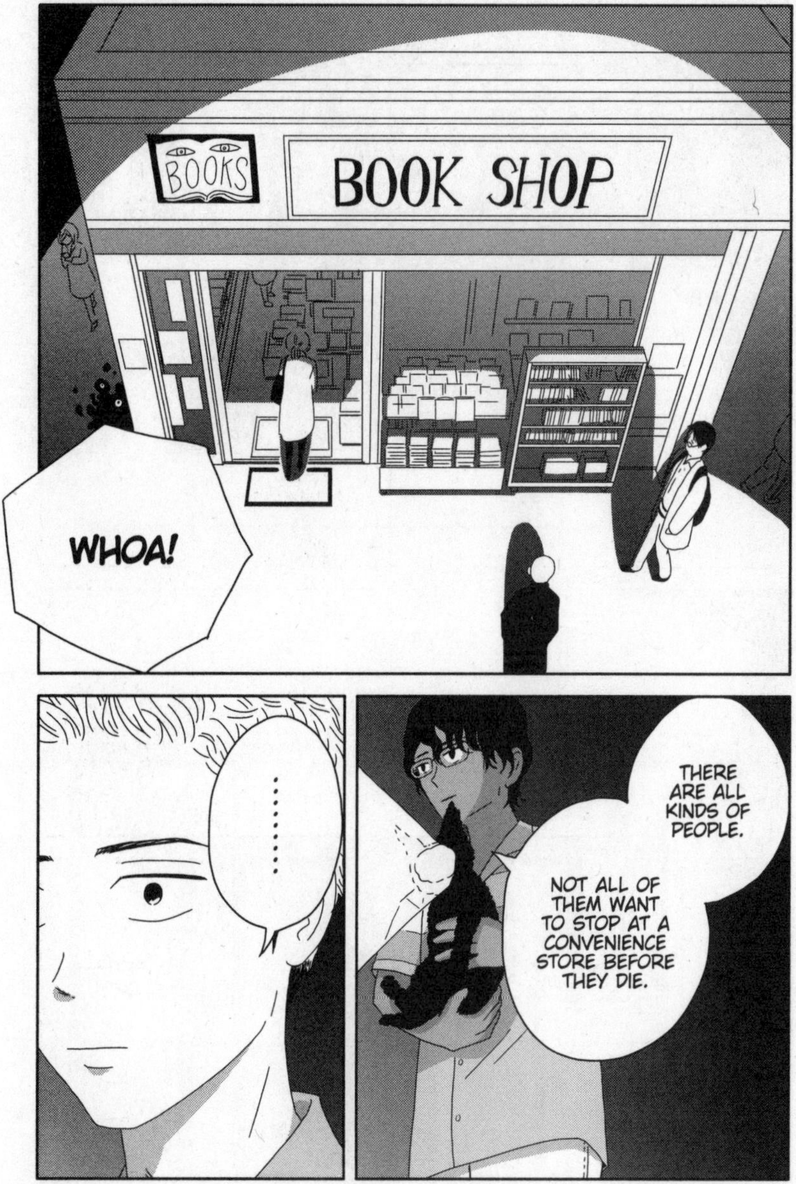
BOOKS
BOOK SHOP
WHOA!
THERE ARE ALL KINDS OF PEOPLE.
NOT ALL OF THEM WANT TO STOP AT A CONVENIENCE STORE BEFORE THEY DIE.
....

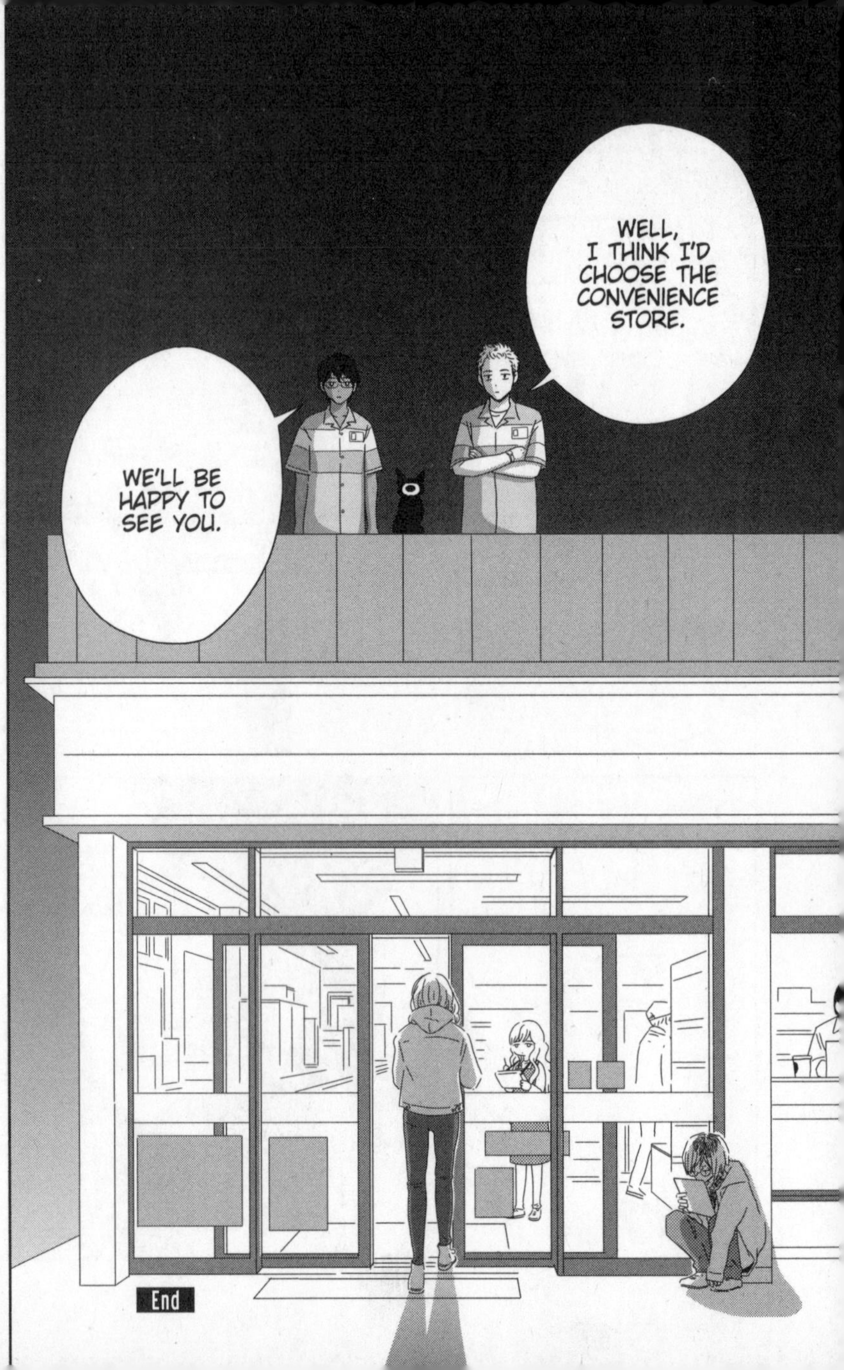
WELL, I THINK I'D CHOOSE THE CONVENIENCE STORE.
WE'LL BE HAPPY TO SEE YOU.
End

PROFILE

Seiko Erisawa

Born October 13. From Tokyo.
Notable works include *Seifuku
Nusumareta*, *Chizuka Map*,
*Veranda wa Nankou Furaku no la
France*, and *Uchi no Class no
Joshi ga Yabai*.

SEVEN SEAS ENTERTAINMENT PRESENTS

BOX of LIGHT

story and art by **SEIKO ERISAWA**   **VOLUME ONE**

TRANSLATION
Daniel Komen

LETTERING
Brendon Hull

ORIGINAL COVER DESIGN
en to kyu-

COVER DESIGN
Nicky Lim

PROOFREADER
Kurestin Armada

SENIOR EDITOR
J.P. Sullivan

COPY EDITOR
Dawn Davis

PRODUCTION MANAGER
Lissa Pattillo

PREPRESS TECHNICIAN
Melanie Ujimori

PRINT MANAGER
Rhiannon Rasmussen-Silverstein

EDITOR-IN-CHIEF
Julie Davis

ASSOCIATE PUBLISHER
Adam Arnold

PUBLISHER
Jason DeAngelis

HIKARI NO HAKO vol.1
by Seiko ERISAWA
© 2020 Seiko ERISAWA
All rights reserved.
Original Japanese edition published by SHOGAKUKAN.
English translation rights in the United States of America, Canada, the United
Kingdom, Ireland, Australia and New Zealand arranged with SHOGAKUKAN through
Tuttle-Mori Agency, Inc.

Seven Seas press and purchase enquiries can be sent to Marketing Manager Lianne
Sentar at press@gomanga.com. Information regarding the distribution and purchase of
digital editions is available from Digital Manager CK Russell at digital@gomanga.com.

Seven Seas and the Seven Seas logo are trademarks of
Seven Seas Entertainment. All rights reserved.

ISBN: 978-1-63858-521-3
Printed in Canada
First Printing: July 2022
10 9 8 7 6 5 4 3 2 1

READING DIRECTIONS

This book reads from *right to left*,
Japanese style. If this is your first time
reading manga, you start reading from
the top right panel on each page and
take it from there. If you get lost, just
follow the numbered diagram here.
It may seem backwards at first,
but you'll get the hang of it! Have fun!!

Follow us online: www.SevenSeasEntertainment.com